The Deviant Pupil

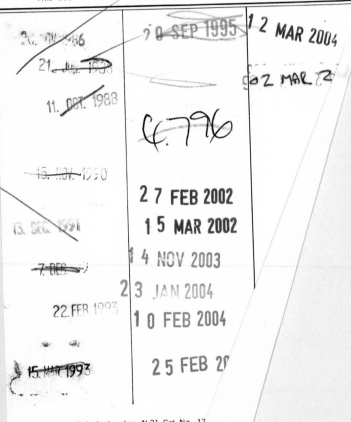

Contents

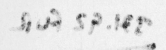

Acknowledgements

I first recognized the need for a book such as this when I was a research fellow in the Educational Studies Unit at Brunel University engaged on an empirical study entitled 'Disaffected Pupils' (1977–1980). I am indebted to the other members of the research team, Catherine Bird, Rosemary Chessum, Daphne Johnson and Maurice Kogan, for their support during two years of intensive fieldwork in schools, and three years of lively debate about the 'real meaning' of what we saw. That practical and empirical experience has proved invaluable in assessing other people's research. For their help, support and interest in the preparation of this present manuscript I am indebted to many friends and colleagues in Cambridge, most particularly Ruth Furlong, Gerald Grace, Felicity Hunt, Sheila Miles and Shirley Willcocks. Their encouragement and critical interest has proved invaluable during the last two years. Finally, I would like to thank John Skelton of the Open University Press for his encouragement at the beginning of this project and his patience at the end.

Introduction

Letter from headteacher to parent:

> I'm sorry to inform you that in spite of the assurances given by your son David at our last meeting there has been a marked deterioration in his behaviour this last week which culminated this morning in his kicking and breaking a door and swearing at a teacher. I have no alternative therefore but to suspend him from school. The subject of his future education is now in the hands of the Local Education Authority and you will, no doubt, hear from them in due course.
>
> I am informing the Director of Education and the Chairman of the governing body and must ask you to make sure that David does not come onto the school premises at any time. Would you note that from this point of time you are legally responsible for David; the school accepts no responsibility for his behaviour.

This letter from a headteacher to a parent marked the end of a stormy school career for David. His records showed that even in his primary school he was a problem, being rude and aggressive to his peers and his teachers. During his first two years at secondary school David seemed to settle down but by the time he was 14 years old he was again regularly in conflict with the school authorities. He would do little work and was a disruptive influence on his peers. When disciplined he was often verbally abusive. Most of his teachers breathed a sigh of relief when, in his fourth year, he began to truant from school.

Why is it that pupils like David are such a problem to their teachers? Why do some pupils play truant? Why are some disruptive or even violent? Indiscipline at school has been examined from many different theoretical perspectives. Some theorists would suggest that pupils like David suffer from inherited personality disorders that make them uncooperative with authority figures, while others would consider such pupils to be emotionally unstable and enquire into their family backgrounds. Were David's parents divorced or unemployed? Were they uncaring when he was a child? Has he regularly been exposed to scenes of violence and aggression at home?

A quite different approach has been to look to the experience of school itself for the explanation of difficult behaviour. For example it has been suggested that pupils reject school because they feel rejected by it; disruptive behaviour may be a way of coping with the humiliation of academic failure, with the fact that teachers seem uncaring or are ineffective. Alternatively it has been suggested that teachers themselves are inpart to blame. If David's teachers 'labelled' him as troublesome and constantly treated him with suspicion, this may have encouraged him to live up to those expectations. Labelling, it is argued, can make pupils' behaviour worse rather than better.

Yet another group of researchers have looked beyond the school for explanations, suggesting that pupils challenge school because they feel the values it projects are incompatible with the world they inhabit outside. The moral authority of teachers, with their emphasis on conformity and commitment to academic achievement is, for some pupils, felt to be irrelevant to their present and future lives; school therefore seems like an imposition. Given that it is experienced as an imposition, it is argued, pupils resist in the only way they know how, by being disruptive and playing truant.

All of these explanations, and many others besides, have been put forward in order to try to understand difficult behaviour at school. As was implicit in the examples given above, the explanations offered cover a wide spectrum of academic disciplines — biology, psychology, social psychology, sociology. In this book I will be concerned primarily with the latter two. My purpose is to clarify the range of different theoretical perspectives commonly employed by sociologists and social psychologists to study indiscipline at school. After an historical introduction, four major research traditions are introduced: positivism, anomie and status deprivation theory, interactionism and theories of reproduction. In each case the central tenets of the perspective are presented, its strengths and weaknesses considered, and the major empirical studies exemplifying the tradition are discussed. In the final chapter a summary and synthesis is proposed.

Although a great deal of substantive research is discussed, the purpose of the book is therefore primarily theoretical. My objective is to clarify the theoretical assumptions underlying different research studies so that their strengths, weaknesses and different policy implications can be more readily assessed. Although the substantive examples of research are almost exclusively drawn from the British context it is therefore hoped that the book will have a broader appeal. In North America or Australia, for example, the body of substantive research on indiscipline may be somewhat different, but the underlying theoretical models utilized are largely the same.

That violence, disruption and truancy are important topics for the teaching profession is best illustrated by the dramatic growth in specialist provision that has been made for difficult children during the last 40 years. When historians come to write the history of Britain's post-war education, one factor they are likely to emphasize is the rapid growth in the number of pupils formally or informally classified as 'maladjusted' and therefore removed from mainstream schooling. Although as early as 1913 some Local Authorities had established what were called 'psychiatric clinics' for the purpose of diagnosing children who were considered incapable of benefiting from normal education (Underwood, 1955), it was not until 1945 that the category of 'maladjustment' was formally enshrined in legislation.[1]* From that date all Local Education Authorities (LEA's) had a responsibility to establish special educational treatment, either in ordinary or special schools, for pupils who were so defined. Since that time the growth in numbers of pupils in special schools for the maladjusted has been startling.

During the first 15 years of the operation of the new regulations the number of children in England and Wales officially classified as 'maladjusted' rose from nil in 1945 to 1742 in 1960. Such an increase was probably to be expected given the new responsibilities imposed on L.E.A.s. What was perhaps less to be expected was the literally exponential growth in the number of maladjusted pupils over the next 15 years. During that period the number doubled, doubled again and then doubled again. By 1975 there were 13 000 pupils classified as maladjusted and that number has remained more or less stable since (Ford *et al.*, 1982).

Because of the framework of legislation, maladjustment is a formal term. Before a child is transferred to a special school, he or she must be formally assessed. That assessment is usually undertaken by a representative of the local schools psychological service. At the same time as the number of places in

---

*Superscript numbers refer to numbered notes at the end of each chapter.

maladjusted schools stopped expanding another, more informal, network of educational provision for difficult pupils began to grow. 'Sin bins', 'support centres' and 'special units' appeared for the first time in the late 1970s and have already attracted considerable comment and research (Grunsell, 1979; Advisory Centre for Education, 1980a; Mortimore *et al.*, 1983.). Such units may be attached to a single school although more frequently they draw pupils from a number of schools in a particular locality. Although educational psychologists may be involved in the referral procedures, assessment is more informal and referral often remains more in the hands of ordinary teachers and unit staff. The 1970s saw a rapid increase in the number of such units. In 1978 a survey undertaken by Her Majesty's Inspectorate (H.M.I.) revealed 239 units in England (H.M.I., 1978a). Two years later the Advisory Centre for Education carried out their own survey throughout the U.K. and identified 439 units (A.C.E., 1980b). Ten years earlier such special units were almost unheard of.

Whether difficult pupils are eventually sent to special schools, special units, or, as in the case of David referred to above, simply remain in their ordinary classrooms, the most common explanation for their behaviour is that they are 'maladjusted'. Those who are assigned to special schools are presumably the most seriously disturbed but many other pupils are considered maladjusted too[2].

As a concept, maladjustment is a psychological one. Some psychologists concerned with maladjusted children work in a Freudian tradition of psychiatry while others draw on behaviourist learning theories. Whatever their theoretical allegiances, psychologists have had a profound impact on policy and practice with difficult pupils. Their influence stretches back into the last century (Sully, 1896, 1913; Underwood, 1955) and is today firmly established in the profession of educational psychology.[3] As has already been noted, the main foci for this book are the more recently established sociological and social psychological theories of school deviance. However, because psychology has been and remains such an important influence on educational thought in this area, some preliminary discussion of this tradition, and particularly the concept of maladjustment, is necessary.

Maladjustment — Its Nature and Aetiology

Maladjustment is a notoriously vague term. In 1950 the Underwood Committee, set up to inquire into the medical, educational and social problems of maladjusted children, failed to come up with any precise definitions or give an accurate estimate of the size of the 'problem' (Underwood, 1955). The nearest the Committee came to a definition was as follows:

> In our view a child may be regarded as maladjusted who is developing in ways that have *a bad effect on himself or his fellows* and cannot without help, be remedied by his parents, teachers and other adults in ordinary contact with him. (p. 22, my emphasis)

The Committee emphasized that maladjustment was not a medical term diagnosing a medical condition, rather it was a relative term referring to modes of behaviour or habits that fell outside the limits of what was accepted as 'normal'. It was easier to recognize by its symptoms than to accurately define. Any or all of the following were considered as possible symptoms indicating maladjustment:

(i)   nervous disorders,
(ii)   habit disorders,
(iii) behaviour disorders,
(iv)   organic disorders,
(v)   psychotic behaviour, and
(vi)   educational and vocational difficulties.

Given that the term maladjustment was relatively new in educational circles it is perhaps not surprising that the Underwood Committee failed to give a more precise definition. As we have seen, at the time of their Report, the numbers of pupils officially defined as maladjusted was relatively small. However, 20 years later (perhaps partly as a result of the very vague and broad definition adopted by the Underwood Report) provision had increased dramatically. Interestingly, however, Laslett (1977a) in his important book *Educating Maladjusted Children* was unable to be any more precise on the nature of maladjustment. For him a maladjusted child was one

> whose behaviour and emotional difficulties, however caused, had prevented the child from benefiting from the ordinary social and educational experiences of home and school, and whose difficulties will persist unless help is given by those with appropriate skill — a child for whom failure in learning and in socially approved situations is more probable than success. (p. 3)

Once again Laslett emphasized that there were many different symptoms of maladjustment. All sorts of abnormal and antisocial behaviour could be seen as indicating an underlying problem. As Wilson and Evans (1980) admit, it is easy enough to identify the seriously disturbed child who fails to function with even minimal competence, yet the majority of those who are assessed as maladjusted do not fall into this category 'and we are far from certain about the cause and nature of their difficulties' (p. 21). Given the very real difficulty of defining maladjustment with any accuracy, it is perhaps not surprising that some commentators have come to the rather cynical conclusion that maladjusted pupils are those who end up in maladjusted schools.

Despite the difficulty of accurately defining maladjustment, a great deal of sophisticated theoretical inquiry into its aetiology has been undertaken by psychologists. As was noted above, these theories fall into two broad traditions. First, there are psychodynamic theories, derived at least in part from the work of Freud and, secondly, there are behavioural learning theories derived originally from writers such as Pavlov, Thorndike and Skinner. Each will be considered briefly in turn.

Psychodynamic Theories of Maladjustment

Psychodynamic theorists consider maladjusted behaviour to be a symptom of deep-seated pathology arising from repressed psychic energy. The many different symptoms which we interpret as maladjusted behaviour are the ways in which children find some outlet for these repressed feelings. Writers such as Winnicott, Horney and Bowlby, drawing as they do on the work of Freud, lay great emphasis on the fact that it is during infancy that the foundations of emotional health are laid. Inadequate or interrupted parenting at this critical stage can, at a later date, lead to antisocial behaviour.

For example, Bowlby, (1953, 1971, 1973) has argued that maladjustment can be the result of 'maternal deprivation'. He suggests that children do not become attached to a particular adult until they are about six months old. If a child is deprived of his or her mother (or mother substitute (Rutter, 1972)) then this can be emotionally devastating. It can leave the child insecure, anxious, hostile and angry and these feelings may at a later stage be directed at other adults in the child's life. Winnicott (1957) also emphasized the importance of continuity of 'mothering' during the critical dependency stage. It is when a child has started to build a relationship and is then deprived of it for some reason that the experience is traumatic and can lead to maladjustment. As a result, maladjusted children may not only engage in antisocial behaviour, they may also be excessively demanding, claiming emotional support from any adult who shows an interest in them.

For Bowlby the critical factor leading to maladjustment was the loss of the 'mother' figure. Stott (1963, 1982), on the other hand, has emphasized that children do not have to be physically deprived of those who 'mother them' to suffer from maternal deprivation. If parents are unwilling or unable to engage in close emotional relationships with their children then this can be just as much of a form of 'deprivation' as if those parents leave physically. Other writers have also emphasized the importance of the quality of parenting. For example, Winnicott suggested that parents should provide unconditional love for their children even when they express hostility. A child who does not experience this unconditional care may, at a later stage, come to disown his or her own feelings of frustration and anger and project these onto others. The child, in Winnicott's terms, is 'unintegrated'.

Horney (1949) also emphasized the nature of parenting that children experience. If a child is constantly exposed to anxiety or hostility during his or her early years then that child is unlikely to develop the emotional resources to cope with stressful situations in the future. For example, some children will be excessively compliant, having no emotional resources of their own, while others will be constantly aggressive even when this is inappropriate. Yet others will become detached. Stott describes similar responses in maladjusted children. Because of their inadequate parenting, these children are unable to learn from their experiences about how to respond more appropriately to those around them.

Learning Theory

In contrast to psychodynamic theorists, learning theorists (Bandura and Walters, 1969; Bandura, 1971) do not believe that maladjusted behaviour is the product of an underlying pathology or emotional difficulty. Deviant behaviour is not indicative of anything else except that children have learnt such inappropriate behaviour through 'imitation' or 'reinforcement'. Learning theorists argue that behaviour is learnt. Children will imitate the behaviour of those around them and they are particularly susceptible to learning when they are emotionally aroused. If they witness violent and aggressive behaviour at home there is a strong chance that they will learn it because of the emotional arousal it creates in them.

Learning theorists also argue that behaviour can be learnt through reinforcement. Acceptable behaviour may be reinforced by attention, praise or reward, but unacceptable behaviour can also be learned in this way too. For example, some 'inadequate parents' may not respond to their children when they make reasonable demands for attention, yet they may respond when those children become aggressive or violent. In this way parents may be rewarding and reinforcing antisocial behaviour patterns. Even worse, according to Laslett (1977a), are parents who covertly reinforce unacceptable behaviour (for example, laughing with the child at authority figures) and then punish the child when their patience runs out.

One further factor which learning theorists argue often leads to antisocial behaviour at school is that some children have not been taught to 'discriminate' appropriate 'cues' for behaviour. If they have learnt that some authority figures are unreliable and inadequate (again these may be parents) then they may see all adults in this way and display hostility and suspicion towards them. Some children may also have not learned how to discriminate social contexts adequately. Aggressive or assertive behaviour may be acceptable in some situations, for example on the football field, but quite unacceptable in the classroom. Pupils have to be taught, if they have not already learned, how to discriminate social contexts in order to adapt their behaviour appropriately.

As one might imagine, the strategies for dealing with maladjusted behaviour advocated by psychodynamic theorists and social learning theorists are rather different. For the psychodynamic theorist it is inadequate to concentrate on unacceptable behaviour alone. If a child is stopped from being violent in the classroom, then it is assumed that his or her psychic energy will have to find an alternative outlet through, for example, truancy or theft. The only real cure for maladjusted behaviour is to address the causes themselves. In extreme cases this may demand psychotherapy, but in more moderate cases it can be achieved by providing the child with the emotional warmth or security he or she was missing in early childhood. Those working with such children have to learn to 'live through' the child's aggression and hostility until they learn to trust themselves and the adults in their lives (Dockar-Drysdale, 1968; Pringle, 1974; Rutter, 1975).

Learning theorists by contrast, concentrate explicitly on the deviant behaviour itself. They try to establish more satisfactory forms of behaviour through a programme of behaviour modification. For example, teachers may be urged to ignore unacceptable classroom behaviour and reward any signs of more positive response. Pupils may be taught new 'social skills' so that they have a wider repertoire of responses especially when dealing with authority figures, and they may be taught more efficient skills of discrimination in order to help them behave more appropriately (Bandura, 1971; Poteet, 1974; Leach and Raybould, 1977).

These then are the dominant psychological theories used to explain and treat maladjusted behaviour in school. Such theories have for many years been widely influential on educational policy and provision. However, during the last 25 years sociological theories have gained increasing acceptance and have, to some extent, challenged the hegemony of the psychological perspective. As in other areas of educational debate (for example on educational achievement) the psychological perspective on indiscipline was first challenged in the 1960s by the results of large-scale positivist studies which revealed social patterning in disruption and truancy (Douglas and Ross 1964, 1965; Davie *et al.*, 1972). Such studies showed that disruption and truancy were systematically associated with low social class, with educational under-achievement and with areas of residence, particularly inner cities. Such findings challenged the idea that the relationship between indiscipline at school and the child's psychological development was as straightforward as had been assumed. Many people felt that the results challenged the very notion of maladjustment itself. The hunt for sociological explanations was on.

During the 1970s and 1980s theoretical developments within the sociology of education itself have encouraged the elaboration of a variety of explanations of difficult school behaviour. In the early 1970s sociological research tended to concentrate on the internal working of schools themselves (this could perhaps more appropriately be characterized as social psychology). More recently, largely through the influence of neo-Marxist theories, debate within the sociology of education has broadened to include a discussion of the relationship between education, the economy and the state. In each phase of development within the sociology of education, positivism, institutional studies, and neo-Marxist studies, the topic of school deviance has been a central one. The result is a rich variety of theory and research.

Outline Of The Book

In the first chapter indiscipline at school is placed in an historical context. By examining such evidence as is available from three historical periods, it is argued that school deviance has been a permanent feature of mass schooling. Whether one looks at the secondary modern in the years after the last war, the elementary schools at the turn of the century, or early forms of provided schooling before compulsory attendance was introduced, there is plenty of evidence that pupils and their parents have always challenged the moral authority of their teachers. What is distinctive about the contemporary period, it is argued, is the continuity of public concern about indiscipline. This public concern is not only reflected in the massive increase in specialist provision for maladjusted pupils already described, it is also reflected in the wide variety of theory and research that is the main focus of this book.

Closely allied with the psychological theories of maladjustment outlined above have been positivist approaches to research. Positivism is the application of principles and methods derived from the natural sciences to social phenomena. These methods have been used to study biological, psychological and sociological dimensions of deviant behaviour. In Chapters 2 and 3 the main principles of positivism are presented and two forms of positivistic research are considered. In Chapter 2 'individual positivism' is discussed. In this tradition researchers have attempted to identify the 'causes' of school deviance by plotting correlations between its incidence and other factors in pupils' lives (personality, family break-up, academic achievement, social class background). Whatever the nature of the initial causes, individual positivists argue that it is in the child that the underlying pathology is located. Any attempt to reduce indiscipline in school must therefore be directed at the pupils themselves. In Chapter 3 a more recent form of positivist research, entitled 'institutional positivism', is considered. In this tradition different dimensions of school procedures and organization (forms of discipline, teaching methods, etc.) have been operationalized, measured and systematically related to the incidence of indiscipline in different schools. The promise of institutional positivism is that by the application of rigorous scientific research methods, those factors of school organization and procedure that cause indiscipline can be isolated. From this perspective it is the school, rather than the child, that is 'pathological' and any intervention should be addressed in the first instance to the school itself.

As has already been noted, a distinctive feature of much psychological and positivistic writing is that disruption and truancy are seen as abnormal. Indiscipline may be indicative of an underlying pathology or inadequate learning, but whatever the cause, it is assumed that as a form of behaviour it is fundamentally different from that adopted by the majority of the population. By contrast, most other sociological perspectives assume that deviant behaviour is essentially 'normal'. Violence, disruption or truancy may indeed be *unacceptable* but they are 'normal' forms of behaviour in the sense that they are attempts by pupils to come to terms with the specific circumstances they face: they are ways of coping. Such a perspective necessarily broadens the focus of theory and research to include an analysis of the context in which pupils find themselves as well as an analysis of their forms of response.

In Chapter 4 two interrelated theories that have been widely influential in establishing the legitimacy of a sociological perspective on school deviance are considered. These are anomie theory and status deprivation theory. Anomie theorists argue that deviant behaviour is one way people adapt when they are frustrated in the achievement of their goals. A range of different adaptations can be adopted by pupils (for example, intransigence, ritualism, rebellion) depending on the degree to which they remain committed to the goals of the school and the conventional means of achieving them. In status deprivation theory (which is a development of anomie theory) it is argued that some pupils, especially those who are academically unsuccessful, develop a deviant response to school because they are 'status deprived' in a context that confers and emphasizes status and achievement. In this tradition the social nature of the deviant response to school is emphasized. Groups of pupils, it is argued, who find themselves in the same low status position develop a common response to school; they produce a 'subculture' with its own anti-school values. Such subcultures have the twin purpose of conferring status on those who conform to their anti-school values and allowing the pupils to hit back at the very educational system that deprived them of status in the first place.

In Chapter 5 symbolic interactionist theories of school deviance are presented. As a sociological theory, symbolic interactionism emphasizes the importance of subjectivity. Pupils are seen as active agents in constructing their own interpretation of the world. *They* choose how to interpret their experience of schooling and in the light of their interpretation they 'negotiate' various forms of behaviour. Even conformist behaviour has to be negotiated between pupils and teachers. Deviance occurs when pupils refuse to accept their teacher's definition of what is appropriate. In this chapter two groups of interactionist studies are considered. First, 'appreciative studies' are presented which attempt to document the subjective views of schooling of different groups of pupils. The second group of studies focuses on classroom interaction itself analysing the process of negotiation through which conformist and deviant forms of behaviour are established by pupils.

Chapter 6 introduces labelling theory. Labelling is distinct from other approaches to indiscipline at school in that it does not focus on the 'causes' of such behaviour but on the way in which teachers respond to it. Researchers in the tradition argue that if teachers constantly and publically label pupils as disruptives or truants this can, in certain circumstances, influence the child's self-concept. Pupils who accept their teacher's view of them as deviant may try to live up to these labels and engage in more rather than less challenging behaviour. Most research on labelling in school has been undertaken within a symbolic interactionist perspective. However, in recent years other theories and perspectives on this process have been developed. Both phenomenologists and neo-Marxists have analysed labelling at school though they necessarily highlight different aspects of the process. All three perspectives (symbolic interactionism, phenomenology and neo-Marxism) are considered.

In Chapters 7 and 8 indiscipline at school is placed in a broader context and the issues of race, class and gender, occasionally touched on by other theoretical traditions, are considered more systematically. In exploring the relationship between school deviance and these wider dimensions of social structure, contemporary neo-Marxist writing on social and cultural reproduction has been extremely influential. In Chapter 7, a number of theories of social and cultural reproduction are briefly outlined and some early attempts to locate school deviance as a form of conscious class resistance are considered. In Chapter 8 a more sophisticated approach to reproduction, developed particularly by Willis (1977), is presented. From this perspective, school deviance is not necessarily seen as a form of conscious class resistance, rather it is a form of 'cultural production'; a creative response which is nevertheless located in a specific institutional and class cultural context. Willis' work is primarily concerned with social class as a fundamental factor in structuring the lives of the boys he studied. Other research has employed a similar perspective to analyse issues of race and gender and these studies are also discussed within this chapter.

In the final chapter of the book a summary and synthesis is presented. By drawing on and extending Willis' notion of 'cultural production' it is argued that deviant behaviour at school can be used to explore and express many different factors that impose on pupils' lives. Pupils, especially as they grow older, may indeed use disruption and truancy to explore issues of gender, race and social class which structure their lives. However, indiscipline can also be used to explore many other issues as well. It can be used to explore and express emotional difficulties deriving from personal relationships outside school, it can also be used as a response to institutional life, especially the experience of academic failure. Disruption and truancy can have many meanings for pupils and these meanings can become cumulative. Pupils may initially reject their schooling because of the inadequacies of a particular teacher or because they are experiencing some emotional difficulties at home. If the child is an academic failure as well, challenging the authority of teachers will have an added valency. As pupils grow older they can use indiscipline to explore their feelings about the relationship between schooling and the lives they see themselves leading when they leave school. For some pupils such experimentation may show that school has little or no utility. Once again, indiscipline which may have begun for quite different reasons, can come to have added potency. Given the cumulative nature of the meaning of school deviance it is argued that it is not surprising that indiscipline is such persistent feature of school life.

Notes

1. The 1944 Education Act established the principle that all children should be educated in accordance with their age, ability and aptitudes and recognized that some children (those who were handicapped) would require special educational provision. Initially five categories of handicapped pupil were proposed: educationally subnormal, physically handicapped, blind, deaf and epileptic. In 1945 a further six categories were added including the category 'maladjusted'.

2. This was certainly the view of the headteacher quoted at the beginning of this chapter. He considered that 10% of the pupils at his school were to some degree maladjusted.

3. For examples of two early psychological investigations of maladjusted behaviour at school see McFie (1934) and Milner (1938).

CHAPTER ONE

Lessons From History

Most pupils believe that they and their teachers have different interests. In their view it is his business to exact of them hard service, theirs to escape from it. It is his privilege to make laws; theirs to evade them. He is benefited by their industry, they by their indolence; he is honoured by their obedience, they by their independence. From the infants school to the professional seminary this moral warfare exists. (*English Journal of Education*, 1858:373)

Indiscipline at school is a complex phenomena; children may be violent, disruptive or play truant for a multitude of different reasons. Sometimes it may be because they are actively encouraged to do so by their parents, at other times because they are hitting back at parents. Alternatively, disruption and truancy can be directed at a school system which is considered to be irrelevant, unfair, unnecessarily oppressive or, it can be a form of expression when pupils are unhappy or emotionally disturbed. It can also be an expression of sheer fun.

In this book it will be argued that all of these motivations can be seen in contemporary forms of disaffection from school, yet it is also important to recognize that indiscipline amongst school children is nothing new; pupils have always posed a challenge for their teachers. In the seventeenth century they were apparently often armed, and violent mutinies were not uncommon (Ariès, 1960). All of the best public schools seem to have been razed to the ground by their pupils at least once in their history (Ogilvie, 1953). This book is concerned with less dramatic events. It focuses on the truancy, classroom disruption and occasional violent outbursts that occur at some stage in most schools. How frequent such occurrences are today is hard to gauge.[1] What is certain is that indiscipline is a recurrent feature of school life though its nature and form are necessarily historically and institutionally specific.

During the last 20 years there has been something of a 'moral panic'[2] about disruption and truancy. Features have regularly appeared in the press documenting the 'growing tide' of indiscipline in our schools;[3] teachers' unions have conducted regular surveys of their members documenting their continued anxiety;[4] policies have been established at national and school level[5], and a vast body of writing and research has been undertaken.

The objective here is to provide some limited sense of history for this contemporary concern about school deviance. A full and systematic history of the topic remains to be written;[6] this chapter is less ambitious. Its purpose is simply to assess such evidence of indiscipline at school as is readily available in three historical periods — the first half of the nineteenth century, the beginning of the twentieth century and the 1950s.[7]

One of the difficulties of providing such an historical account is that until the 1960s there was little systematic investigation of the topic. One might speculate on the reasons for this neglect. It may be that there was a conspiracy of silence amongst those in authority concerned to protect their reputations (Boyson, 1975, suggests that this is still the case). Alternatively, it may be that teachers and inspectors 'distorted' the real meaning of children's behaviour by writing it off as moral depravity, emotional disturbance or even original sin (Humphries, 1981). Yet again it may be that the disaffected minority were thought of as inevitable — like the poor, always with us but deserving little serious attention. Whatever the reason, neglect there was and recovering the history of school deviance therefore poses serious problems. As a consequence we must turn to less conventional sources of evidence than those favoured by contemporary sociologists; oral histories, diaries, biographies and semi-fictional accounts of schooling must, at least in part, form our evidence in order to recover some of this 'history from below'. Whether such evidence gives a 'true' picture of disruption and truancy in earlier periods is impossible to say. All that can be said with any certainty is that challenging behaviour at school is nothing new. As will be shown in the first period to be considered, it has a history as long as mass education itself.

Unwelcome Charity? Challenges to Pre-compulsory Schooling

National Education the Great Need

The discipline of slavery is unknown
Amongst us; hence the more do we require
The discipline of virtue; order else
Cannot subsist, nor confidence nor peace.
Thus duties rising out of good possessed
And prudent caution needful to avert
Impending evil, equally require
That the whole people should be taught and trained;
So shall licentiousness and black resolve
Be rooted out and virtuous habits take
Their place; and a genuine piety descend
Like an inheritance from age to age

With such foundations laid, avaunt the fear
Of numbers crowded on their native soil,
For the prevention of all healthy growth,
Through mutual injury! Rather in the law
Of increase, and the mandate from above,
Rejoice!
(Wordsworth, quoted in the *English Journal of Education*, 1844:116)

The rise of mass schooling in Britain was intimately bound up with the development of the modern industrial city. The great movement of population at the end of the eighteenth and the beginning of the nineteenth centuries from the land to the town proved irreversible. The foundation of the industrial working class in its characteristic environment — the industrial city — was accomplished at this time. Industrial capitalism may have made England the 'Workshop of the World' but in the same movement it created the urban working class as a massive social, political and economic force.

As many commentators have suggested (Williams, 1961; Johnson, 1970; Grace, 1978) it was middle class concern about the new urban poor that was one of the main forces behind the expansion of mass education in the first half of the nineteenth century. That concern focused on a variety of issues, but two were particularly important. First, the massive growth in juvenile crime and, secondly, the growing politicization of the working class exemplified in the 1840s by the Chartist movement. Pearson (1983) links the two in his evocative phrase 'the artful Chartist dodger'.

That the industrial working class was a *political* force to be reckoned with was something that was noted by social analysts of vastly different political persuasions. Engels wrote in 1845:

> If the centralisation of population stimulates and develops the property holding class, it forces the development of the workers yet more rapidly. The workers begin to feel as a class as a whole ... the great cities are birthplaces of labour movements; in them the workers first began to reflect on their own condition and to struggle against it; in them the opposition between the proletariat and bourgeoisie first made itself manifest .... Without the great cities and their forcing influence on the popular intelligence the working class would be far less advanced than it is today. (Engels, 1969:152)

For both Engels and Marx (Marx and Engels, 1969) the industrial city was a good and an evil. It was to be condemned because it symbolized all the evils of capitalism, but at the same time it constituted the necessary conditions for the development of the workers' movement to overthrow it.

Many other commentators were equally aware of the growing politicization of the urban working class. For example, James Kay Shuttleworth (later to become the first Secretary to the Privy Council's Committee on Education) like Engels, carried out a detailed study of that epitome of new industrial towns — Manchester. What he saw alarmed him. In 1839 he wrote:

> A great change has taken place in the moral and intellectual state of the working classes during the last half century. Formerly they considered their poverty and suffering, in so far as they thought about its origin at all, as inevitable, now, rightly or wrongly, they attribute their sufferings to political causes; they think that by a change in political institutions their condition can be enormously ameliorated.[8]

Many sections of the Victorian middle classes saw the new urban poor as a potential threat to the established order, and believed education to be the way of staving off such insurrection. Education became one of the strongest early Victorian obsessions. Repression was not enough, some means had to be found of establishing an inner attachment of the urban poor to society's goals. What was needed was a positive commitment to social order and that was to be achieved through education. As one commentator wrote in 1831:

> The foundations of real security are beyond and above the law. Outrage and attack may and ought to be put down; but no severity of punishment will prevent them from breaking out anew. And hence, if we were to have perfect security ... we should show the people that it is for their advantage that it should be preserved inviolate.[9]

The threat of political insurrection was not the only reason schools were needed. There was also a major concern about the rapid rise in juvenile delinquency. For example, in about 1845, an advertisement appeared in ten London newspapers offering a £100 prize for the best essay on 'That fearful and growing prevalence of juvenile depravity'. The result was the publication in 1849 of Henry Worsley's prize winning essay 'Juvenile Depravity' which documented both the rapid growth of juvenile crime and the reasons for it. His statistics revealed that crime generally had increased five-fold since the beginning of the century, while the population had not doubled. Juveniles (those between 15 and 20 years of age) who accounted for not quite one-tenth of the population made up one-quarter of those convicted. This over-representation by juveniles in the crime statistics was the same in any district town or country, but overall it was the cities that revealed the most serious problems. 'Crime is more precocious in the neighbourhood of large towns, but most of all so in the metropolis' (Worsley, 1849:7). Clearly something had to be done.

> The overwhelming mass of vice and crime, now deluging our land ... the increasing degeneracy of our juvenile population — the frightful statistics of intemperance as well as the inherent connection of drunkenness with far more than half our misery, destitution and sin — constitute a most powerful warrant of appeal to every class of our fellow countrymen. (Worsley, 1849:247)

What was needed was firstly a national temperance movement with the example being set by those in authority and secondly an extended education system.

Worsley was not alone in his observations about the rapid rise of crime. As Pearson (1983) points out his was one of dozens of books, pamphlets and letters to be published at the time on this topic. The statistics varied somewhat but the underlying message was the same — juvenile crime was dramatically increasing and education should form a central part of the policy for combating it. As one essayist wrote in 1867: 'Which is best — to pay for the policemen or the schoolmaster — the prison or the school?'[10] Education and crime were considered two sides of the same coin.

As a consequence of these twin concerns about crime and political insurrection a primary objective of the education that was to be offered to the new urban poor was moral training. As Kay Shuttleworth himself put it:

> In every English proprietor's domain there ought to be, as in many cases there are, school-houses with well-trained masters, competent and zealous to rear the population in obedience to the laws, in submission to their superiors and to fit them to strengthen the institutions of their country by their domestic virtues, their sobriety, their industry and forethought.[11]

This concern with moral training ran throughout educational developments of the first half of the nineteenth century. It was implicit in the missionary spirit of the Sunday School Movement that became so important in the industrial north and Midlands at the end of the eighteenth century; it was explicit in the Ragged School Movement that focused on the children of the 'depraved and vicious' poor in the inner cities 30 years later. It was also implicit in the structure and organization of Bell and Lancaster's monitorial system with their emphasis on real and mechanical discipline as well as in Kay Shuttleworth's more liberal notions of the morally superior pupil teacher. In all of these movements a concern with moral training, and most particularly religious moral training, was to the fore. Teachers were expected to 'save and gentle, elevate and refine, make rational and efficient the urban working class' (Grace, 1978:21). Given such an agenda it is not surprising that there is at least circumstantial evidence to suggest that to begin with some working class children and their families resisted this imposed education both through their behaviour and through non-attendance.

Behaviour

At this historical distance the degree of opposition and indiscipline that teachers faced in their classrooms at the beginning of the nineteenth century is very difficult to gauge. However, from such evidence as is available we might surmise that some children were unwilling to be 'civilized' without a struggle.

One rare insight into the life of a Ragged School in 1849 is provided by a teacher whose diary was published a year later in order to 'convince some who need to be instructed in the great work to be done before the education of the people is effected'.[12] Reflecting on his first day the teacher noted:

No school can possibly be worse than this ... the very appearance of one's coat is to them a badge of class and respectability — although they may not know the meaning of the word, they know very well or at least feel, that we are the representatives of beings with whom they have ever considered themselves at war. This is not theory but fact. (p. 5)

Opposition to this new teacher often came in the most startling form:

I had occasion to punish a boy slightly this morning; he swore and blasphemed most horribly and rushed from the school. I took little notice of this display and sat down calmly to hear the class with which I was engaged ... I was suddenly startled by a large stone passing my ear ... I got out of reach of the stones thrown into the window and continued the lesson. Several followed, half a dozen at least. He was ready in the court with a brick in his hand to have his revenge when I came out. With some difficulty I got out to the lane without being obliged to run ... I considered it best to call at the police station to ask for a convoy. This was readily granted. (p. 6).

Other attempts at discipline by this teacher brought down the wrath of the mothers who would rush into the classroom and abuse him in 'no measured terms'. Not surprisingly he soon learned that he had to treat his pupils in a more circumspect manner. Severe punishment could result in an instant rebellion 'and we could not get over the storm'. Kindness was also ineffectual, 'rather a mixture of all kinds of legitimate expedience must be used.' (p. 13).

The Ragged Schools were intended by their very nature 'to boldly go' amongst the most 'depraved' and 'vicious' sections of the urban poor. Opposition was to be expected. In other schools teachers were able to administer more traditional forms of punishment but the degree and severity of punishment imposed provide circumstantial evidence that some children in ordinary schools were difficult to contain. Joseph Lancaster, for example, argued that his 'Monitorial System', which became popular in the first 30 years of the nineteenth century, was such an efficient 'machine' that the personal authority of the teacher was replaced by the authority of 'the system'.

However, indiscipline was still expected as is implied in the elaborate system of punishment devised by Lancaster. In the first place monitors were to give out a card to each offender on which was written the nature of the offence.

On a repeated or frequent offence, after admonishion has failed, the lad to whom he presented the card has liberty to put a wooden log around his neck, which serves him as a pillory and with this he is sent to his seat. This machine may weigh from four to six pounds, some more and some less. The neck is not pinched or closely confined — it is chiefly burdensome by the manner in which it encumbers the neck, when the delinquent turns to right or left. While it rests on the shoulders, the equilibrium is preserved; but, on the least motion one way or the other, it is lost, and the log operates as a dead weight upon the neck. Thus, he is confined to sit in his proper position. If this is unavailing, it is common to fasten the legs of offenders together with wooden shackles: one or more, according to the offence. The shackle is a piece of wood about a foot, sometimes six or eight inches long, and tied to each leg. When shackled, he cannot walk but in a very slow, measured pace: being obliged to take six steps, when confined, for two when at liberty. ... Frequent or older offenders are yoked together sometimes, by a piece of wood that fastens around their necks: and, thus confined, they parade the school, walking backwards — being obliged to pay very great attention to their footsteps, for fear of running against any object that might cause the yoke to hurt their necks or keep from falling down. Four or six can be yoked together in this way. (Lancaster, 1805:101–2)[13]

Lancaster, not surprisingly, was able to boast that with this system of education corporal punishment was unnecessary — indeed as a Quaker it was against his principles! Corporal punishment was certainly alive and well in other schools during the period. In 1845, an H.M.I. survey of 163 schools revealed that 145 used corporal punishment — canes, sticks, ferules, rulers, straps or taws (straps with three, five or seven tails) and birch rods. The comments of some of the teachers who used corporal punishment most frequently are very revealing.

> 'Strap very often' — a tolerable school rather deficient in discipline.
> 'Cane very often' — a very bad, undisciplined and ignorant school.
> 'Cane very frequently' — the worst school (I think) in moral tone and discipline in the whole district.
> 'Cane and strap frequently' — a fair village school but the children are inattentive and nervous.

These comments by teachers are brought to life by a rare pupil's view of school life at the time.

> One did not learn much, but the place was full of feeling. It was so easy to get a beating for one thing. Some boys could not sit through a day without 'holding out their hands' or a week without a real thrashing. While the thrashing proceeded, the school simmered. Would a boy cry? Was the master hitting harder than usual? It might be oneself soon. Life was uncivilised in school . . . [15]

Clearly schools in the early nineteenth century were for many children harsh and unpleasant places to be. If the teachers had a civilizing mission it would seem that with some children it had to be achieved by the strap or the cane. Such children probably considered it fortunate that their parents did not expect them to attend school regularly or for very long.

Attendance

In considering the evidence for school deviance in the early stages of mass schooling it is important to recognize the role of parents as well as children. For parents attendance was often a major issue. For example, Laqueur (1976) reports that many parents continued to opt for their own forms of private education at least until the middle of the nineteenth century. In a testimony to the Parliamentary Inquiry into the Education of the Poorer Classes in 1837, Kay Shuttleworth had to admit that publicly funded schools often met with little success in attracting pupils even when they paid a bounty. A case in point was the National School at Granby Row in Manchester built to accommodate 500 but actually half empty. Yet it was not that the people rejected education; what they rejected, at least for a while, was the formal education provided through state and church support. As Laqueur comments, Kay Shuttleworth did not tell the Committee about the real educational ecology of the area around Granby Row. While the National Schools stood half empty it seems that at least seven other private venture schools flourished within a 500-yard radius of its door: 'with free schooling on the back door, parents nevertheless preferred to pay 4–8d per week to send their children to the allegedly inferior private schools' (Laqueur, 1976: 197).

Why was it that parents at first resisted these free or at least subsidized schools? Laqueur suggests a number of reasons. Working class families, it would seem, were suspicious of something provided for nothing; they suspected ulterior motives and an eventual increase in their taxes. They also resented teachers who self-consciously placed themselves above and outside the community. More significant from our point of view, the discipline they sought to impose was thought to be either obnoxious or at best irrelevant to elementary education. As the Secretary to the National Society commented:

> Parents will, in their ignorance, not value the school according to the kind of instruction they give, but they will take into account whether they are allowed to break the rules or not. They resist the discipline of our schools to a surprising extent; they do not like the obligation of attending fixed hours and conforming to rules, having clean dress and short and tidy hair.[16]

By contrast, private schools, Laqueur argues, took their clients' poverty into account. Without adequate heat, soap or clothing, standards of appearance and cleanliness, however desirable in themselves, were difficult to maintain. These schools were more closely attuned to the rhythms of working class life than their public competitors. Attendance was sporadic for the working class child, often totalling no more than 18 months to two years of education between the ages of five and 11. Pupils would attend for a few days here and a couple of weeks there when their family could afford the school pence or when they were not working. Private schools accepted and understood this pattern, their informal structure and organization responding to the poverty of the communities that they served.

However, publically financed schools eventually won the day

and by the middle of the nineteenth century provided the majority of school places. Nevertheless, parents still tried to use these schools in their own way. Attendance remained brief, the average length of time spent in school not rising above two and a half years until after 1870. Education was also mainly confined to the young. The chances of a thorough education were further diminished by the high turnover of pupils, children staying no longer than three months in some schools. As the prize essayist Worsley (1849) noted:

> There is also observable in manufacturing neighbourhoods a great readiness on the part of parents to shift children from one school to another so that at the end of two years very few of the original scholars in any school will be remaining. (p. 15)

Education was further interrupted by irregular attendance. In 1854 it was suggested that pupils on average lost one-quarter of their time at school by ill attending.[17] One teacher writing in 1843 estimated that she spent one-third to one-half of her time following up irregular attenders.[18] As a Government Inspector of Schools said at the time, 'We may be educating more, but they are, I believe younger children and stay with us less time.'[19]

So if by the middle of the nineteenth century large numbers of working class children were receiving *some* publically funded education, it was usually of short duration, confined to the young, interrupted by frequent transfers between schools and by irregular attendance. The reasons for parents not displaying the commitment to education expected of them are not difficult to find. To many parents struggling to earn a living education was a real luxury. It was not that they could not afford the school fees, rather that they would have to forego the child's wages. 'It is not for the sake of saving a penny per week but for the sake of gaining a shilling or eighteen pence that the child is transferred from school to the factory or the field.'[20] The facility with which the children could augment the family income also explains differences in attendance between the sexes and in country versus industrial areas. In agricultural districts, work was only available at particular times of the year even for older children, so parents found it worthwhile to register their children at school and withdraw them when the need arose. Their attendance was consequently seasonally erratic. By contrast, in industrial areas, permanent work could be found at a very early age, so as children grew up they were withdrawn progressively from school in increasing numbers. In both town and country, girls were more vulnerable to parental withdrawal than boys. Particularly in larger families, older girls were considered an invaluable help to their parents and even those on the registers of schools attended extremely infrequently especially as they grew older.

It would be wrong to suggest that children were never sent to school — they were in large numbers, though often it seems the families took schools on their own terms. In some cases the attraction was the free clothing provided.[21] At other times even simpler motivations seemed to operate. As one teacher noted in his diary: 'Had fires today which was a great attraction.'[22]

By and large general education in the first half of the nineteenth century was neither efficient, nor did it necessarily lead to any greater financial reward in later life. If one were going to be a farmer or a miner in adult life then the best education one could have was on the farm or down the mine working from the earliest years. It was therefore not surprising that many parents only sent their children to school as and when it suited them. In this period at least, there is therefore some evidence to show that the education system was troubled by indiscipline and a lack of support from parents. It remains to be seen if things were much better 50 years after compulsory attendance had been established.

Indiscipline and the Elementary School — The Early Twentieth Century

The Move to Compulsion

During the early Victorian period non-attendance was one of the most significant forms of resisting school. At that time most children not in school were placed in paid employment by their parents[23], but throughout the last quarter of the nineteenth century a complex series of factors served to increase school attendance. In 1870 universal provision was established but even before that attendance had started to rise. Successive Factory Acts had placed increasing restrictions on the employment of young people which had the effect of encouraging parents to send their children more regularly to school. Teachers too were more concerned with regular attendance once the revised code of 1862 linked their salaries to a system of payment by results. However, it was not until the Mundella Act of 1880 that the first real attempt was made to regulate the situation by granting Local Authorities the power to frame bye-

laws to establish compulsory attendance. From 1880 onwards it
was stipulated that no child could be absent from school
without a certificate of educational achievement unless
specifically exempted. However, until 1918 a complicated
system of exemptions existed that were finally abolished by the
Fisher Act in 1918. The same Act also raised the school leaving
age to 14.

The move to compulsion was therefore slow and confused and
the educational bye-laws were subject to continuing disputes
throughout the last two decades of the nineteenth century. Yet
the attempt to introduce compulsion was real and, therefore,
marked a major watershed in the history of mass education.
Parental opposition to schooling could no longer be open. To
challenge overtly the school authorities by removing one's child
had legal consequences. From this point on deviance at
school became marginalized. Parents might covertly support
their children when they were disruptive or played truant but
the law placed increasing constraints on them doing so openly.

Throughout the end of the nineteenth century registration
and attendance slowly increased. Table 1.1 shows the increase
in numbers of children on school registers from 1873 to 1900
which rose continually even before the Mundella Act. Actual
attendance did not rise so fast and the rate of 70% was not
achieved until 1895.

Two further aspects of school attendance which are of interest
are the length of time children spent in school and their punctuality. The length of attendance increased dramatically during
the last 30 years of the century. In 1870 the average length of

Table 1.1   Registration and attendance of children at English schools,
1873–1900.

Year	Children on the registers (%)	Children in average daily attendance (%)
1873	2 218 598 (73·95)	1 482 480 (49·42)
1880	3 895 824 (77·92)	2 750 916 (55·02)
1885	4 412 148 (80·22)	3 371 325 (61·1)
1890	4 804 149 (81·61)	3 717 919 (63·2)
1895	5 299 469 (87·12)	4 325 030 (71·13)
1900	5 705 675 (87·78)	4 687 646 (72·12)

Source: Ellis (1973).

school life was only two and a half years, by 1897 it was seven years. Those who came to school were apparently more punctual too for there was a significant reduction in the volume of complaints of unpunctuality in inspectors' reports and school logs.[24].

Such changes did not always go unopposed by parents and their children. For example, proposals to raise the school leaving age in 1914 met with strong opposition in the form of school strikes in north-east Warwickshire and the striking pupils were supported by their parents and the local people. This struggle lasted for several weeks with protest meetings and a petition signed by almost 6000 people (Humphries, 1981). Humphries also reports that until 1914 there was still evidence of what he calls 'subsistence' truancy where pupils were withdrawn from school and sent to work by their parents. But despite these protests, by the beginning of the First World War the majority of the country's children were on the register of a school, and attended with reasonable regularity and punctuality. By 1922 the Chairman of the School Attendance Officers' Association was able to report to his Annual Conference that things had improved very considerably in recent years. There was less poverty, less uncleanliness, less evasion of the law and less truancy.

> Young persons do not generally object to attendance *if one excludes those who have been waiting impatiently for the day when they will be released from attendance.*[25]

By 1927 the same association argued that things were felt to be so good that 'many people questioned whether School Attendance Officers were even needed any more.[26] However, despite growing official complacency, attendance officers continued to be necessary and teachers continued to struggle with their difficult pupils though once again the nature of that struggle received little publicity.

Some of the best insights into deviance at school from the 1880s to the beginning of the Second World War are provided by Stephen Humphries (1981) in his book *Hooligans or Rebels?* Given a lack of more official forms of evidence Humphries has utilized oral histories to gain some insight into life in school at the time. He draws material from three archives of oral history plus his own interviews in order to present examples of old people reminiscing about the conflict of their school days. The result is a colourful, if highly selective, account of the working class response to school at the time.

Elementary Resistance

Humphries discusses a number of different strands of deviant behaviour at school all of which he interprets as evidence of class conflict or resistance. For example, truancy remained an important form of expression. 'Subsistence' truancy, where pupils were sent to work by their parents, was still important until the First World War; even more important were 'opportunist' and 'retreatest' truancy. These were activities children pursued with, at best, only tacit support from their parents. Opportunist truancy, Humphries suggests, was an occasional form of resistance practiced by many working class children who, several times a year, would attempt to abscond from school and play in the fields and on the beaches, to poach, to go to fairs, markets, etc., and later swimming baths and picture palaces. Although detection meant certain punishment, Humphries argues that many children were periodically lured away from the classroom by the promise of adventure, entertainment and food for free in the surrounding streets and countryside.

> If it was a glorious day, a great thing us kids used to do was to go out into the countryside . . . in those days most of the vehicles were horse-drawn and mainly flat, trolley-type on four wheels, and what we used to do was to wait for one to come along and jump on the back and go wherever that one was going. Or you would go wandering round the dock and get on the barges and try to pinch the monkey nuts that used to come in on the boat. That's what used to get you going on the mooch. I mean you did not do it very often because the punishment was fairly severe.[27]

By contrast, retreatist truancy tended to be incessant and deeply ingrained, derived from a profound aversion to school. Humphries suggests that it was usually a solitary activity, inspired by a variety of motives such as desire for independence and adventure, fear of a particular teacher, victimization because of poverty, difficulties with learning as a consequence of poor health, or a search for freedom away from the regimentation of school routine. The crucial difference between the retreatist truant and the opportunist was that the retreatist experienced such deep feelings of discontent that regular attendance became impossible.

Although truancy was important, Humphries suggests that the most potent and persistent form of opposition to schooling occurred in the classroom itself. He provides numerous examples of children subverting their school teachers by their reluctant and apathetic approach to work as well as many instances of 'larking about'.

I remember more than once a girl would go out to the front of the class and start mimicking the teacher, imitating her voice and attitude whilst someone kept 'kye' by the doors. They used to do it in the playground too when the teachers weren't around, little mincing walk, shoulders back, you know. And we'd all be killing ourselves laughing.[28]

At other times pupils' classroom opposition took on a more serious face with acts of disobedience and disorderly conduct. Amongst the boys, disobedience usually took the form of a spontaneous and volatile outburst of physical aggression and they would disrupt lessons or seek immediate revenge on authoritarian teachers by throwing ink pots or by kicking or punching them. Girls, however, tended to rely less on physical strength than on trickery and evasion to resist control. When they were drawn into conflict with authority they were more likely to resort to verbal than physical abuse, often making loud and sarcastic comments on their teacher's personal appearance. When, as a consequence, girls were caned for their insolence, they would often call on their considerable resources of artfulness in order to convince their parents that the punishment was unjustified.

Parents apparently did sometimes protest about unfair treatment of their children, particularly girls: they also challenged teachers when they used severe indiscriminate punishment against either sex. Humphries argues that such punishments did not crush resistance but in fact aggravated the tension between the working class community and the school. While parents usually accepted and approved of mild and occasional punishment, the injuries inflicted were sometimes so severe that the parents summonsed the teachers involved.

Well, we'd 'ad one teacher an' he was a big pig, a sadistic pig. He delighted in rapping kids' knuckles if you weren't paying attention, day dreaming instead of writing (respondent bangs on table) "wake up boy!, wake up boy!" Anyway, one of my pals, their name was Been, and he 'ad a younger brother Arnold in a lower class. And a kid rushed into our class an' said, "Eh, Tommy Burrows i'n't 'alf 'itting your Arnold, Wilf." So Wilf Been and Wilf Williams and me got out of our seats and rushed into Tommy Burrows' class and he was doing little Arnold and we jumped on him and we had'n down and we was going "we'll have you, leave our Arnold alone!" In the meantime someone had rushed round the next street, Water Street, and my mother was doing her washing. She was a tiny woman. She always wore my father's cap and a sack apron. She rolled 'er sleeves up, round the school into the classroom. "I'll kill you if you 'it my son!" He had hit both of us, marked us, wealed us, marked all our legs with the stick. We could 'ave sued the Education, because we were marked. It made me the worst boy in the class for hitting the teacher.[29]

School Strikes

Perhaps one of the most dramatic acts of resistance to schooling was the pupils' school strike. School strikes are rare, though some such as the Burston school strike are widely known. Others such as the nationwide protest of school children in 1911 have recently been 'rediscovered'. By scanning the press and speaking to and corresponding with elderly people, Humphries himself has discovered over 100 other school strikes between 1880 and 1939, a few of which continued for long periods. Humphries records that strikes focused on one or more of five key issues: corporal punishment; regulations concerning school hours, holidays and school leaving age; provision of free education and welfare services and payment of scholars; the appointment of teachers; and the organization of the school itself. The most common school strikes were protests against corporal punishment. Such strikes were inevitably initiated by pupils and tended to be extremely short-lived often collapsing within a few hours. Isolated protests often went unrecorded, but the nationwide wave of strikes in 1889 and 1911 aroused widespread public interest and concern.

In 1889 the schools' strike originated in Hardwick Roxburgh as a protest against discipline and rapidly spread throughout the Scottish lowlands and Tyneside areas and as far south as London, Bristol and Cardiff. The 1911 strike began in Bigyn School, Llanelli when pupils deserted their classrooms and paraded the streets after a boy was punished for passing round a piece of paper urging his friends to strike. During the following two weeks the strikes spread to 60 major towns and cities throughout Britain and aroused considerable press comment.

By and large spontaneous school strikes about corporal punishment had little support from parents. Strikes to oppose the raising of the school leaving age on the other hand received broader support. Parents also sometimes supported teachers on trade union issues. One of the most prolonged and powerful strikes by pupils was in Herefordshire in 1914 where children supported the county's National Union of Teachers' demand for salary increases. The children's resistance began at the beginning of February when in response to the union's strategy of mass resignation the Local Education Authority appointed new teachers, many of them unqualified, to replace those involved in the dispute. Pupils in towns and villages throughout the county expressed sympathy for their teachers who were, Humphries reports, amongst the lowest paid in the country. Pupils refused to be taught by the new members of staff and 70 schools were forced to close. A bitter conflict ensued in which the former members of staff enjoyed the popular support of parents, pupils and school managers and in the following weeks the Board of Education was forced to intervene to settle the dispute in the teachers' favour.

Perhaps the most famous strike of all was at Burston in Suffolk where parents eventually established an alternative strike school. The strike originated as a protest against the dismissal of Kitty and Tom Higdon from their teaching posts. The Higdons were Christian socialists and trade union activists and deeply involved in politicizing and unionizing the agricultural labour of the area. However, both pupils and parents were incensed by their victimization and a strike began on the day when the new members of staff replaced the Higdons. A strike school was set up in a local carpenter's shop but the strike attracted so much attention that it became the celebrated cause of the labour and trade union movement. As a result, enough contributions were forthcoming to build a new school which continued for two decades in opposition to the state system.

Through the use of oral histories, Humphries provides a unique insight into working class schooling at the beginning of this century. One limitation of his work is of course that we do not know how widespread the instances that he describes actually were. While it is clearly true that *some* working class children became actively involved in challenging their teachers and *some* parents prosecuted the teachers for an excessive use of corporal punishment we do not know whether these were occasional or frequent events. These are perhaps questions that must be tackled by using a rather different methodology from that adopted by Humphries. There are also important questions to be raised about his interpretation of events. Many people would question his suggestion that all forms of deviant behaviour at school should be interpreted as evidence of class resistance. This is an issue which is considered in more detail in Chapter 7.

Whatever the limitations of his work, however, Humpries' evidence does most effectively show that popular schooling at the turn of the century was not without its problems. For some pupils at least it was profoundly unpopular and that minority expressed their feelings just as clearly as disaffected pupils do today.

One factor which characterizes a great deal of today's more popular writing on the subject of indiscipline at school is the sense of 'loss'. Journalists, teachers and politicians often complain that pupils are much worse behaved today (whenever 'today' actually is) than they were five, ten or 20 years ago. One of the periods that is most frequently the focus of nostalgia, particularly for today's older teachers, is the post-war period — the 1950s. It is this period that forms the subject for the final section of this chapter.

Halcyon Days? The Case of the Post-War Secondary Modern

The passing of the 1944 Education Act was accompanied by high hopes. The new educational policy of a genuine secondary education for all would, it was hoped, produce major changes in the structure of British Society — indeed the phrase 'revolution' was used by some commentators. As Mays wrote in 1962:

> Possibly no single piece of legislation has been so charged with social and political significance as the Education Act of 1944 which is generally accepted as an important milestone on the way to the achievement of a more egalitarian society, being firmly based on the democratic belief in the necessity of full equality of opportunity. (p. 4)

The Act itself was largely based on another belief which fundamentally influenced the structure of the secondary education which was established by the Act. That was, if children do well at school, it is because they have the ability to do so and this ability can be measured.

Post-war educational provision was based on the idea that there were two main categories of pupil, those with a superior and those with an inferior intellectual ability. This concept of two types of child or two types of mind was first suggested in the Haddow Report of 1926. The Spens Committee on Secondary Education which reported in 1938 endorsed the general distinction between the more theoretical and the more practical types of mind and proposed a third category, those suitable for technical education. By 1943 when the Norwood Committee published its findings the doctrine was widely established and the tripartite system of secondary education was born. Each child was to be educated according to his or her own 'measured' ability.

In the event the social revolution was unforthcoming. During the 1950s and 1960s it slowly became apparent that the psychological model of ability and particularly of educational achievement on which the legislation was based was faulty. A series of widely publicized studies[30] demonstrated that selective secondary modern school places were more likely to be given to children from families who were better off. As Byrne *et al.* (1975) wryly commented:

> This raised the question of just how far God had favoured the middle classes when he gave out intelligence or whether to be more realistic, there were factors in the home environment or social position of children which enhanced or depressed ability. (p. 19)

Of the three types of secondary education established by the 1944 Act, grammar, technical and modern, the secondary modern schools were overwhelmingly the most significant in numerical terms. In 1956 there were 303 secondary technical schools, 1357 grammar schools and 3636 secondary modern schools. In all 67% of the country's children were being educated in secondary moderns. Given that contemporary research had repeatedly demonstrated that disruption and truancy are disproportionately associated with the educationally less successful, the post-war history of school deviance necessarily points to the secondary modern. Yet despite the fact that for nearly 30 years secondary moderns were the dominant form of secondary education in England and Wales (they still are in Northern Ireland) comparatively little has been written about them. What is clear, however, is that in many ways they were seen to be inferior to the grammar schools.

The 1944 Act had promised all three forms of education 'parity of esteem', though in 1947 the Ministry of Education stated:

> The modern school will be given a parity of conditions with other types of secondary schools; parity of esteem it must secure by its own efforts.[31]

Yet as Taylor commented in 1963:

> The promise of the first part of this statement has not been fulfilled and ... the injunction of the second is incapable of fulfilment. (Taylor, 1963: 42)

Taylor identified seven characteristics of the secondary modern all of which compared unfavourably with the grammar schools.

1. The pupils were those who had not been selected for grammar or technical school education.
2. Although many modern pupils did take public examinations their curricula were not primarily directed towards this goal.
3. The staffs of modern schools were on the whole less well qualified than those of other types of secondary schools.

4. A disproportionate number of children at secondary modern schools came from the working class, particularly semi and unskilled homes.
5. The majority of pupils left at the statutory minimum age of fifteen.
6. Because of the lower average age of the secondary modern school population their teachers received on average a lower salary than their grammar school counterparts. By the same token such schools were generally less well equipped.
7. A higher proportion of secondary modern school leavers entered semi-skilled and unskilled work.

If this characterization is correct it is not surprising that secondary moderns found it hard if not impossible to achieve the parity of esteem they were promised. It also seems possible that they would have suffered at least some degree of indiscipline amongst their pupils.

One insight into life in secondary modern schools in the 1950s is provided by a series of novels written by ex-teachers that were published at the time. Michael Croft's *Spare the Rod* published in 1954, Edward Blishen's *Roaring Boys* in 1955 and E. R. Braithwaite's *To Sir With Love* in 1955 are the best known. All three novels painted a 'blackboard jungle' image of the inner-city secondary modern. Yet each author claimed that their novels were drawn directly from their own experience as teachers and from those of friends and colleagues.

All three novels have a remarkably similar plot. In each case a young, middle class teacher (in Braithwaite's novel it has the added twist of being a black middle class teacher) takes up teaching after the war and arrives, somewhat by mistake, at an inner-city secondary modern. After the shock of the appalling behaviour of the teachers and pupils alike the hero grows wiser, recognizing the humanity buried within his fellow teachers and even the most hostile of pupils. The following extract from Michael Croft's novel illustrates the genre. John — the hero — has just arrived at the head's office on the first morning of his appointment.

> The head rose from his desk and picked up a box of pen nibs. "I'm starting you off the hard way", he said. "You'll be in charge of Class 2. That can't be helped I'm afraid. They are a first-class crowd of dyed-in-the-wool-heartbreakers. Half of them are as likely to land in borstal as anywhere else, and where the other half will land doesn't bear thinking about. I'm not putting you there because I want to but because there's no-one else to do the job. Mr. Murray has his hands full with the top class — they're a year older and a year sillier, though not so vicious —

Mr. Gubb has enough on his hands already and I daren't let Mr. Bickerstaff have them, so it falls on you."

John was disturbed at the head's description of the class, but he was even more surprised by the attitude it expressed. "I don't care what method you use with them", the head continued, "so long as you hold them down. Believe me if you can keep this lot down, you'll keep any class down."

He indicated the cupboard on the left. "There's a cane in there which I'll let you have. Only, when you use it, there are certain things you must bear in mind. First, make sure they've got their fingers stretched out to the full, and then see their thumbs are put right back out of the line of flight. Never catch them across the thumbs. We don't want any of them going home with bruised thumbs. Then remember always to cane on the left hand. They want the other hand to write with — unless you have to give them two strokes, and then it can't be helped."

John was shocked at the callousness of the head's tone. He considered caning an admission of weakness, but he dare not voice his disgust. If he did so he would show that already he despised the head.

"The other important thing", said the head "is to make sure that the boy's arm is held out full stretch. It must be stretched right out horizontally. That prevents the risk of catching him across the knees if you happen to miss the hands. You won't do that of course if you swing outwards away from the body, but with the crafty little beggers we have here you can't be too careful. Some of them wouldn't quibble over a gash in the leg if they could get us into court on the strength of it." (Croft, 1954:12—13)

Croft, Blishen and Braithwaite's novels caused something of a 'moral panic' in the mid-1950s. A similar theme was taken up by a number of newspaper articles and questions were asked in Parliament[32]. The National Union of Teachers undertook an investigation of the various allegations of indiscipline that were made although they could find no evidence to support them. Taylor (1963) suggests that the moral panic about secondary moderns in the 1950s was relatively short-lived. The popular imagination of a mainly middle class audience had been caught for a while but after everyone had frightened themselves most of them lost interest arguing that concern had been over-emphasized.

A survey of the *Times* and the *Times Educational Supplement* would certainly seem to suggest that Taylor is correct about popular opinion. During the first half of the decade (1950—6) there were increasing numbers of news items on indiscipline and truancy and regular features outlining their aetiology. For example, in 1956 the *Times Educational Supplement* reported the following speech by the Director of Education for Leicestershire.

It is far too often true that modern school pupils fail to discover any incentive and merely drift along, resentful of discipline and longing to escape. Far too often in the final year the drift away at Christmas and Easter has an unsettling effect on those who have to stay on. There is a particular difficulty too, in the education of girls. There have been many comments in recent months on the implications of the fact that adolescent girls appear to mature physically at a far earlier age than hitherto; many of them are preoccupied with sex and envying the ease with which their older friends earn high wages and buy a good time, they seek less legitimate excitement. In consequence, school and all it stands for becomes a bore, teachers are held in contempt and their boastful attitude demoralises their less adventurous classmates. It is not surprising that many teachers, particularly the unmarried ones, find themselves helpless in the face of a situation which was largely unknown to their predecessors. (Thomas, 1956)

These sorts of reports were common in the first half of the decade, yet from 1956 to 1960 there were virtually no references to difficult behaviour at all.[33] Instead of the images of the blackboard jungle the *Times Educational Supplement* in particular promoted a different view of the secondary modern with a series of glossy articles in order to show 'what is being done in our secondary modern schools and which may offer suggestions to others who work in them' (*Times Educational Supplement*, May 1957)

Yet it would perhaps be wrong to write off the earlier 1950s concern about the secondary modern as lightly as does Taylor. A middle class moral panic it may have been but that does not necessarily mean that it had no foundation in reality. Some slight support for the blackboard jungle image is provided by a case study of a boys secondary modern school made in 1962 by Partridge (1968). In many of its features the school described is identical to the fictitious ones of Croft, Blishen and Braithwaite:

The headmaster and his deputies may use a cane but other members of staff are only permitted to use a "whacker". A typical whacker is a round-edged piece of wood about two feet long with grooves carved at one end as a handle ... the prescribed way of using a whacker is to give the culprit one or two sharp strokes across the behind. It is considered to do this with such a flat piece of wood hurts the boy in an instant, but this soon leaves off and leaves no prolonged bruise. It is thought important to avoid unduly hurting or marking the child, because this may make for complications and rows with certain parents. (Partridge, 1968: 112)

Partridge asserts that in his school every member of staff used a whacker or some form of corporal punishment particularly with the lower stream boys — many teachers used it daily when boys were caught smoking, stealing, playing truant or were uncooperative in class. Partridge suggests that the problems facing young teachers in school were enormous. They needed the whacker more than anyone else.

> To inspire any awe he must administer a pretty good walloping at the first opportunity so that the boys understand from the word go that he means business. (p. 115)

If he did not the boys would 'destroy' him — fighting, throwing things and refusing to do even the simplest task.

Rather more systematic evidence on difficult behaviour in school was provided by two major studies undertaken at either end of the decade. The first was a survey of rewards and punishments in school undertaken by the N.F.E.R. (Highfield and Pinsent, 1952), the second was a survey conducted for the Newsom Report 1963. The N.F.E.R. survey was commissioned as a result of the suggestion in Parliament that corporal punishment be abolished. Out of the 724 teachers surveyed, 90% of them were strongly in favour of corporal punishment being retained at least for use with the 'difficult minority'. The wish to retain corporal punishment is unsurprising amongst British teachers; perhaps more revealing are the suggestions that teachers gave for what they saw as the five most urgent reforms necessary for the improvement of their teaching conditions. These were in rank order:

(1) Stricter parental control.
(2) Smaller classes.
(3) Better provision for retarded children.
(4) More special schools for persistently difficult children.
(5) Improved training of teachers in psychological observation and early detection of behaviour difficulties.

There is clear evidence here of a concern for discipline.

The N.F.E.R. survey also provided evidence of the number of children considered 'difficult' by their teachers. Nine county and borough divisions were surveyed and out of the 44 490 children in all types of schools in these areas approximately 7·5% were considered to be difficult. On analysis into types of schools these children were distributed as follows: primary 9·07%, secondary modern 6·88%, secondary technical 4·61%, grammar 3·96%. The analysis also indicated that in the school system as a whole the difficulties were greater in the town than in country schools and greater in lower streams. In the secondary modern sample, for instance, the incidence of difficult children was: A stream 3·47%, B stream 8·39%, C stream 11·02%.

Further evidence of the difficulties being faced by secondary modern schools was provided by the Newsom Report (1963). As part of the report on the secondary education of children of 'average and below average ability' a survey of 6000 children in 150 schools was undertaken. Pupils were divided into three ability groups — the upper quartile, the average and the lower quartile. Head teachers were asked to answer a range of questions about randomly selected pupils.

From the survey, indiscipline at school was shown to be overwhelmingly associated (at least in the eyes of head teachers) with the lowest ability group. For example, 18% of boys in this bottom group were considered to neglect their homework; 15% were thought to truant; 51% did not wear school uniform though expected to do so; and 10% were thought to be 'thoroughly difficult' in their behaviour. Amongst the girls the figures were similar. They were 22%, 18%, 36% and 7% respectively.

Although the report does not emphasize the fact in its conclusions, it also demonstrated that these 'lower ability' children were disproportionately concentrated in 'Problem Areas', that is 'areas of bad housing with a high concentration of social problems' (Newsom, 1963:186)

It would seem perhaps that the heroes of the 'blackboard jungle' novels had strayed by mistake into these difficult and often forgotten schools. As Castle (1958) commented at the time:

> In urban situations where social stability and tradition are weakest . . . where slum conditions provide no stable basis for home discipline, where classes are larger and buildings inadequate, the teacher experiences the greatest strain and is inclined to resort to severe forms of punishment in sheer self-defence. In justice to teachers in these difficult schools we must always remember that they are faced daily with disciplinary difficulties hardly known to their more fortunate colleagues. (p. 368)

Conclusion

From the evidence suggested in this chapter it is clear that the popular images of lost innocence so frequently employed by contemporary commentators on indiscipline in school are at least an exaggeration of the truth. They may even be considered a distortion. There is plenty of evidence from even a superficial survey of different historical periods to suggest that a minority of pupils have always challenged the moral authority of their teachers. It is perhaps generalizing too far from this initial survey to claim that there was *never* a golden age of pupil behaviour when children attended with regularity and did their teacher's bidding without question. Such a period may have existed. What is clear is that this golden age did not exist in the mid-1950s, in the first part of this century nor in the first half of the last century. These have been periods which in the popular mind have often retrospectively been thought of as peaceful and calm. Yet it takes only a little scratching of the surface to show that like today some pupils played truant, some were rude and disruptive and some were aggressive towards their teachers; indiscipline at school is a permanent not a purely contemporary phenomenon.

What is also apparent is that in each of these historical periods there was some form of popular moral panic about the behaviour of young people. In the mid-1950s it focused on the secondary modern following the 'blackboard jungle novels'. In 1911 it followed the national wave of school strikes and in 1840 it focused on the growing tide of juvenile crime and political insurrection. Yet significantly it would seem that on each occasion these moral panics by the respectable middle classes were relatively short-lived. The behaviour itself may not have abated but public concern certainly did. What is therefore distinctive about the modern age of schooling is that the moral panic has continued now for more than two decades. Not only has indiscipline at school aroused concern in the media, amongst M.P.s and amongst teachers themselves, it has also spawned the vast body of social research and theorizing that are the main focus of this book.

It is interesting to speculate why a concern with indiscipline is so permanent today — presumably the reasons are complex. It may indeed be that things are much worse than they ever were before, though whether this is actually the case is impossible to say. Wright (1977) provides an alternative plausible explanation which will serve as a fitting conclusion to this historical introduction.

> There are innumerable accounts of dreadful secondary modern schools in the past, and of elementary schools before the war. But the public opinion makers — the journalists, broadcasters, politicians, and one might suggest, the middle classes generally — were not usually conscious of it, or worse, did not care. It is with the coming of the comprehensive schools that these things have begun to 'crawl out of the woodwork'. Journalists, politicians and broadcasters now find *their* children are going to schools alongside youngsters who would always in the past have been hidden from sight and sound in some back-street sink school. This is no consolation to those of us who are faced with having to send our children next September to a local school. But being aware of a problem is the first step towards doing something about it and in this sense the public concern is to be welcomed. (p. 106)

Notes

1. The difficulties involved in measuring school deviance with any accuracy are explored in Chapter 2.

2. Cohen (1973) defines a 'moral panic' in the following way:

> Societies appear to be subject, every now and then, to periods of moral panic. A condition, episode, person or group of persons emerges to become defined as a threat to societal values and interests; its nature is presented in a stylised and stereotypical fashion by the mass media; the moral barricades are manned by editors, bishops, politicians and other right-thinking people; socially accredited experts pronounce their diagnoses and solutions; ways of coping are evolved or (more often) resorted to; the condition then disappears, submerges or deteriorates and becomes more visible. Sometimes the object of the panic is quite novel and at other times it is something which has been in existence long enough, but suddenly appears in the limelight. Sometimes the panic passes over and is forgotten, except in folklore and collective memory; at other times it has more serious and long-lasting repercussions and might produce such changes as those in legal and social policy or even in the way the society conceives itself. (p. 9)

3. See, for example, the *Guardian*, Friday 16 April 1982: 'Assaults "have risen to one a day" in city schools.'

4. For the latest example see the Assistant Masters and Mistresses Association Report (A.M.M.A., 1984) which reported an alarming rise in indiscipline amongst five and six-year-old pupils. See also National Association of Schoolmasters (1974, 1976).

5. See, for example, the sudden growth in the provision of sanctuaries or 'sin bins' (H.M.I., 1978).

6. One of the factors which a more systematic history of the topic would have to address is the historical relativity of moral judgement about particular forms of behaviour by pupils. To put it crudely, what may have been labelled inappropriate behaviour in the 1830s may have been simply interpreted as self-expression in the 1960s. Whitehead and Williams (1976) provide some interesting evidence on the way in which teachers' judgements about what counts as unacceptable behaviour have changed during this century.

7. This survey is in no way intended to be exhaustive. These three periods have been selected in order to illuminate indiscipline in three different types of educational context: pre-compulsory elementary education (the first half of the nineteenth century); post-compulsory elementary schooling (the beginning of the twentieth century); and in secondary education (the 1950s secondary moderns).

8. *Recent Measures for the Promotion of Education in England*. J. K. Shuttleworth. Quoted in Smith (1923:87).

9. *Quarterly Journal of Education,* 1831

10. Education, crime and pauperism. *English Journal of Education,* 1867.

11. *Recent Measures for the Promotion of Education in England*. J. K. Shuttleworth. Quoted in Smith (1923:87).

12. *English Journal of Education,* 1850, 4:5–14.

13. Such evidence is of course circumstantial. Standards of punishment and indeed discipline were very different from today. We cannot necessarily assume that because harsh discipline was used pupils were particularly badly behaved. However, what is clear is that despite the severity of the punishment a minority of pupils still challenged the authority of their teachers.

14. *Report of the Committee of Council on Education for 1845*, Vol. 2:164–6. Report by the Reverend F. Watkins, H.M.I. Quoted in Goodsen (1969).

15. Ashby (1961), quoted in Goodsen (1969).

16. *Select Committee on the Education of the Poorer Classes 1837–38*, Vol. 11:747. Quoted in Laqueur (1976).

17. Compulsory education. *The School and the Teacher*, 1845:162–5.

18. A simple method of assuring regular attendance at school. *English Journal of Education*, 1843, 1:15–7.

19. Quoted in Worsley (1849:13).

20. Registrar General's Report for 1851. Quoted in Pallister (1969:388).

21. See Pallister (1969).

22. The Ragged School teacher's diary. *English Journal Of Education*, 1850, 4:5–14.

23. The Newcastle Commission of 1861 estimated that 66% of children not in school were in paid employment.

24. See Humphries (1981:50).

25. *Times Educational Supplement*, 17 June 1922, p. 279. Emphasis added.

26. *Times Educational Supplement*, 11 June 1927

27. Humphries (1981:123). Respondent born 1898.

28. Humphries (1981:63). Respondent born 1913.

29. Humphries (1981:86). Respondent born 1912.

30. See, for example, Douglas (1964).

31. Quoted in Taylor (1963:42).

32. See Taylor (1963)

33. An interesting exception is the case of teachers' annual conferences where concern about declining standards of behaviour still remained a prominent issue. See, for example, *Times Educational Supplement*, 18 April 1958, Report on the Annual Conference of the National Union of Women Teachers. The longest discussion was provided by a Central Council motion which viewed with 'grave and increasing apprehension the ill effects that some aspects of the moral climate of our time is having on children and young people' (p. 606).

CHAPTER TWO

Measurements and Correlations

The unity of all science consists alone in its method.[1]

Indiscipline at school was bound to become a cause for concern from the moment the education service became universal, free and compulsory.[2] From 1870 onwards the numbers of children attending school increased sharply with a consequent awareness that a surprisingly large number were ineducable because, in the phrase of the time, they were either morally or mentally 'defective'. It is therefore not surprising that the period that saw the move to compulsion also saw the birth of what we now call educational psychology. In 1884 Francis Galton opened an 'anthropometric' laboratory which was devoted to the scientific study of individual children and shortly afterwards Sully established the British Child Study Association, which aimed at investigating the common causes of minor deviations among normal children. In 1896 Sully went a stage further and opened the first 'laboratory' in Great Britain exclusively devoted to psychology to which teachers were invited to bring their most difficult pupils.

Medicine was an important influence on the new discipline of educational psychology. Galton, a cousin of Darwin's, trained as a doctor and Burt, who was to dominate British educational psychology for 30 years had applied to study medicine at Oxford but had been refused a place.[3] Sully, although himself a philosopher, argued that the pioneers who struck out in the new research were all 'medical men', and what these medical men brought to the study of psychology was their scientific training — the training to observe, to classify and to measure. In short they brought with them the principles and procedures of positivism. Positivism has remained one of the dominant intellectual forces in the study of school deviance ever since.

There are many varieties of positivism but perhaps the most important form is 'individual positivism': 'This theory admits that biological, psychological and social influences all contribute to the creation of the criminal, but that it is in the individual that the fundamental disposition to crime is situated' (Young, 1981:267). In the case of school deviance, behaviour such as violence, disruption and unjustified absence have been variously attributed to, for example, low intelligence, inadequate parenting, underachievement at school and low social class. The purpose of positivistic research is to try to isolate the particular constellation of factors that are causal. In each case such factors are seen as affecting the individual child's response to school. Any form of intervention is necessarily directed at the individual child.

Individual positivism is today the dominant approach in academic as well as professional circles. However, in the last ten years, a growing body of research that might be termed 'institutional positivism' has emerged. Here, the characteristics of particular schools are operationalized and measured and related to indices of institutional deviance such as attendance rates or official delinquency figures. Clearly school differences have important consequences for individual pupils, but in these studies it is the school that is the primary focus and any intervention is to be directed at the school and not the child.

In this chapter the basic tenets of the positivist perspective will firstly be outlined and then some of the main findings from individual positivist studies will be presented. In the next chapter, four important institutional studies will be discussed and some criticisms of the positivist approach will be considered.

The Positive Approach

Burrell and Morgan (1979) have suggested that all social scientific paradigms can be seen as involving assumptions about four fundamental issues: assumptions about the nature or reality (ontology), assumptions about human nature, assumptions about how one can begin to understand the world and communicate this to fellow human beings (epistemology), and assumptions about appropriate methods of study. In each of these assumptions, positivist social science borrows directly from the natural sciences, because positivism is in essence the application of methods and principles derived from the natural sciences to the social world. As we will see, this borrowing from the natural sciences has a profound influence not only on the way positivists study something like school deviance, but it also affects the nature of their findings and the explanations they are able to offer.

Let us consider these assumptions in more detail beginning with ontology. For the positivist the world is made up of social facts which are 'real' and external to the individual; they exist as relatively immutable structures whether or not we perceive them as such. For example, the truancy rate of a particular school exists independently of whether or not the pupils or the teachers are aware of it. As such it is something that can be measured by the application of appropriate scientific procedures. As will become apparent in subsequent chapters, other sociological paradigms adopt a rather different approach to this question, arguing that reality is the product of individual consciousness and it is this that must be investigated by the social scientist. From this latter perspective the fact that two pupils who are absent from school without their parents' permission are both officially classified as 'truants' is of less interest than the pupils' own subjective reasons for staying away. Even though they are officially classified in the same way, their subjective reasons may be very different. For the positivist, however, such subjective feelings, meanings and purposes are irrelevant. Their analyses focus exclusively on data that can be validated because it is objectively available and verifiable by other observers.

Closely interrelated with this realist view of the world are assumptions about human nature, in particular the degree to which human behaviour is the product of voluntarism or determinism. All social scientific paradigms take up a stance with regard to this issue and positivists adopt a determinist position. In positivism, behaviour, however this might violate our view of our selves, is seen as the determined product of circumstances. The idea that our behaviour is the product of autonomous free will is rejected outright. Whether a pupil is a deviant or not will depend on the influence of a large variety of factors — biological, psychological, social — of which the pupil may be largely unaware. The purpose of positivist research is to discover these determining factors. It is because we are all determined in our behaviour that the study of deviance at school, or anywhere else, demands the intervention of an external scientist who is above the individual actor. The scientist has privileged information and can explain the *real causes* of behaviour better than the individuals themselves.

The third important assumption of positivism relates to epistemology — the ways knowledge is acquired, the form knowledge can take and how 'truth' can be distinguished from 'falsehood'. Once again positivists draw directly on a traditional natural scientific perspective in that they seek to explain and predict what happens in the social world by searching for regularities and causal relationships between its constituent elements. Positivists may differ in terms of detailed approach. Some would claim, for example, that hypothesized regularities can be verified by an adequate experimental research programme. Others would maintain that hypotheses can only be falsified and never demonstrated to be 'true' (Popper, 1963). 'However both "verificationists" and "falsificationists" would accept that the growth of knowledge is essentially a cumulative process in which new insights are added to the existing stock of knowledge and false hypotheses eliminated' (Burrell and Morgan, 1979:5).

From this point of view, knowledge is advanced when one set of objective data (truancy rates, convictions in juvenile courts) is shown by valid and reliable research procedures to be related systematically to another set of objective data (divorce rates, educational underachievement, etc.). It is the production of these sorts of correlations that is the final objective of positivist research, though as we will see many studies of school deviance in this tradition have concentrated on the more limited objectives of definition and measurement.

Assumptions about valid and reliable research procedures constitute the final defining characteristic of positivism in social science. In contract to anti-positivists who deliberately choose techniques such as participant observation[4] that will allow the description and analysis of pupils' and teachers' subjective accounts, positivists mainly employ standardized research instruments (questionnaires, personality tests, rating scales) to generate their data and quantitative techniques in their analyses. Their objective, as far as possible, is to follow the canons of scientific rigour established in the natural sciences. As we will see below, positivists studying school deviance have expended a great deal of energy in trying to produce reliable and valid research procedures in order to generate the 'objective' data necessary for their research.

These then are the defining characteristics of the positivist approach to research on school deviance. It is assumed that truancy, disruption and violence at school are the product of a variety of determining factors (biological, psychological, social) of which the individual pupil is largely unaware. The ultimate hope of the positivists is that by utilizing standardized research techniques and by following rigorous research procedures that particular constellation of factors which are causal can be revealed.

Given the multiplicity of variables that might be significant in causing indiscipline at school, different researchers have focused on different dimensions of the problem. For example, some have sought the causes in social factors (class, race and gender) while others have looked at the families of school deviants for evidence of family discord, divorce rates, separation from parents at an early age. The argument here is that these factors often interrupt the normal psychological development of the child. Yet others have focused on educational factors (IQ., verbal reasoning, underachievement) and another group (to be considered in the next chapter) have concentrated on the structure and organization of schools themselves. However, whatever the approach, positivism depends first and foremost on accurately defining and measuring school deviance. If correlations with other factors are to be rigorously tested, truancy, disruption and violence at school must themselves be accurately quantified; a great many positivist studies have concentrated purely on this process. As will be shown below, measuring indiscipline at school with any accuracy is not as easy as it may seem.

Studies of unjustified absence from school have traditionally been treated somewhat differently from studies of violence and disruption. Each will be considered in turn. At the end of the chapter those studies that have gone a stage further and systematically explored the correlations of school deviance will be discussed.

Measuring Unjustified Absence From School

In studies of absence from school it is usually considered appropriate to distinguish between three different groups of pupil. First, there are those who are absent for legitimate reasons, for example because they are ill; secondly, there are those who are unjustifiably absent but with the knowledge of their parents; finally, there are those pupils who are unjustifiably absent but without the knowledge of their parents. The term 'truant' is normally confined to this latter group.

A number of studies have investigated the incidence of absence from school. For example, the Plowden report in 1967 found that on average the overall attendance in primary schools in 1964—5 was 93%, though primary school teachers estimated that only about 4% of those absent at any one time were illegitimately away. On Thursday, 17 January 1974 the Department of Education and Science (D.E.S.) asked all middle and secondary schools in England and Wales to submit data on pupils who were away from school. This data showed that 10% of pupils were absent and the schools could find no legitimate reasons for 23% of these, that is about 2% of pupils in all. While only 2% of 12-year-olds were estimated by their schools to be absent without good reason, the percentage at 15 was 5%.

Other evidence of attendance rates on a national scale is provided by the National Child Development Study which followed 16 000 children born in England, Scotland and Wales during one week in 1958. In 1974 Fogelman and Richardson reporting on the children's primary school attendance commented that rates had remained remarkably constant at around 90%. However, when the children were 14, attendance rates had dropped to 89·4% and a year later the average attendance for the same pupils had dropped again to 87·5%. Fogelman *et al.* (1980) concluded that absence from school was therefore less of a problem than is often assumed, but they commented that the absence rate of 12·5% of 15-year-olds is hardly a cause for complacency.

Some of the most reliable and consistent data on attendance rates is provided by the Inner London Education Authority (I.L.E.A.). Since 1972 the I.L.E.A. have undertaken an annual survey of attendance in their primary and secondary schools on a single day in the summer term. In primary schools the average attendance rate has remained constant at around 92%, though this average hides considerable variations between schools. For example, in 1983 one school had an attendance rate as low as 75%, while others had a 100% rate. At secondary schools the average has remained at around 85% since 1972[5] though there are marked differences in attendance by age and sex as is revealed in the 1983 figures shown in Fig. 2.1.

All of the above studies use formal attendance rates as their main source of data. However, this procedure can be criticized on a number of counts. For example, Baum (1978) and Billington (1978) both argue that spot checks like the D.E.S. and I.L.E.A. surveys are inadequate because rates vary systematically throughout the week and throughout the year — no one day is therefore typical. A more important criticism is that a school's rate of attendance tells us very little about the pattern of individual attendance. As has been pointed out by Galloway (1976), a 90% attendance rate could indicate that 10% of the school's population were persistently absent, or that

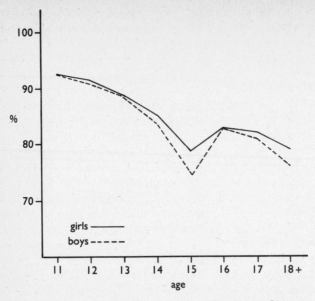

Figure 2.1. I.L.E.A. attendance rates for 1983 by age and sex.
Source: I.L.E.A. (1983)

every pupil missed one session a week. A report by an
anonymous L.E.A. official (Anon, 1973) suggested that when an
inquiry was made into the percentage of children who were
absent from 10 secondary schools in his authority, the evidence
was far from reassuring. While attendance rates varied from
84·8 to 92·4%, the percentage of children actually involved in
absence in any one school varied from 11 to 54%. A further
doubt is cast on the accuracy of attendance registers in that a
number of pupils may register at the beginning of a session and
then 'skip' classes. However, in 1971 an I.L.E.A. survey found
that only 300 out of their 150 000 pupils left after registration
(0·2%). The number involved may therefore be rather small.

Attendance figures clearly have to be considered with some
caution and as a consequence many studies of unjustified
absence supplement data from attendance registers with information from teacher questionnaires. For example, the National
Child Development Study asked the teachers of all their 16 000
pupil sample whether or not they thought the pupils truanted.
At the primary level the number of pupils estimated to have
truanted at least once or twice during the term was 1:100
(Fogelman and Richardson, 1974). Among the 14—16 year olds
the figure increased to 1:10 (Fogelman *et al.*, 1980). Their find-

ings also clearly demonstrated that teachers report more truancy amongst boys than girls, a factor corroborated by other studies.[6]

However, even teacher estimates of unjustified absence have to be treated with caution. Williams (1974) points out that parents from working class homes tend to keep children at home for more minor illnesses than those from middle class homes. This would make absence rates difficult to compare.

In addition, Farrington (1980), reporting findings from the Cambridge Longitudinal Study of Delinquent Development, suggests that when pupils completed self-report questionnaires one-quarter of all bad attenders who were thought by their teachers to be absent because of illness were in fact truanting. Such findings are supported by Reynolds and Murgatroyd (1974) who used participant observation techniques to investigate unjustified absence. They report that in many cases the children they investigated were not in fact ill as their teachers thought but were away for illegitimate reasons.

Each of these studies lends support to Galloway's (1980) conclusion that real truancy — that is absence without parental knowledge — is a relatively minor problem in comparison with the number of children who are away from school with their parents consent or at least knowledge. In his study of 30 comprehensives and their feeder primary schools in Sheffield, Galloway followed up all pupils who had missed at least 50% of their attendance during a seven-week period. The educational welfare officers who knew both the children and their parents were asked to state what they thought were the reasons for the pupils' absence. All cases of absence that were considered by the educational welfare officers to be solely due to organic illness were excluded from the findings. As in other studies, Galloway reports a steady rise in illegitimate absence as children get older, with a peak in the final year of comprehensive schooling when 4% of children in his survey fell into this category. The reasons for absence as rated by educational welfare officers are presented in Table 2.1.

The most frequently cited reasons for absence were 'mixed reasons' (where children were considered to be suffering from some, but probably not serious organic illness) 'parents unwilling or unable to insist on return' and 'with parents' knowledge, consent and approval'. In each of these cases some form of parental support or at least knowledge was therefore involved.

The reliability and validity of Galloway's data as he himself admits is not above question. Nearly 30 educational welfare officers were involved and they would have differed in how well

Table 2.1. Reasons for persistent absenteeism in percentages (excluding prolonged organic illness)

	Primary schools		Secondary schools	
	1973	1974	1973	1974
With parent's knowledge, consent and approval	24·2	19·2	24·3	15·4
Socio-medical reasons — child is excluded from school for reasons such as infestation, scabies, etc.	10·5	6·6	2·7	3·0
'School phobia.' Non-attendance is associated with severe relationship difficulties in the home	1·2	4·0	4·2	3·5
Parents unable or unwilling to insist on return — child is at home with parents' knowledge but not with their active consent	16·1	18·6	26·0	31·3
Truancy — child is absent without parent's knowledge or consent	2·4	2·0	11·2	15·4
Psychosomatic illness	4·4	1·3	3·8	4·7
Mixed — part of the child's absence is due to illness but one or more of the other factors is also relevant	41·2	48·3	27·8	26·7
Total	100·0	100·0	100·0	100·0

Source: Galloway (1980)

they knew the families and children. However, their contact with families would mean that their estimates were more likely to have been accurate than those of teachers. It seems likely therefore that teachers underestimate the true rate of unjustified absence.

Measuring Violence and Disruption

If measuring the real incidence of truancy seems difficult, the problems are compounded dramatically when it comes to examining violent and disruptive behaviour. At least with truancy it is possible to begin with the attendance records — it is (relatively) easy to determine whether a child is at school or not. When it comes to violence and disruption things are more difficult. What is acceptable behaviour for one teacher may be quite unacceptable for another — there is no publicly available quantifiable data to use as a starting point and many positivist studies have foundered on the initial problem of measurement. Four approaches to measuring violent and disruptive behaviour have been attempted: teachers' estimates; recording incidents; rates of suspensions and exclusions; teachers' rating scales. It is only the final approach, i.e. teachers' rating scales, that has produced data of any reliability.

Teachers' Estimates

One approach to measuring violence and disruption has been to ask L.E.A.s, head teachers and teachers to give their own subjective assessments of their incidence. For example, the Head Teachers' Association of Scotland surveyed 200 of its members in 1975.[7] Eighty four per cent of head teachers admitted that they had some experience of disruption in their schools but only 20% regarded it as a moderate or severe problem. A similar sort of study, but on a national scale, was undertaken by the D.E.S. in 1973,[8] which examined the incidence of violence, indiscipline and vandalism. The survey involved the completion of a questionnaire by L.E.A.s reporting their view of the problems over the period 1971–2. A statistically usable response was received from 60% of L.E.A.s covering all forms of state schools in England and Wales. The relevant findings of the survey were as follows:

(1) The number of pupils in schools involved in misdemeanors was proportionately very low, although noticeably greater in secondary than in primary schools.

(2) About 60% of the responding Authorities thought that there had been no significant increase in misdemeanours.
(3) Over three-quarters of the responding Authorities thought that boys were more involved in misbehaviour than girls.
(4) There were proportionately three or four times as many incidents reported in more densely populated areas.
(5) The average size of primary and secondary schools involved in incidents was greater than the national average for these schools.
(6) Much of vandalism affecting schools occurred out of normal hours.

More recently, Dierenfield (1982) has reported a study of 465 teachers from 41 L.E.A.s representing typical schools throughout England. In response to the question, 'How would you assess the extent of classroom disruption in comprehensive schools?', the responses were as follows:

Not really a problem	7·7%
Only a mild difficulty	19·3%
A problem, but one with which it is possible to cope	67·8%
A severe situation	33·6%
Totally out of control	0·0%

Of these teachers 8·7% thought that classroom disruption was becoming a less serious problem, 49·3% thought that it had remained at the same level, while 14·4% thought the problem was becoming more severe.

The main difficulty with all of these studies from a positivistic perspective is that they are indeed subjective. The fact that 7·7% of teachers thought that classroom disruption was 'not really a problem' tells us little or nothing about the actual rate of school deviance. What is acceptable behaviour in one school might be quite unacceptable in another. Such subjective judgements are flawed further when one recognizes that teachers, schools and L.E.A.s are all likely to be somewhat defensive about reporting that they are facing serious problems. Many teachers find it unnecessary or are unwilling to refer classroom disruption on to senior staff. Head teachers are therefore unlikely to be aware of the true rate of disruption and violence. The same applies to the L.E.A.s. Heads refer only the most serious cases, though as Galloway *et al.* (1982) have shown, the frequency with which they do so varies considerably from school to school.

Recording Incidents

If surveys of subjective judgements of rates of disruption and violence are inadequate then one obvious alternative is to try to record the number of actual incidents of challenging classroom behaviour that occur within a given period. This has been attempted on a national scale by Lowenstein (1975) and within a single school by Lawrence *et al.* (1981).

Lowenstein asked all members of the National Association of Schoolmasters to record incidents of violence and disruption in their schools over a two-month period. He defined violent behaviour as 'fairly vicious attacks on other pupils or members of the school staff'. Disruptive behaviour was 'any behaviour, short of physical violence, which interferes with the teaching process and/or upsets the normal running of the school'. Completed questionnaires were returned from 825 primary schools (5% of the total), 141 middle schools (15% of the total) and 846 secondary schools (18% of the total). Lowenstein's findings are summarized in Table 2.2 (p. 40).

Lowenstein concludes that the incidence of violent and disruptive behaviour is more frequent in secondary schools than in middle and primary schools, that overall violent and disruptive behaviour is more common among boys than girls and that the peak age is 15 plus years.

Lowenstein's findings must, however, be treated with considerable scepticism. Apart from the extremely low response rate there are also more profound difficulties with the research procedure. First, there is the fact that we have no knowledge of the way in which teachers selected incidents to report. Once again it could be that some teachers reported only the most serious incidents while others reported comparatively minor ones — not all evidence will therefore be of equal weight. A more profound criticism of the study is made by Laslett (1977b) who questions whether such a survey could *ever* produce reliable evidence on such a scale. He argues that any assessment of problem behaviour is to some extent contingent upon place, circumstance and the personality of the teacher. 'Any attempt to roll up into one large mass all of the various types of violent and disruptive behaviour as reported by a variety of teachers in a wide variety of different areas and then to measure and comment upon this totality seems a very dubious procedure' (Laslett, 1977b:156). Laslett does not challenge the positivistic approach, rather he pins his hopes for more precise studies of the rate of school deviance on small-scale local research.

Table 2.2. Violent and disruptive incidents in different types of school

	VF	F	S	I	VI	Total
Violent incidents						
Primary	7	18	52	51	420	548
Middle	2	2	17	10	77	108
Secondary	13	44	159	200	351	767
Total	22	64	228	261	848	1423
				Not tabled		421
						1844
Disruptive incidents						
Primary	15	36	62	86	377	576
Middle	2	12	14	23	55	106
Secondary	70	175	192	167	176	780
Total	87	223	268	276	608	1462
				Not tabled		382
						1844

Schools were asked to report whether incidents of disruptive behaviour were: Very Frequent (VF), Frequent (F), Sometimes (S), Infrequent (I), or Very Infrequent (VI).
Source: Lowenstein (1975).

One of the most systematic small-scale studies of the incidence of deviant behaviour[9] is by Lawrence *et al.* (1981) in which a study was made of a single comprehensive in outer London with 1200 pupils and 100 staff. All teachers were asked to file report forms on all incidents of disruptive behaviour that took place in one week preceding half-term in the spring term. A total of 144 different incidents were reported in all during the week, some by teachers who had experienced them directly and others by senior staff to whom individual pupils had been referred. Twenty one per cent of the incidents reported by staff were considered to be very serious, 54% serious and 16% not serious. The most frequently complained of behaviours were, in rank order: rowdy behaviour, refusing authority, talking/chatting, abuse or bad language, extreme lateness, dumb insolence, sudden tantrums, bullying or violence to peers.

In one sense this study represents an improvement on that of

Lowenstein in that all of the incidents took place within a single institution and the researchers were therefore able to take considerable care in introducing the reporting scheme and conducting follow-up interviews. However, the highly selective nature of the reports filed still remains a problem. It is simply not possible to tell when and why teachers chose to report an incident. This difficulty is well illustrated by the fact that of the 100 staff, two submitted 10% of the incident sheets while only three sheets were completed by probationers and supply teachers. We are left to speculate on the motivation of these two groups.

Rates of Suspension and Exclusion

If recording the incidence of disruptive behaviour within schools presents problems an alternative approach has been to research the rate of children who are removed from school by expulsion, suspension or exclusion.[10] York *et al.* (1972) report that in their study of Edinburgh, 31 out of a total school population of 67 500 were either suspended or excluded during a two-year period. They conclude that the problem of very serious misbehaviour at school is therefore a relatively minor one. Grunsell (1979), however, casts doubt on the accuracy of statistics reported by L.E.A.s. In a study of an L.E.A. he calls Baxbridge the recorded number of permanent suspensions from school was 42 in 1975 and 40 in 1976. In November 1976 instructions were issued to schools insisting that in future the procedure of notifying the L.E.A.s of suspensions was to be strictly observed. In 1977 permanent suspensions rose to 63 and the number of temporary exclusions doubled. Grunsell therefore argues that reporting of exclusions and suspension rates is unreliable and cannot be taken as hard evidence of the incidence of difficult behaviour at school. He further suggests that such figures are unreliable because schools exclude pupils at very different rates. Out of the 74 comprehensives in Baxbridge, Grunsell reports that the top three suspending schools in all three years contributed 45% of the total and the top five, 60%. The top three schools suspended seven times as many pupils as the bottom three schools in a league table. More recently, Galloway *et al.* (1982) have pointed to similar inconsistencies in their study of suspensions and long-term exclusions from schools in Sheffield. Suspension rates may not, therefore, reflect the degree of deviant behaviour within a school so much as the school's willingness to contain or exclude its own problems. Once again we find that hard data from which we can generalize is difficult to come by.

Teachers' Rating Scales

Because of the difficulty of assessing the incidence of disruptive and violent behaviour at school in a direct way, many researchers have turned to indirect means by using, for example, teachers' rating scales. The best known scales of this type are the Bristol Social Adjustment Guide (Stott, 1963) and the Rutter Scale (Rutter, 1967). The Rutter scale will serve as an example. This scale involves a list of 26 statements describing behaviour often shown by children at school, for example: 'Very restless. Often running about or jumping up and down' or 'Frequently sucks thumb or finger'. The items are nearly all behavioural descriptions involving little or no interpretation by the teacher. After each statement are three columns: 'Doesn't apply (scores 0)', 'Applies somewhat (score 1)' and 'Certainly applies (score 2)'. Teachers are asked to place a cross in the appropriate box for each item when rating a child. Rutter (1967) argues that a score of more than nine identifies children with some form of 'psychiatric disorder'. The behavioural items included are also intended to discriminate between different types of disorder. Items such as 'Often worries, worries about many things' and 'Often appears miserable, unhappy and tearful' are intended to identify children with 'neurotic disorders'. Other statements such as 'Often destroys own or others belongings' or 'Is often disobedient' are introduced to identify children with 'behavioural disorders'.

During the last 30 years a number of studies have utilized such rating scales as a means of assessing the incidence of 'maladjusted behaviour' or 'psychiatric disorder' among large groups of pupils. Table 2.3 (pp. 44–5) summarizes some of the most significant of these epidemiological studies. They show that teachers rate anywhere between 8·1 and 19·1% of their children as showing signs of serious deviant behaviour.

One of the best known series of studies utilizing rating scales such as this has been undertaken by Rutter himself in a large comparative examination of 10 and 11-year-old children in the Isle of Wight and an Inner London Borough (Rutter *et al.* 1975). The procedures adopted involved two stages. First, all teachers completed a questionnaire for the sample of children, and then those with a score of nine or above were given a follow-up standardized psychiatric interview. The proportion of children showing 'psychiatric disorder' as revealed by the teacher questionnaires is shown in Table 2.4 (p. 46).

The incidence of deviant behaviour as reported by teachers in the Inner London Borough was therefore almost double that of the Isle of Wight.[11] There was also a much higher incidence of deviant behaviour among boys in comparison with girls. However, as the figures in Table 2.5 on p. 46 suggest, teachers observed a far higher incidence of 'conduct' disorder for boys than girls, 'neurotic' disorders having a similar incidence across both sexes. From the teachers' point of view, therefore, a significant proportion of children are seen as displaying behaviour which causes them concern, the largest group being disciplinary conduct disorders, for example fighting, disobedience, lying, stealing and bullying.

In an interesting sub-study comparing teachers' perceptions of indigenous London children with those of Afro-Caribbean descent (Rutter *et al.*, 1974) the ratings in Table 2.6 (p. 47) were recorded. Once again the degree of estimated neurotic disorder was seen to remain constant throughout all four groups — girls, boys, Afro-Caribbeans and non-immigrants. However, there was very considerable variation between the four groups in terms of teachers' ratings of conduct disorders. The greatest problems from the teachers' point of view lay with Afro-Caribbean boys, of whom 40% were reported as showing behaviour indicating conduct disorders.

Clearly, behaviours like lying, disobedience and stealing present problems for teachers but whether these can legitimately be considered evidence of psychiatric disorder of some kind is clearly open to debate. In the study of Afro-Caribbean children reported above follow-up research with parents showed no significant differences between rates of disorder in children of Afro-Caribbean families and the rest of those from non-immigrant families. In fact from the parents' point of view there was slightly more deviant behaviour reported among the non-immigrant group (25% as opposed to 18%). An earlier study (Graham and Rutter, 1970) also showed that when a similar rating scale was completed by parents as well as teachers for the same children there was comparatively little overlap between the disorders perceived by both groups. A child might be considered a problem at school but behave perfectly acceptably in the home or vice versa.

Therefore, while it may be true that between 10 and 20% of children engage in behaviour that causes their teachers concern, for many children such behaviour may be more a product of their response to school than evidence of some psychiatric disorder. The possibility of considerable over-estimation of psychiatric disorder in rating scales of this kind is suggested by Rutter's own study of the Isle of Wight. When children with a

Table 2.3. Epidemiological studies using teacher rating scales to measure serious deviant behaviour

Researchers	Rating scale	Age (years)	N	Prevalence (%)	Assessment
Pringle et al. (1966)	Bristol Social Adjustment guide, completed by teacher	7	3244 boys 3223 girls	15·6 8·1	'Maladjusted' 'Maladjusted'
Graham and Rutter (1970)	Rutter scale completed by teachers and parents followed by psychiatric interviews with child and parents	10–11	2199 boys and girls	6·8	'Psychiatric disorder'
Jones (1975)	Bristol Social Adjustment test completed by teachers	5–10	1000 boys and girls	13·7	'Maladjusted'
		11–15	1330 boys and girls	11·7	'Maladjusted'
Shepherd et al. (1971)	Own teacher rating scale	Primary Secondary	6463 boys and girls	9·8 (boys) 4·0 (girls) 7·1 (boys) 4·2 (girls)	'Very restless' 'Not interested in school work'

Davie et al. (1972)	Bristol Social Adjustment guide completed by teacher	7	16000 boys and girls	14·0	'Maladjusted'
Fogelman (1966)	Own teaching ratings scale	16	Same sample as for Davie et al. (1972)	16·0 15·0	'Very restless' 'Irritable. Is quick to fly off the handle'
Rutter et al. (1975)	Rutter scale completed by teachers and parents followed by psychiatric interviews with child and parents	10–11	1279 Isle of Wight boys and girls	10·6	'Psychiatric disorder'
Rutter et al. (1975)	Rutter scale completed by teachers and parents followed by psychiatric interviews with child and parents	10–11	1689 Inner London boys and girls	19·1	'Psychiatric disorder'

Table 2.4. Percentages of children with deviant scores on Rutter's behavioural rating scale (Rutter, 1967) in the Isle of Wight (IOW) and an Inner London Borough (ILB)

	Boys	Girls	Total	N
ILB	24·5*	13·2*	19·1*	1689
IOW	13·8	7·1	10·6	1279

*Difference between areas significant at 0·1% level.
Source: Rutter *et al.* (1975).

Table 2.5. Percentages of children showing different types of deviant behaviour as revealed by Rutter's behavioural rating scale (Rutter 1967) in the Isle of Wight (IOW) and an Inner London Borough (ILB)

	Boys			Girls		
	'Neurotic'	'Conduct'	'Mixed'	'Neurotic'	'Conduct'	'Mixed'
ILB	7·7**	14·2**	2·6*	6·5*	5·1	1·6
IOW	3·9	9·0	0·9	3·3	3·0	0·8

*Difference between areas significant at 5% level.
**Difference between areas significant at 1% level.
Source: Rutter *et al.* (1975a).

score of nine or more on the teachers' rating scale were given a standardized psychiatric interview only 20% of those interviewed were diagnosed as positively abnormal, 32% as definitely normal and 48% as undefined.

Clearly a small minority of children do suffer from problems of personal social adjustment stemming from neurotic disorders. These problems may be exhibited, as implied in the rating scales, in behaviour such as nail biting, bed wetting and speech difficulties. However, it would seem that such pupils are a very small minority and should not be confused with the rather larger group characterized as presenting behavioural problems at school.

In conclusion it is apparent that estimates of the actual rate of deviant school behaviour vary considerably. Whilst the number of children who are formally suspended or excluded from school may be very small (e.g. York *et al.*, 1972; Grunsell,

Table 2.6. Percentages of children from different ethnic backgrounds showing specific types of deviant behaviour as revealed by Rutter's behavioural rating scale (Rutter, 1967) in one Inner London Borough

	Boys			Girls		
	'Emotional'	'Conduct'	'Mixed'	'Emotional'	'Conduct'	'Mixed'
Children from 'non-immigrant' families	7·7	14·2	2·6	6·5	5·1	1·6
Children from Afro-Caribbean families	6·4	40·1*	2·3	6·6	25·8*	1·7

*$P < 0.001$.
Source: Rutter et al. (1974).

1979) there is some evidence that teachers find difficulty with containing and controlling a much larger group of pupils (Rutter *et al.*, 1975), though we should not overlook the findings of Dierenfield (1982) that most teachers feel that they can cope with the challenges they experience. Perhaps one of the most realistic estimates of the size of the problem is made by Mills (1976)[12] who made a study of 61 secondary schools in a single L.E.A. using questionnaires and follow-up interviews. He concluded that a hard core of seriously disturbed 13–16 year olds numbered only about 3% of the school population in any one school — clearly very much a minority. However, this 3% was supported by a further 10% of other pupils who were occasionally involved in disruption. He also found evidence that disruptive pupils were often encouraged by outsiders — older pupils who had left school and influenced school events from a distance. He reports that on average urban schools had two and a half times more seriously disruptive pupils than rural schools.

Correlations and Causes

Despite difficulties in precisely defining and measuring any form of deviant behaviour in school a large number of studies have attempted to explore the 'causes' of school deviance through statistical correlation. In the area of unacceptable classroom behaviour the most frequent correlational studies have utilized data from teacher rating scales (e.g. Rutter, 1967) as a means of measurement. In studies of non-attendance, researchers have utilized teacher assessments as a way of identifying truants. However, comparatively few studies have made a precise differentiation between different types of 'maladjusted' children or between different types of unjustified absence; truancy and maladjustment are usually treated as unitary concepts.

Correlational studies can be grouped under three broad headings: those investigating social factors (e.g. race, class and gender), those concerned with family relationships (in particular their impact on the child's psychological development), and those focusing on educational factors.

Social Factors

The relationships between truancy, age and gender have already been highlighted and these are some of the most consistent findings in this body of research. Children seem to engage in unjustified absence (however defined) with far more frequency as they get nearer school leaving age and at every age boys seem to truant and disrupt more frequently than girls (Davie *et al.*, 1972; Mitchell and Shepherd, 1980; I.L.E.A. 1983). There is also some evidence that Afro-Caribbean children, particularly boys, are seen as more problematic by teachers than their peers (Rutter *et al.*, 1974).

An equally consistent finding is the relationship between school attendance and social class. As far back as 1953 the Scottish Council for Research in Education noted that while 80% of children of small employers attended school regularly, only 57% of the children of agricultural workers did so.[13] Many other studies have since confirmed that children from manual working class homes attend school less regularly than their middle class peers (Tyerman, 1958, 1968; Douglas and Ross, 1965; Mitchell and Shepherd, 1980). The most authoratative evidence is provided by the National Child Development Study with its sample of 16 000 children. Attendance was shown to be strongly related to class at age seven (Davie *et al.*, 1972), at age 11 (Fogelman and Richardson, 1974), and at age 16 (Fogelman *et al.*, 1980).

The same study also provided evidence that 'maladjusted behaviour', as assessed by teachers, was strongly related to social class. Davie *et al.* (1972) report a relatively homogeneous non-manual or middle class group which has a much lower incidence of 'maladjustment' than all of the manual or working class groups. The highest incidence of 'maladjustment' is among children from social class five — the manual working class. As they note, the situation is not unlike their finding for ability and attainment where the lowest levels of measured ability and attainment were found among the children of the manual working class. Davie *et al.*'s (1972) results are presented in Fig. 2.2.

Other studies have examined the correlation between deviance and more specific social factors. For example, Mitchell (1972) presents evidence to suggest that there is a correlation between family size and truancy, while Tibbenham (1977) argues that there is a clear correlation between housing conditions and truancy which apparently persists even when social class is taken into account. Farrington (1980) provides a long list of social factors positively correlating with teachers' suspected as well as self-reported truancy. These include low family income, large family size, slum housing, 'criminal' parents and erratic job record of father. Similar correlations are provided by Rutter *et al.* (1975) in his study of 'maladjusted behaviour' in Inner London and the Isle of Wight. Clearly many

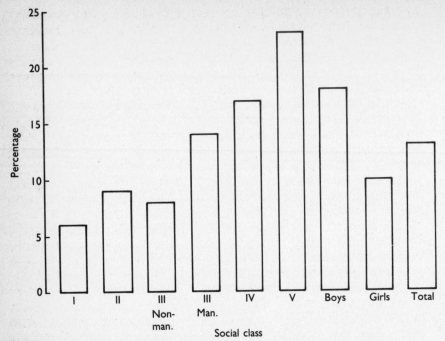

Figure 2.2. Percentage of 'maladjusted' children by social class and sex at age seven.
Source: Davie *et al.* (1972).

of these factors are interrelated with the concept of social class. It is the lower working class who are poorer, have larger families and are more prone to unemployment. These studies therefore simply serve to reconfirm the general trend.

Family Relationships

Other studies have sought the causes of deviance in the psychodynamic relationship between parents and children. Children from broken or unhappy homes where normal child–parent relationships are disrupted have been shown to be more likely to engage in antisocial behaviour at school. For example, Tyerman (1958) in his classic study of a sample of truants reported to him by school attendance officers, concluded that: 'Few truants have a happy and secure home influence'. He found that most of the truants he studied came from broken homes or homes where there was open disharmony. In general, the parents 'set poor examples' and were 'unsatisfactory characters'. They neglected their children, were ineffective in their supervision and took little interest in their welfare. He concludes: 'The view of many writers that truants are born into an inferior environment seems confirmed' (p. 219).

In a comparative study of two different 'types' of truant referred to the Maudsley Hospital, Hersov (1960) concluded that children whose school refusal was one part of a psychodynamic syndrome (e.g. school phobics) came from families with a higher incidence of neuroticism and over protectiveness. The result was children who were passively dependent but who exhibited high standards of work and conformity when they could be persuaded to go to school. By contrast, children who were referred to the clinic because their behaviour was one aspect of a 'conduct disorder' came from larger families where discipline was inconsistent and where there was a record of paternal or maternal absence during infancy or early childhood. For these children, truancy was one aspect of a wide variety of anti-school and delinquent behaviours. When they attended school their conduct and work there was uniformly unsatisfactory.

Other studies have pointed to similar correlations. Farrington (1980) reports that a high incidence of separation, marital disharmony, poor parental supervision and poor 'child rearing behaviour' are common among 'truant families'. In the National Child Development Study (Davie *et al.*, 1972) four out of ten parents felt that their child's maladjustment behaviour was attributable to the loss of a father or mother and similar correlations are presented by Rutter *et al.* (1975). Wadsworth (1979), in a longitudinal study of 15 000 delinquents, reports an above average chance of their coming from homes that were broken before the age of five.

Educational Factors

Turning to correlations with educational factors there is a generally noted relationship between attendance and attainment though there is some evidence that this is modified by class. Thus Douglas and Ross (1965) in their national longitudinal study of 3273 primary children noted that school performance was directly affected by attendance except in the case of upper middle class children. Fogelman (1978) reporting the findings of the National Child Development Study concluded that there is a 'Fairly straightforward relationship between school attendance and attainment and behaviour' (p. 157). Children with high attendance levels attained on average higher test scores on reading, comprehension and mathematics and were less often indicated by their teachers as showing deviant behaviour. The same sample has also shown that truancy is more frequently associated with certain types of school, most particularly secondary moderns and comprehensives. Selective schools for the academically successful would appear to be less frequently affected (a finding corroborated by Tyerman, 1968). Berger *et al.* (1975) report that specific reading retardation overlaps markedly with conduct disorders in school, while Lunzer (1960) reports a similar relationship with difficulty in mathematics. Shepherd *et al.* (1971) report that over half the boys and nearly two-thirds of the girls in their study of 6463 pupils in Buckinghamshire, who were rated by their teachers as having below average attainment, had at least one reported behaviour problem compared with only about one in four for those rated above average in each sex. All of these studies therefore suggest that indiscipline at school of all types is more frequently associated with the educationally unsuccessful, though whether this is a cause or simply an effect of frequent absence and disruption is hard to determine.

Perhaps one of the most consistent findings in studies of the relationship between indiscipline and school factors is that deviant pupils do not like school. In Mitchell and Shepherd's (1980) study in Buckinghamshire, pupils were asked whether or not they liked school. Forty one per cent of boys who reported that they did not like school had been absent for more than ten sessions during the term while among girls, only 6% of those who did not like school had achieved a perfect attendance record. A number of reasons have been suggested for truants, in particular, disliking school. It may be as Tyerman (1958) suggests that they are socially incompetent and inadequate or it may be that they are unable to build good relationships with their teachers (Eaton, 1979) or because they have no friends (Croft and Grygier, 1956). Other studies suggest that truants simply reject the whole idea of having to spend time in an educational system which has no particular value for them and whose aims they cannot support (Mitchell, 1972).

Conclusion

Positivistic research offers a wide variety of possible causes of indiscipline at school. Disruption and truancy have been shown to correlate with a range of social factors, particularly age, gender and class. Working class boys nearing the end of compulsory schooling apparently present the most consistent problems for their teachers. There are also consistent correlations between indiscipline at school and various indicators of family discord — divorce, 'inadequate parenting', early separation from parents. Finally, there are consistent correlations between school deviance and educational factors, most particularly underachievement at school.

However, it is clear that these findings must be taken with considerable care. Apart from the difficulties of classification and measurement, a factor on which all these studies depend, there is a further difficulty that most researchers treat truancy and maladjustment as unitary concepts. Hersov (1960) would appear to be unusual in distinguishing between children suffering from 'conduct disorders' and those suffering from 'psycho-neurotic disorders'. This is a distinction that is frequently acknowledged by practitioners but seldom seems to have been considered by researchers. However, it is clear that even this distinction is not sufficient. As will become apparent in subsequent chapters, pupils may play truant or be disruptive for a wide variety of reasons and to lump them together in a single category because they present similar problems for their teachers is unsatisfactory. Once again it seems that we are confronted with the problem of definition.

A more fundamental problem concerns the degree to which correlations can be considered causal. It may be that it is working class adolescent boys who are educationally unsuccessful who are the most problematic for their teachers, but this correlation does not necessarily offer a causal explanation. Indeed it may be more appropriate to see this correlation as the starting point for research rather than the conclusion. Why is it that girls are less frequently reported as problems than boys? Why is it that the educationally unsuccessful so frequently reject what is on offer to them? These are questions that have been taken up by researchers subscribing to different theoretical traditions from that of positivism. However, before moving to a consideration of alternatives, a further important form of positivistic research — institutional positivism — needs to be considered in more detail. Institutional studies, together with some more systematic discussion of difficulties associated with the positivist perspective, form the main focus of the next chapter.

Notes

1. Pearson, K. (1882).
2. Ford *et al.* (1982).

3. Ford *et al.* (1982:38).

4. A more detailed discussion of participant observation as a research technique is presented in Chapter 5.

5. There was, however, a sharp drop in 1973–4 coinciding with the raising of the school leaving age.

6. See, for example, I.L.E.A. (1983), Mitchell and Shepherd (1980).

7. See Pack Report (1977).

8. See Department of Education and Science (1973).

9. Laslett (1977b) provides some interesting references to unpublished material.

10. Pupils may theoretically still be *expelled* from school although in practice very few L.E.A.s allow their head teachers to do this. Far more frequent is the practice of *suspension*. This is an official procedure of which the school governors and Chief Education Officer have to be notified. Parents may formally appeal against suspensions. The principal characteristic of suspension is that the head teacher sees no immediate possibility of readmitting the pupil and very often it is the functional equivalent of expulsion. A final, and more informal procedure, is *exclusion* in which the head teacher temporarily excludes the pupil for a few days in order to 'cool off'. This is an informal procedure between the school and the pupil's parents. It involves no official notification and there is no possibility of appeal.

11. For a review of the findings across all London boroughs see I.L.E.A. (1973).

12. Mills (1976) quoted in Laslett (1977b).

13. See Tyerman (1958).

CHAPTER THREE

The Deviant School?

The search for the *causes* of delinquency in school has become what Reynolds (1976b) has called the criminological equivalent of the quest for the Holy Grail. As was demonstrated in the last chapter, positivistic researchers have explored the correlations between delinquent behaviour and a bewildering variety of different factors — I.Q., family size, physical characteristics, overcrowding at home, gender, social class, etc. However, until comparatively recently, very little systematic research had been undertaken on the impact of the school as an institution on rates of school deviance. Plenty of studies had demonstrated that school factors such as educational achievement were strongly associated with all forms of disaffected behaviour, but no-one had seriously pursued the question of whether it made any difference as to which school a child attended. As Phillipson noted in 1971:

> The implicit assumption (in much research) is that all schools are sufficiently alike to produce a standardized response from their pupils. The idea that there may be considerable differences between overtly similar schools, that some schools may facilitate and other schools hinder the drift to delinquency does not seem to have occurred to writers on delinquency. (p. 239)

In the first part of this chapter four major studies which have attempted to redress this imbalance are considered. Three of them support the conclusion that schools are highly significant in influencing whether or not pupils become delinquent; the fourth study challenges that conclusion. At the end of the chapter some of the difficulties of the positivistic theory and

methods that underlie these studies and those outlined in the
last chapter are considered.

It was the work of Phillipson, Power and their various co-
workers in the late 1960s that first raised the question as to
whether schools made a difference in the degree to which pupils
became delinquent. Their study of Tower Hamlets in London
demonstrated that there was at least a prima facie case to be
answered about the differential impact of schools. However,
their study remained incomplete as they were prohibited from
making a more in-depth analysis of exactly what it was about
a particular school that engendered or prohibited delinquency.
Attempts at this more detailed analysis of the correlation
between specific school processes and delinquency rates had to
await the studies of Reynolds in South Wales and Rutter in
Inner London in the mid-1970s.

These three studies of school differences have had a considerable impact on educational thought in recent years. They
therefore deserve some detailed consideration. Each (in theory)
involves the same three steps. First, a sample of schools within
a particular locality is chosen and a differential rate of delinquency associated with each school is measured using some
objective criteria such as appearances in juvenile court or
official cautions. By using such indices it has not proved difficult
to show that schools do indeed have very different delinquency
rates. However, if these differences in outcome are to be attributed to the school rather than the children who enter them
then a second step to control for the intake is necessary. Controlling for intake is a complex problem and, as we will see
below, has been subject to considerable controversy. In these
three studies it has been attempted by various means, for
example measuring pupil performance on a variety of tests
(I.Q., educational achievement, personality) and then examining
the differential intake of the sample schools. To the extent that
school outcomes are indeed seen to vary *independently* of the
intake it is then possible for researchers to undertake a third
step exploring the correlations between specific school
processes (methods of teaching, use of rewards and
punishments, etc.) and variations in the adjusted delinquency
rate for each school.

Tower Hamlets

The first study undertaken by Power and his co-workers (Power
et al., 1967, 1972; Phillipson, 1971) was of 20 secondary modern

schools in the London Borough of Tower Hamlets. This borough, they emphasize, is a largely self-contained cohesive district of mainly manual workers, 'a stable homogeneous community' (Power *et al.*, 1972:117).

By the time the boys (no mention is made of girls) in the district were 17, one in every four had made at least one court appearance — delinquency, they say, was therefore a normal activity for boys in the Borough. However, they report that among the 20 secondary modern schools which took 85% of all 11–14 year olds, the conviction rate varied dramatically. At one extreme only 0·7% of the pupils at one school were convicted by the juvenile court each year. At a school at the other end of the spectrum 19% of boys each year were convicted. These differences in delinquency could not be explained by variations in school size, sex, ethnic composition, age or type of building. The team also report that there were no significant differences with regard to verbal reasoning and maths scores of the pupils entering each school at the age of 11. Furthermore, as most pupils did not have a delinquency record at the age of 11, they argue that differences did not occur because the schools were selecting or refusing to select particular pupils. Clearly there was at least a prima facie case suggesting that the schools themselves made some difference in the drift towards delinquency.

In order to explore this hypothesis further, Power and his colleagues computed the delinquency rates for each of the census enumeration districts in the Borough — these too varied dramatically. In some districts the court appearance rate was 12% while in other districts it was only 1%. Yet, they argue, the schools did not have set catchment areas relating to either high or low delinquency districts — equal numbers of pupils from both sorts of districts attended the same schools. They assert that it is therefore not possible to explain the variation in school rates in terms of the schools' intake. 'Thus the conclusion is that the variation between schools in delinquency rates is not accountable for by the variation in the district rates. Some Schools apparently protect pupils from delinquency while others may put them at risk of it' (Phillipson, 1971:283).

As has already been noted, Power and his team were refused permission to take their study a stage further to explore what it was about particular schools which 'caused' such variations. It may be, as others have emphasized, that the educational authorities were defensive and short-sighted (Reynolds, 1976, Hargreaves, D., 1980) but it is clear that the Tower Hamlets study is not above serious criticism, most particularly with regard to the study of pupil intake (Baldwin, 1972). We are told that the schools had relatively open catchment areas drawing pupils from different census enumeration districts, some with high and some with low rates of delinquency. The team conclude that because the schools drew pupils from a variety of different areas in roughly equal quantities the schools obviously varied independently of their intake. However, such a conclusion seems highly suspect. It assumes that families living in a high or low delinquency district will all have consistent attitudes with regard to education or delinquency. In fact it would seem likely that, for example, some families living in a high delinquency district would wish to protect their children from the influence of their neighbourhood and therefore select schools with a 'good reputation'. Other parents might not be so concerned and content to send their children to whatever school was convenient. Schools develop a particular reputation and where there is an element of choice, 'non-deviant' families may well opt for high reputation schools. This might have played an important part in producing the different delinquency rates that the team observed.

South Wales

The second major study of school differences was carried out by Reynolds and various co-workers (Reynolds, 1976a, 1976b; Reynolds *et al.*, 1980) in a former mining district of South Wales. As in the study of Tower Hamlets, Reynolds emphasizes the social homogeneity of the district — it was almost uniformally working class. He therefore concludes: 'Within this community historical and social accident means that we have effectively controlled the effects of intake on our schools' (Reynolds *et al.*, 1980:92). Nine small secondary modern schools served this district taking 65% of the full ability range; these schools formed the basis of the study.[1] Reynolds examined three measures of 'output' from these nine schools — attendance, academic achievement (assessed in terms of numbers of places gained at the local technical college) and officially recorded delinquency. Once again he found wide variations in his nine sample schools. The school with the top attendance rate averaged 89·1% attendance over the years 1966–7 and 1972–3 and the bottom school only 77·2%. One school got over one-half of its pupils into the local technical college (regarded locally as the key to obtaining an apprenticeship or craft) and another managed to get only 8·4%. The school with the highest delinquency rate had 10·5% of boys recorded as officially delinquent each

year and the school with the bottom rate had only 3·8% each
year. When an overall ranking of the schools on the three
measures was produced, Reynolds found a direct correlation
between a school's rank position and the unemployment record
among school leavers. Clearly there was something to be
investigated.

Reynolds' evidence as to the intake of the different schools is
contradictory. In his 1976b article he reports that the overall
rank positions of the schools on 'outputs' was not related to the
proportion of social class 4 and 5 families in the catchment area.
He also reports that the intake of boys to the schools showed no
marked differences on intelligence tests (Raven's Standard
Progressive Matrices). He therefore boldly concludes that there
was no significant difference in the intake at the nine schools:
'The reasons for some schools' evident success and other
schools' manifest failure can hardly lie in the relative ability of
a pupil intake' (p. 222). However, in a more recent article,
Reynolds *et al.* (1980) present further evidence on the intake
differences of the schools and draw more cautious conclusions.
Subsequent tests have shown that schools with high attendance
figures received pupils with higher maths and reading scores.
Oddly enough, however, the pupils at the more 'successful
schools' had on average slightly lower intelligence and slightly
higher extroversions/neuroticism scores (a factor sometimes
associated with school failure).[2] The evidence as to intake is,
Reynolds concludes, therefore confusing. However, it is clear
that as regards educational achievement the successful schools
were recruiting more successful pupils and 'a substantial
amount of variation in output resulting is explicable by school
intake differences' (Reynolds *et al.*, 1980:94).

One of the major difficulties with Reynolds' work is that it
provides almost no evidence on the different catchment areas
that the schools served. Each catchment area was quite specific
and the intake would therefore be drawn from a particular
district, yet Reynolds simply asserts that the area was an
homogeneous working class community. Uniformly working
class it may have been, but this does not necessarily mean that
it was homogeneous with regard to attitudes to education and
delinquency. Some clue to the character of the different districts
is provided in the age of the schools. Those with the lowest
delinquency rate had the oldest buildings (were these the more
stable working class communities?) and the school with the
worst record on all forms of 'outcome' was built in 1966 (was
this a redevelopment area?). As Power *et al.* (1967, 1972)
demonstrate, even in an overtly homogeneous community there

is considerable variation in the delinquency rate. Where schools have fixed catchment areas it is likely they will reflect the attitudes and values of the communities they serve but Reynolds reports very little investigation of these possibilities.

The final part of Reynolds' work is an assessment of the relationships between the schools ranked on the three outcomes and a variety of different organizational factors and disciplinary procedures. He concludes that the more successful schools were smaller (though all of the schools were very small indeed, ranging from 136 to 355 pupils), had lower staff turnover, had smaller classes and were situated in older and less adequate buildings. Perhaps his most widely canvassed and controversial finding is that the more successful schools had reached some form of 'truce' with their disaffected pupils (Reynolds, 1976a). Observation and interview data were collected on the degree to which schools enforced the 'no smoking' and 'no chewing gum'[3] rules and it was found that the more successful schools enforced these rules less rigidly and used less punitive sanctions against offenders. While admitting that the more tolerant schools perhaps did not need to attempt such strong control, because they had a more able intake who did not truant or challenge the rules, Reynolds concludes that it seems likely that in part less rigid control functioned as a *cause* of lower deviance: 'In our research area, schools that attempted significantly to delimit large areas of the pupils' behaviour as deviant are simply unlikely to be pleasurable places for the pupils and the pupils are therefore more likely to truant' (1980:100) and engage in other forms of rebellion. However, given that the schools did indeed have different intakes, this seems an unwarranted conclusion. Rigid law enforcement is just as likely to have been a response to a challenging school population as it is to have been a cause. Repression is a familiar coping strategy for harassed teachers.[4]

The more successful schools were also characterized by two further factors, high co-option of pupils onto the school's organization by the use of prefects etc., and a closer school–parent relationship. Reynolds' findings on pupil co-option are corroborated by Rutter *et al.* (1979: see below). Making pupils feel part of the school and committed to it may indeed be an important fact in success. However, once again such factors cannot be seen to vary independently of intake. The most significant form of incorporation is academic success itself but academic success, high attendance and low delinquency may all be a product of high parental cooperation and interest.

Since Reynolds has made no systematic attempt to control for the variations in school intake, it is difficult to assess the validity of any of his conclusions. Those conclusions must therefore remain at the level of interesting (if not always logical) speculations. By contrast, Rutter *et al*'s (1979) study has attempted to measure school intake differences and to control for their effect. It is to a consideration of this work that we now turn.

Fifteen Thousand Hours

Rutter *et al.*'s (1979) work was based on an earlier study (Rutter *et al.*, 1975) comparing all ten-year-old children living in the Isle of Wight with those in one Inner London borough. In that study, carried out in 1970, it was noted that family variables such as parental mental disorder, family criminality, large family size, etc., accounted for much of the high rate of behavioural and educational problems that were recorded among the Inner London borough group. However, they also found that some primary schools in London differed in both their rates of behavioural problems and educational achievements, yet 'as far as could be determined these differences between schools were not wholly due to variations in the sorts of children admitted to each school' (Rutter *et al.*, 1979:23).

Rutter and his team therefore decided to follow up the cohort of London children into their secondary schools, in order to determine how far any changes in behaviour and achievement were a consequence of what the children were like when they entered their secondary schools and how far they resulted from some kind of school influence.

Two-thirds of the children from the 1970 London survey entered 20 schools in South London. Every child entering these 20 schools was assessed for non-verbal intelligence, reading ability and school behaviour (assessed on the Rutter Behaviour Scale). A total of 3485 children were assessed in all of which 1487 were in the earlier survey. No differences were found between the initial cohort and the larger group, though there were significant differences in the intake of the schools. Some schools admitted as few as 7% of children with behavioural or reading difficulties whereas others took as many as 48–50%. Yet when the pupils were tested again at the age of 14 it became clear that 'the differences between the scores and their intakes did not explain the differences between them ... the schools with the most advantaged intakes were not necessarily those with the best outcomes' (Rutter *et al.*, 1979:27). They suggest that some schools therefore appeared to be able to exert a positive and beneficial influence on their pupils' progress, to some extent protecting them from difficulties, while others were apparently less successful at doing this. They therefore decided to examine 12 of these 20 schools in more detail in order to determine exactly what the differences were.

The basic strategy of the research involved an evaluation of the ways in which the 'outcomes' of schooling were related to specific school processes and 'ecological' factors after due allowance had been made for the effect of individual intake characteristics. The intake measures used were verbal reasoning at age ten, parental occupation, immigrant status and score on the Rutter Behaviour Scale. 'Outcomes' were operationalized in five ways: (1) children's behaviour (assessed by staff interviews, children's questionnaires and systematic classroom observation); (2) attendance returns; (3) examination success at 16; (4) delinquency rates; (5) employment record.[5] Forty six 'process variables' were assessed by a variety of means including interviews with teachers, pupil questionnaires and systematic observation. Finally an assessment of 'ecological' factors affecting the schools such as area influences, balance of intake and parental choice of schools was computed.

As in the Reynolds and Power studies the schools were found to vary considerably in terms of chosen outcomes. For example, fifth-year attendance over a two-week period varied from $12 \cdot 8$ attendances out of a possible 20 in one school to $17 \cdot 3$ in another. The delinquency rate (juvenile convictions and official cautions) for the schools varied from 16 to 44% for boys and from 1 to 11% for girls. In each case Rutter *et al.* argue that the variations between the schools could not be explained entirely in terms of the intake and they therefore turned to an examination of the schools themselves.

In contrast with Reynolds' findings, Rutter *et al.* (1979) report that school size, teacher—pupil ratio and quality and age of school premises were all unassociated with outcomes. However, they report very considerable and statistically significant differences between the schools on the 46 'process' variables which they studied. Factors as varied as the degree of academic emphasis, teachers' actions in lessons, the availability of incentives and rewards, good conditions for pupils and the extent to which children were able to take responsibility for their books, were all significantly associated with outcome differences between schools.

For example, they found that children's classroom behaviour was much better where the teacher had prepared lessons in advance, so that little time was wasted at the beginning in setting up apparatus or handing out papers. Good pupil behaviour was also strongly associated with the teacher's style of discipline. The amount of formal punishment made little difference but frequent disciplinary interventions were linked with more disruptive behaviour in the classroom. Conversely, pupils' behaviour was much better when teachers used an ample amount of praise in their teaching. They also report that children had better academic success where homework was regularly set and marked and where the teachers expressed expectations that a high proportion of their children would do well in national examinations. Schools which expected the pupils to care for their books and papers had better behaviour, better attendance and less delinquency. In a similar way, giving pupils posts or tasks of responsibility (such as the post of form captain or participation in school assembly) was associated with better pupil behaviour.

The models provided by teachers to their pupils were also seen to be significant — when teachers appeared to take good care of the buildings and were willing to see their pupils about problems at any time, they conveyed a *positive* image to their pupils which was associated with better outcomes. Negative models conveyed by teachers, such as starting lessons late, ending them early, using unofficial physical sanctions, etc., were associated with lower outcomes.

At the end of the analysis these and other variables were combined to give an overall measure of process (rather than processes) which Rutter *et al.* (1979) entitle 'ethos'. The association between this combined measure and outcome was much stronger than any of the associations with individual process variables and they therefore suggest that there was a *cumulative* effect of these various social factors in the running of schools.[6]

Rutter *et al.*'s findings lead them to make some bold conclusions about 'good schools'. They suggest that their research has identified key *causal* variables and conclude that the results 'carry the strong implication that schools can do much to foster good behaviour and attainments and that even in a disadvantaged area schools can be a force for good' (1979:205). The emphasis in their conclusion is therefore on school process factors that are open to modification by school staff rather than on those factors fixed by external constraint. Yet such a conclusion overlooks their own very significant findings on the impact of 'ecological' factors, particularly the balance of academic intake on school outcomes. The balance of academic intake is clearly beyond the scope of any individual school to change but as Table 3.1 shows it was highly significantly related to three of the four outcomes. As Acton (1980) suggests, balance of academic intake can provide an equally plausible explanation for all of the variations in outcome apart from behaviour at school, yet the school process variables receive far more emphasis in the conclusions drawn.

Because *Fifteen Thousand Hours* was so widely publicized and debated it is not suprising that it has been the subject of some serious criticism. As a statistician, Goldstein (1980) talks of a 'less than fully competent expertise' (p. 23) in the analysis of intake adjustment, while Acton (1980) criticizes the book for raising false hopes about the ability of schools to help improve the position of lower class and disadvantaged children. Two further criticisms seem particularly important. The first relates to the selection of intake variables and the second concerns the choice of schools utilized by the study.

The use of intake variables is significant, because the major claim that the study makes over that of Reynolds, is that by measuring the intake of the 12 schools, variations can be controlled for and significant school processes isolated. Rutter *et al.* (1979) used only limited input indices (verbal reasoning, behavioural ratings, father's occupation and immigrant status) but as both A. Hargreaves (1980) and Goldstein (1980) point out, many other studies have shown that a multitude of input indices such as family size, parental education, parental income, etc., are correlated with academic success. As Goldstein comments: 'It remains an open question as to how much of the subsequent differences between schools could be attributed to additional variables not used' (1980:22). A. Hargreaves (1980) also criticizes the very limited 'parental occupation' indices. Only three categories were used (non-manual, skilled manual and semi-skilled/unskilled), and 'all manner of different occupations from professor of sociology to filing clerk with the accompanying differences in reward, prestige, working conditions etc. are subsumed under the label of 'non-manual' (p. 213). With such a broad category the effects of background on pupil outcomes are likely to be inconsistent and therefore tend to cancel each other out thus reducing the force of the final correlation. Also excluded from the input indices are mothers' occupations, yet as Jackson and Marsden (1962) revealed many years ago, the 'white bloused' mother in the formally working class family is very significant in pulling children towards more middle class schooling patterns. All of these factors, Hargreaves argues, serve seriously to undermine the influence of background

Table 3.1. Correlations between 'academic balance of intake' and four measures of 'output'

Academic balance	Correlations with behavioural outcomes	Correlations with delinquency		Correlations with attendance		Correlations with academic attainment	
% Band 1	0·19	0·75	$P < 0·05$	0·76	$P < 0·01$	0·61	$P < 0·05$
% Band 2	0·09	0·57	N.S.	0·84	$P < 0·01$	0·48	N.S.

Source: Rutter (1979).
N.S., not significant.

characteristics of pupil outcomes and therefore dramatically to over estimate the effects of school *per se*.

A more general criticism relates to the choice of schools used in the study. Rutter *et al.* (1979) admit that the schools they studied were narrow in their curricula and pedagogic practice. The same admission is made by Reynolds about the schools in his sample. Both studies have considered it more important to examine a coherent set of schools serving a particular community than to select schools that are in any way educationally interesting. In other words, the sampling frame for the schools studied has been the catchment area rather than educational factors. The selection of schools becomes particularly significant when they are used as a source of information about successful practices. The somewhat conservative prescriptions that both Reynolds' and Rutter's studies produce are undoubtedly a product of the schools that were chosen (perhaps unwittingly) for the study. As A. Hargreaves (1980) concludes: 'My fear is that "good practice" (including the frequent setting of homework, spending more time on subject matter, having neat and tidy classrooms and assigning positions of responsibility) all of which ... (were) identified as being present in this sample of twelve less than innovatory schools, will be used as a blueprint for "effective" education and that even modestly different alternatives will be nudged further into the periphery of educational debate' (p. 216).

The 'schools make a difference' thesis advanced by Power, Reynolds and Rutter has attracted considerable interest in recent years. The notion that even with a disadvantaged intake schools can be a 'positive force for good' is an attractive one. However, enthusiasm should not be unqualified for some serious doubt about the impact of schools, particularly on the development of juvenile delinquents, has been cast by another major study — the Cambridge Study of Delinquent Development (West, 1982).[7]

The Cambridge Study of Delinquent Development

The Cambridge study took place over a 20-year period and involved a regular and systematic survey of 400 young males recruited at the age of eight from a working class neighbourhood in London. The boys, who attended six primary schools were followed until they were 25, by which time one-third of the group had gained a criminal conviction record. The study is of major importance because a wide variety of indices were documented comparing those who were eventually convicted with those who were not. These indices include items from the boys' personal background as well as information on their schooling.

Five key factors were shown to correlate with delinquent development: (1) coming from a low income family; (2) coming from a large sized family; (3) having parents considered by social workers to have performed their childrearing duties unsatisfactorily; (4) having below average intelligence; (5) having a parent with a criminal record. West (1982) reports that each of these factors was present in about one-quarter of the sample and the possession of any one of them effectively doubled the likelihood of a boy becoming a juvenile delinquent.

In addition to these background factors, school behaviour was also assessed. When the boys were eight and again when they were ten, their teachers were asked to complete a questionnaire on their behaviour in class. At the age of ten their class peers were also asked to rate the four most troublesome boys in the class. From these measures the boys were divided into three groups — most troublesome, average and least troublesome. Of the 92 boys categorized as most troublesome during their later primary school years 44·6% later became officially classified as delinquent compared with only 3·5% of the 143 boys classified as least troublesome and 21·6% of the 176 moderately troublesome group. 'Thus being perceived as an above average nuisance by teachers and peers (whose ratings were significantly congruent) was much the best single predictor of juvenile delinquency'(West, 1982:31).

The six primary schools from which the boys in the study were drawn each produced roughly the same proportion of delinquents. However, as in the studies described above, it was found that there were marked differences in the delinquency rates of the secondary schools to which the boys transferred. Most of the sample[8] went on to one or other of 13 different local secondary schools. The education authority provided data on the numbers of boys age 11—14 attending each of the 13 schools and also on the number of appearances in juvenile courts by boys of this age from each of the schools over a one-year period. From this information three of the schools were identified as having a high delinquency rate, six as having a low delinquency rate and four as being intermediate. The schools with a high delinquency rate contributed nearly four times as many court appearances in proportion to the number of boys in the school compared with schools with a low delinquency rate. This much is similar to the other studies of school differences.

However, in the Cambridge study, it emerged on closer examination that the differences between the schools were more closely connected with the different kinds of boys joining each school than with anything that may have happened to them at school.

As was noted above 'troublesomeness' at primary school was shown to be highly predictive of later juvenile delinquency. Given the proportion of delinquents in each category of 'troublesomeness' (high, medium and low) and knowing the numbers of boys from each category who were attending each school, it was possible to calculate the percentages of delinquents to be expected in each school, assuming that nothing happened in the schools to alter the boys' delinquency potential. The expected percentages compared with the actual percentages of boys who became delinquent are shown in Table 3.2.

Although there were slightly more delinquents than might be expected in the high delinquency schools and slightly less than would be expected in the low delinquency schools, Table 3.2 shows that the majority of the differences between the schools was accounted for by the differences in intake. The high delinquency schools had a much higher proportion of troublesome children sent to them. Similar results were obtained with regard to truancy. Schools did make a minor difference in promoting or prohibiting truancy, but more significant was the intake of the school.

In comparing these results with those from the other institutional studies outlined above, it is important to remember that the Cambridge study only dealt with officially recorded delinquency, whereas Rutter and Reynolds took a much broader definition of 'outcomes' including academic success and

Table 3.2. Comparison of expected and actual percentages of delinquent boys according to the delinquency rates of secondary schools

	Expected	*Actual*
High delinquency-rate schools	31·3	35·7
Medium delinquency-rate schools	22·9	22·9
Low delinquency-rate schools	15·2	12·8

Source: West (1982).

behaviour at school. In addition, it must be noted that the Cambridge study is quite small in comparison with the others. It would, therefore, as West points out, be rash to conclude from these results that schools have no effect on delinquent development. However, the Cambridge study does present prima facie evidence to question the conclusions of the other studies. It seems that when detailed information on the intake of schools is obtained, much of the differences between schools seems to evaporate. As West (1982) concludes: 'Rutter did not have the same behavioural ratings of boys as we did, so one possible reason for the differences in results is that his assessments of delinquency potential at intake were less efficient' (p. 100).

The debate about whether schools can indeed make a difference in their pupils' delinquent development is at present unresolved. What has been learned so far though is that the business of studying institutional differences with any degree of sophistication is highly complex. Not only are there important difficulties in successfully operationalizing school processes and pupil outcomes, but there are still many complex problems to be overcome in effectively controlling for intake. Until that methodological issue is successfully resolved the results of this form of research will have to be treated with considerable caution.

In addition to these controversies within the positivist camp, there are of course many other questions that can be raised about positivist methods and assumptions themselves. It is to a consideration of some of these more fundamental criticisms that we now turn.

Problems in Positivism

Since its emergence at the end of the last century, *individual* positivism has become a major influence in the field of indiscipline at school. The notion of the 'maladjusted child', which is at least in part based on the findings of positivist research, is today granted a central place in educational policy and provision. Teachers as well as other professionals in the educational welfare network (Johnson *et al.*, 1980) overwhelmingly subscribe to a pathological view of school deviance. Children reject their education because of some deficiency in themselves, in their families or in their social milieux. That rejection is illogical for it denies the validity and importance of what schools have to offer.

More recently, *institutional* positivism has achieved considerable notoriety with its promise that rigorous scientific analysis can isolate those particular features of school organization and practice that can positively promote better behaviour and results at school. Rutter *et al.*'s (1979) study in particular perhaps holds a unique place in contemporary educational research in that it has been widely read by teachers throughout the profession.

Why is it that this form of research has become so influential in the sphere of policy with disaffected pupils? Perhaps one of the reasons is that positivism tends to serve the interests of practitioners, administrators and politicians and is in a sense conservative. By writing-off pupil opposition to schooling as irrelevant or illogical, positivism reconfirms teachers' own perceptions of the world and their place within it. It also provides the politician and planner with a model of human behaviour which is comforting; it leaves the central aspects of society unchallenged but, through the notion of determinism, allows some hope for progress.

However, the fact that positivism has achieved virtual hegemony within the sphere of professional involvement with the school deviant does not mean that its principles and procedures have gone unchallenged. At the level of epistemology contemporary philosophers of science[9] frequently dismiss many of the claims of classical positivism. In particular, the notion of neutral scientific observation — absolute objectivity — is considered by many to be an impossible goal. Facts do not speak for themselves — scientific observation and scientific theories are inextricably linked and in reality social scientists have to choose which 'paradigmatic universe' they wish to enter. This casts considerable doubt on the claim of positivists to be able to validate a particular theory by an appeal to objective evidence. For many contemporary analysts there is no objective evidence, no one truth, only a variety of truths which vary according to one's initial theoretical assumptions.

At a general level, therefore, positivism's claim to follow natural scientific procedures has been challenged. It is based, many argue, on a false understanding of the nature of science in the first place. But in addition to these general criticisms, positivism's more specific assumptions — the assumed consensus of values, the determinacy of behaviour, deviance as a product of undersocialization — have not escaped critical comment either.

Determinism and the Denial of Freedom

Positivism's most central assumption, the notion of determinism, is for many its most profound difficulty. In searching for the causal laws of school deviance, positivists deny the consciousness of the individual pupil. Pupils are seen as reacting to causal factors whether these are in their own make up and personality, their family or in their school; they do not decide how to act for themselves. Yet for many contemporary writers this determinism denies the most important element of human behaviour — that of consciousness. Pupils do not simply react, they *act*. The world has a subjective meaning for them and those subjective meanings are critical in influencing how they decide to behave. As we will see in later chapters, some theorists consider subjective perspectives to be critical in explaining why pupils behave as they do. Sociology's central task for these writers is therefore to discover the meanings pupils attach to their behaviour. For others of less idealist persuasion subjective meanings do not provide the whole answer, rather they are something to be explained in themselves. Yet these analysts too emphasize the importance of understanding subjective meaning. It is only the positivists who rule such meanings out of court as irrelevant or as misleading.

Simply because positivists are able to demonstrate correlations between certain objectively defined external factors (e.g. class, gender, educational achievements, inner city schools) and various forms of formally recorded school deviance does not mean that any of these relationships are causal. It would be absurd to deny that these correlations are significant. The methodology of positivism is extremely powerful in revealing important social facts. However, the determinist *theory* implicit in positivism is simply inadequate as a form of explanation. Rather than explanations, therefore, correlations must be seen as something to be explained in terms of choices and meanings. Why is it that inner-city low-achieving working class boys reject their schooling as a means of coping with their predicament? Should they not logically try even harder than their middle class peers to achieve success? Why are girls less often thought of as a problem by their teachers? Surely they share the same range of objective social facts — family background, educational success, social class — as their brothers? As will be shown in later chapters, for many writers these questions are the starting point of research, not the conclusions.

Cultural Myopia

An interrelated problem to that of determinism is that positivists take a consensual view of human behaviour. Their positivism leads them to become culturally myopic, denying the authenticity of pupils' diverse responses to school. Many pupils' experience of schooling is of constant failure and rejection but the authenticity of any protest they make is denied by positivism. Resistance is written off as poorly socialized or irrational behaviour because it does not support the consensual view of schooling. Yet to take such an attitude is to underestimate the creativity of pupils. The way in which children cope with their world is very diverse. As we will see in the next chapter, children take up a wide variety of different responses when faced with school failure. These responses are not the product of unsocialized behaviour as positivists would have us believe. Rather they are genuine cultural phenomena to be explained in themselves.

Defining the Deviant

As was shown in the last chapter, one of the most intractable problems for positivist research in the study of school deviance is how to define it; how to distinguish the truant from the non-truant, the violent child from the non-violent one and the 'maladjusted' from the normal. Yet discrete classifications are essential if correlations are to be calculated in any meaningful way. As we have seen, one of the responses has been to use officially recorded statistics such as absence rates or prosecutions by the juvenile courts. Another response has been to construct rating scales for use by teachers and psychologists. On the basis of these categorizations, correlations have been established and causes proposed. Yet this sort of classification often conceals more than it reveals, denying the complex and often transitory nature of school deviance. Disruption and truancy are difficult to classify by their very nature. The worst behaved pupils conform for most of the time and the overwhelming majority of all difficult pupils simply 'grow out of it', without any formal intervention or treatment.[10] The strict classification of pupils as deviant or normal that is essential for scientific analysis is therefore artificial.

Whose Categories?

A further problem of definition relates to whose categories are used. In reality it would seem that positivist classification procedures often say more about the classifier than the pupils. Truants may appear as a unitary category for teachers because they have to deal with them as such. Yet that single category might conceal a multitude of realities on the part of the pupils. It can be argued that researchers who treat official statistics and definitions of school deviance as facts and then attempt to explain their causes may therefore simply be revealing the commonsense theories of school deviance employed by those who are agents of social control — teachers, magistrates, educational welfare officers.

This issue becomes particularly apparent if one thinks of the position of girls in positivist research — they are invisible. Because researchers are largely dependent on teachers' categories for the classification and recording of disruption and truancy, the subject of girls and school deviance has seldom been seriously studied by positivists. To put it bluntly, girls are not much of a problem for teachers so they have not been much of a problem for positivistic researchers. Yet the case of girls to some extent points up some of the limitations of positivist procedures in defining who is deviant. Research on girls from different theoretical perspectives seems to suggest that they may be equally disaffected from school as boys but that their means of expressing that disaffection is less overt and therefore leads to less conflict. McRobbie and Garber (1976) suggest that girls talk rather than act and Humphries (1981) suggests that they subvert rather than confront.[11] It is true that these forms of behaviour are less of a problem for most teachers, but this does not prove that the girls are any less disaffected. Yet positivists are largely unconcerned with such subjective meanings. If pupils do not appear in the official statistics then they are not deviant. Cultural meanings are essentially inaccessible to the positivist whose classification and measurement techniques insist that he (!), like the teacher, sees more male than female deviance.

The Individualization of Problems

A final difficulty of positivism is its individualistic approach. In individual positivism the focus is on the study of the pupil, and in institutional positivism it is on the school. However, in both cases the approach is the same; the individual unit is divorced from any wider social context. Pupils fail and become truants and disruptives because of individual differences — it is a discreet problem understandable in terms of the child as an individual. Yet we all know that the opportunities for educational success are not equally distributed. There are substantial differences in social opportunities that structure material possibilities and constrain individual pupils. The same is true of schools. They may face considerable constraints in terms of intake and resources and in their opportunities to respond. Yet positivism reduces all these social problems to the individual pupil or the individual school — wider issues become irrelevant. As Matza (1969) comments, one of the greatest achievements of early positivists was that 'they separated the study of crime from the workings and theory of the state' and, with that done, 'the agenda for research and scholarship for the next half century was relatively clear, especially with regard to what would not be studied' (p. 123). And what was not to be studied was the relationship between school deviance and wider society. It is to a consideration of some of the earliest attempts to reintroduce a more fully social theory of school deviance that we now turn.

Notes

1. Thirty five per cent of the children in the district attended grammar schools reflecting the traditionally high rate of grammar school provision in Wales.
2. See Carroll (1977)
3. These were taken as indices of other forms of rule enforcement.
4. See, for example, Woods (1979), A. Hargreaves (1978).
5. No results on employment are included in the main study as it was published before these were obtained.
6. As a number of commentators have noted, 'ethos' is primarily a statistical rather than an educational concept in this context. It is never defined, being simply an amalgam of all the positively correlating process variables. As Goldstein (1980) comments, by adding variables together it is not surprising that they correlate with outcomes more than any individual variable. However plausible the concept, the authors present little or no evidence for having studied ethos in any meaningful way.
7. The findings of this research have been published in various books and articles over the years. West (1982) provides a useful overview of the main findings.
8. 335 boys out of the original 400.
9. See, for example, Kuhn (1970), Popper (1963).
10. Topping (1983) reviews the literature on the effectiveness of provision for dealing with disaffected pupils and argues that two-thirds of such pupils simply 'grow out of it' without any specific intervention.
11. Davies (1984) has recently made a systematic comparison of the different 'offences' undertaken by boys and girls in one school. Her study shows that:

> Girls are more conformist only in certain areas — the institutional rules of school in terms of attendance, misbehaviour and damage, and the technical goals of achievement in terms of conscientiousness and presentation of work. Rule infringements such as smoking and lack of uniform are however equally likely for both sexes and girls seem to assert *more* independence in the creation of personal time and space around the school. (p. 14)

CHAPTER FOUR

Adaptations And Subcultures

During the twentieth century positivism has become established as the dominant way of understanding indiscipline in school. Its theoretical links with medicine and the emerging profession of educational psychology have aided its rise to ascendency. Today it holds sway in both lay and professional thought and through the concept of 'maladjustment' is widely influential in social and educational policy. As was argued in the last chapter, positivists take a very determinist view of indiscipline. The causes of deviant behaviour may lie in biological, psychological or social factors and however pupils may explain their behaviour it is these objective factors that cause them to be antisocial; it is these factors that make them maladjusted.

The term 'maladjustment' reminds us that from the positivist perspective, deviant behaviour is something that is abnormal — it is viewed as a form of individual pathology. Even when the 'causes' lie in social factors it is in the individual child that the disposition to pathological behaviour is found. Yet the idea that deviant behaviour is irrational or pathological has not gone unchallenged. It was Durkheim (1951, 1966), writing at the beginning of this century, who first advanced the proposition that crime and deviance were not necessarily irrational — they could equally be seen as a rational response to *particular social circumstances*. This view necessarily shifts the search for the causes of deviant behaviour from the individual to society itself. Durkheim was the first writer to argue for a fully social theory of crime and deviance. His influence on contemporary research on school deviance is profound. Indeed, in all of the perspectives explored in the remaining chapters of this book it is taken for granted that deviance is 'normal'. Most sociological researchers accept that indiscipline at school is not necessarily a product of maladjustment; it may equally be seen as a rational response to particular circumstances. As a result the purpose of theoretical and empirical work is to reveal what those particular circumstances are and to document how different groups of pupils respond.

In this chapter two interrelated theoretical perspectives which have generated a number of important empirical studies will be considered. The first is anomie theory, derived from the work of Merton (1938). Research in this tradition is exemplified in the studies of Wakeford (1969) and Woods (1979). The second approach is status deprivation theory — a particular development of Merton's work. This is illustrated by a consideration of studies made by Hargreaves (1967), Lacey (1970) and Ball (1981). At the end of the chapter, some criticisms of this theoretical tradition are considered.

Adapting To School

Merton's Theory of Anomie

Merton was a sociologist writing in America in the 1930s, the depression years. For him the key feature of his society was the contrast between the American dream — the idea that everyone could move from rags to riches, from the log cabin to the White House — and the reality of harsh economic inequality. The promise was of an open society where, given hard work, everyone could realize their ideals. This promise, Merton argued, constituted the central element of American culture; it helped define the goals, purposes and interests of the whole population. But for a society to work harmoniously, common goals were not enough; there also had to be an appropriate social structure to allow the achievement of those goals. In America the social structure could not yield limitless opportunities for all.

In order for contemporary society to function successfully, he argued, an emphasis on success was essential. How else could an individual be encouraged to find his or her own natural level? Yet this emphasis on success also had dysfunctional consequences for it was continually contradicted by the actual opportunities facing people. Not everyone could achieve the same, either because of their natural talents, or more importantly, because of the inequalities of society. Members of the lower social classes seldom had the same opportunites as those higher up the social structure. For certain parts of the population there was, therefore, a disjunction between the *goals* of society and the *means* of achieving those goals and this led to 'strain'; it led to 'anomie'.[1]

In the same society that proclaims the right and even the duty of lofty aspirations for all, men do not have equal access to the opportunity structure. Social origins do variously facilitate or hamper access to forms of success represented by wealth or recognition or substantial power. Confronted with contradictions in experience, appreciable numbers of people become estranged from a society that promises them in principle what they are denied in reality. (Merton, 1964:214)

For Merton, anomie therefore arose because of structural strain generated by differential access to opportunity structures. As Fitzgerald (1980) comments: 'No society can at one and the same time hold out a common goal to all its members and block off access to the achievement of that goal — and not expect problems' (p. 21). According to Merton, crime, deviance and psychopathology were the most common problems; these were ways of adapting to anomie.

Merton argued that the way in which people adapt in the face of anomie depends on two things. First, whether they accept or reject the *goals* of society and, secondly, whether they accept the legitimate *means* of achieving those goals. This can lead to four sorts of adaptation, all of them deviant. They are 'innovation', 'ritualism', 'retreatism' and 'rebellion'. Mertons' model is represented diagramatically in Fig. 4.1.

'Innovation' involves accepting and pursuing the goals of society (for example, money and success) but by illegitimate means such as theft or fraud. Merton argued that those who steal are still committed to the goals of society because they still value money, but they use illegitimate means to achieve them. In the context of the school we might consider that children who cheat in tests or examinations are 'innovators'. They are wedded to the conventional goal of academic success

		Means	
		Positive	Negative
Goals	Positive	Conformity	Innovation
	Negative	Ritualism	Retreatism or rebellion

Figure 4.1. Merton's model of adaptations to anomie.

but try to achieve it by illegitimate means. 'Ritualism', Merton suggested, is the opposite of innovation. It involves an elimination or scaling down of unobtainable goals but an obsessive attachment to the institutionalized means of achievement. Merton saw this as the response of the lower middle classes in society, for example the unsuccessful bank clerk who has given up on the idea of promotion but who is still ritually conformist at work. In school, children who are consistently unsuccessful but still keep on trying could be considered 'ritualists'.

'Retreatism' is a form of adaptation where individuals have dropped out of society. They are no longer committed to the goals or the means of society but have found no alternative. This, according to Merton, is a private response, typical of drunks, tramps and addicts. Interestingly enough he saw this as the least common form of adaptation, yet in the context of the school retreatism is quite common. Many children, especially as they grow older, seem to opt out, some by playing truant and others by being 'mental truants' even though they attend in person. Finally, there is 'rebellion', which involves rejection both of the means and the ends of conventional society and replacing them with some alternative. This might be observed among those pupils who have found alternative values to those sponsored by their teachers. Pupils actively involved in youth culture or petty crime might fall into this category.

The Four Basic Assumptions

In Chapter 2 it was suggested (following Burrell and Morgan, 1979) that all social scientific paradigms involve assumptions about four topics: ontology, or the nature of reality; human nature; epistemology, or the nature of knowledge; and research methods. Positivists, it was argued, derive most of their assumptions on these topics from an idealized version of the natural sciences. If Merton's anomie theory is examined in relation to these four paradigmatic issues it is clear that from a sociological point of view the theory involves a considerable conceptual advance over that of positivism. In terms of ontology, anomie theory focuses, at least to a limited extent, on both subjectivity and objectivity. The theory directs us first to a range of social factors which are seen to structure people's lives (opportunity structures) and secondly to the patterned subjective responses that people make (adaptations). Thus there is a less deterministic view of human nature from that of positivism. People may have internalized a range of culturally defined ideas of success and face a range of opportunities which structure their possibilities of achieving that success, yet within that framework they are seen as making rational decisions in order to solve the problems they face.

Anomie theory also differs from positivism in terms of research methods and epistemology. The approach is a normative one, the theory itself determining what is to count as data (objective evidence of unequal opportunity structures, insights into subjective patterns of adaptation) and a range of different research methods which can document these data are considered appropriate. The aim of the research is more broadly conceived than in positivism. It is not simply to prove or disprove an hypothesized relationship. It is also the function of research to help extend, explore, elaborate and change the theory. Empiricism has a dual function — theory development and theory testing; these two dimensions of research are seen as inextricably linked.

As a result of this more relativistic view of research it must be accepted that the ultimate test of a theory such as anomie is not through empiricism alone. An equally important test may come from other theoretical work focusing on different sorts of data and offering different sorts of explanations. The break with positivism implicit in anomie theory is therefore profound. As will become apparent in subsequent chapters, most sociological researchers accept this more relativistic approach to research and theory. Once one leaves the secure realms of 'hard science' one enters a more problematic world where words like research, theory, evidence and proof take on a new and less clear-cut meaning.

Cloistered Elites

The first major British research to employ Mertons anomie theory was Wakeford's (1969) study of boys' public boarding schools. In this analysis Wakeford used a revised and extended version of the original typology of adaptations arguing that the approach provided a sociological framework within which to consider the connections between pupils' responses to life in school and the schools' 'sociocultural structure'.

> It can be said that the socio-cultural structure of the school will operate to exert pressure on the pupils to adopt one or other of a number of alternative modes of adaptation to school although they may shift from one alternative to another — at different times in their school careers as they engage in different spheres of social activity within the school system. (p. 132)

As a result of his participant observation in one public school, and visits to others, Wakeford sketches five principal modes of adaptation that he viewed: they were 'conformity', 'colonization', 'retreatism', 'intransigence' and 'rebellion'.

'Conformity' involved supporting both the schools' goals, at least as perceived by the head teacher, and the officially approved means of achieving them. Enthusiasm for the school and its reputation and a general willingness to volunteer for anything were its chief characteristics. Contrary to the expectations of many staff and parents, Wakeford reports that this mode was not adopted by most of the boys for most of their school lives. In Wakeford's case-study school there appeared to be only a small core of relatively senior boys at any one time who adopted this mode. Their principal aim seemed to be to achieve a post of responsibility with its attendant privileges. A far more frequent response to school was 'colonization'.

'Colonization' combined an ambivalence about formal rules and regulations with an indifference to school goals. A boy adopting this mode would accept that the school would provide his basic social environment during the term time for five years and would therefore attempt to establish a relatively contented existence within it by maximizing the available gratifications whether officially permitted or not. Such a boy's main objective would be to 'work the system' to make time pass as comfortably and quickly as possible.

An alternative, slightly more deviant response was 'retreatism', which involved a degree of non-involvement in all but the most rigorously enforced school activities. In the case-study school this could be achieved by taking long walks when no compulsory activities were arranged or by making frequent visits to the music room where it was legitimate to practise alone. This strategy, which expressed a rejection or indifference to the school's goals and institutionalized means without replacing them was popular with older boys in particular.

As far as teachers were concerned a more challenging form of adaptation was 'intransigence'. This combined a rejection of the school's institutional means with an indifference to its ends — a cynical indifference to the life of the school. Various names are applied in public schools to such pupils — 'antis' or 'bolshies' — and Wakeford suggests that in his school such pupils typically tried to symbolize and assert their autonomy in their dress which they adapted from contemporary fashion.

The final mode of adaptation was 'rebellion'. Each year a few senior boys would move from the 'bolshie' stance to rebellion, substituting their own goals and means for those of the school.

They would refuse to take positions of responsibility such as being a prefect or employing a fag and would attempt to precipitate leaving the school as soon as they had obtained the standard of education consistent with their immediate substitute goals.

Wakeford's typology of adaptations is set out in Fig. 4.2. It presents the dominant modes of adaptation to school and indicates the stages in boys' school careers with which they appeared to be associated. Wakeford notes that the sequential pattern of adaptation was clearly related to the structure of opportunities for various responses within the school organization and he therefore suggests that the pattern of adaptations may be different in other schools. However, he gives very little detail on what exactly this structure of opportunity within the school actually was, nor is there any discussion, except at the most general level, of the goals of public school education. Wakeford's model is at best only suggestive. One is left to speculate on why any particular pupil adopted one mode of adaptation rather than another. By contrast, a more detailed analysis is provided by Woods (1979) in his book *The Divided School*.

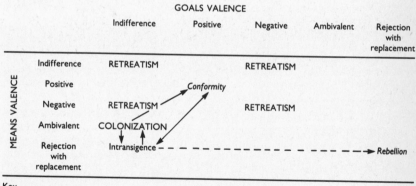

Figure 4.2. Wakeford's typology of modes of individual adaptation showing principal modes of adaptation by boys to a public boarding school.
Source: Wakeford (1969).

A Divided School

In this ethnographic study Woods revised Wakeford's typology in order to apply it to a state secondary modern school. Most of the adaptations he saw were similar to Wakeford's though he provides far more detail. For example, the following quotation illustrates retreatism:

> **Pat:** I think I've been worse behaved the last two years than I 'ave before. It's since that time when they said we couldn't take exams — now we're all misbehaved 'cos they said we couldn't take exams ... we're all just takin' no interest in lessons.
>
> **PW:** Did you have a choice?
>
> **Pat:** Yeah, you had a choice, but when you chose they said you couldn't do it. You know in maths and English an' that, what was some of us like, an' they just went in 'cos they got higher in something else you know....I've got a chip on me shoulder since then,...'Cos in my form I was higher than some of them — and it gets on your nerves when they get on. You know, you think, "Bugger the school I ain't going to do anything for the school now!" If I was taking exams I suppose I'd be a completely different person. I'd be taking more interest in the lessons but I'm not. I'm not taking no exam, so I'm not interested, and that's that! (Woods, 1979:66)

'Colonization', possibly the most prevalent mode of adaptation observed by Woods, was illustrated by Geoff and Martin:

> **Geoff:** It's not really hard work, you get used to it. Maths — you have to do that. Phil never does any homework. Me and Martin copy each other, you see we have different strengths and weaknesses. I do the maths and he does the history. If I could do it pretty easy, I'd do it, or compare the answers with somebody else ... we get things right mostly, we're skilled operators.
>
> **Martin:** It's been a good laugh, mostly. I do a bit of work for teachers I enjoy, like Mr Harvey. He tells us a joke. We get on all right with him and will do some work for him. He's friendly, talks to you, he's more free, lets you do other things, you can ask questions any time. Not like Martell, you can't interrupt him. He's too busy writing on the blackboard and droning on. (Woods, 1979:64).

Like Wakeford, Woods identified 'intransigence' and 'rebellion' as more serious forms of resistance. But where Woods differs from Wakeford is in relation to conformity. Wakeford only provides one space in his typology for conformity while identifying four non-conforming adaptations. Woods, on the other hand, argues that compliance does not necessarily imply 'sucking up', creeping or becoming a 'teacher's pet'. These would be examples of 'ingratiation'. Woods argues that there are other forms of conformity available to pupils such as 'compliance', 'ritualism' and 'opportunism'. According to Woods the 'ingratiators'' main aid is to maximize benefits by earning the favour of those in power. Such pupils are not usually disturbed by their unpopularity with their peers. A more common mode of positive response to school is 'identification', where the pupil identifies with and feels some affinity for the school. Woods suggests that among younger pupils there is often an *optimistic compliance* — pupils take the school's goals on trust in an air of expectancy and hope. In the upper school, pupils on the examination route are more likely to adopt an *instrument compliance*.

Another type of conformity omitted by Wakeford but included in Merton's original typology is 'ritualism'. A pupil adopting this mode is not interested in the school's goals but keeps going through the motions of accepting the official norms of behaviour.

> **PW:** What sort of pupils would you say you were?
> **Derek:** Pretty average really. I do me work. I behave meself.
> **PW:** What do you hope to get out of it?
> **Derek:** Dunno, really. I just do what I'm told.
> **PW:** What do you come to school for?
> **Derek:** Well, you have to don't you. Ain't got much choice.
> **PW:** Why do you have to?
> **Derek:** That's the law, in'it?
>
> (Woods, 1979:73)

A final form of conformity identified by Woods is 'ambivalence', which he suggests is characteristic of second-year pupils. It is a 'trying out' phase often emerging as a reaction against the early optimism of the first year. Pupils are less consistent in their application to work with frequent but momentary leanings to other more deviant modes of adaptation.

Woods also differs from Wakeford in his attempt to make his typology less rigid. With regard to goals he emphasizes that although there may be some agreement on general institutional goals such as 'to teach' or 'to get past examinations', individual teachers have their own goals which can vary considerably. As a result pupils might want to change their mode of adaptation depending on who is teaching them.

> Consider for example a rebellious non examination form in a secondary school — one teacher might aim to 'hammer some sense into them', to achieve some objective standard; another to humour them with a view to teaching them something 'about life'; another simply to pass the time away as agreeably as possible. (Woods, 1979:70)[2]

Because of this sort of variation Woods argues that it is more profitable to think of pupils adapting to individual teachers rather than to their school as a whole.

As a result of this increased sensitivity Woods identifies predominant modes of adaptation for large groups of children, but he emphasizes that individual careers can be very complicated. A pupil might adopt one mode throughout school life, but it is more likely that he or she will move through a series of modes. 'He might employ one mode for one section of the school, one subject or one teacher and another for another. He might have a dominant mode or a mixture of them' (1979:78). For Woods, therefore, the 'retreatist' and the 'ritualist' are not individuals, they are modes of adaptation and there are bits of them in most people. However, despite these caveats, these complexities are not actually included in the model shown in Fig. 4.3. The modes of adaptation may have increased but the basic pattern of dominant orientations still seems to remain.

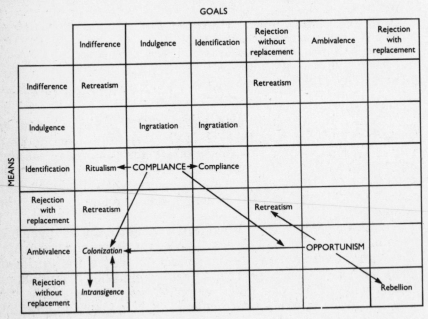

Figure 4.3. Wood's typology of modes of adaptation in the state secondary system.
Source: Wood (1979).

The strength of Merton's anomie theory is the variety of adaptations that can be documented. Subsequent work has seldom been as sensitive. Pupils are often simply lumped together as either conformist or deviant. The notion of adaptation allows the number of positions to be increased, though clearly they could not be indefinitely elaborated without losing the elegance and force of the original typology. The tension in Woods' work is that he realizes that even his revised typology does not capture the multiplicity of reactions to school by deviant and conformist pupils, yet he wants to retain some of the strength of the original model. The result is a rather uneasy compromise in which the typology remains but we are given many caveats about how it works out in practice. The complexities are not actually integrated into the model.[3]

One might also ask of both Woods and Wakeford what has happened to the concept of anomie? Merton's original formulation was based on a serious critique of the society that he observed. It was because there was a tension between the aspirations and opportunities that arose in an unequal society that deviant adaptations were necessary. Yet one finds little of this critique in either Woods' or Wakeford's work. Surely the force of the analysis is lost when children are seen as simply responding to whether they like a particular teacher's teaching style or not. Woods, in particular, with his emphasis on the need to see pupils as responding to teachers as individuals, reduces the theory of anomie to simply that of adaptation. Pupils choose to accept or reject their schooling, not because of the fairness or unfairness of a narrowly selective educational system in which many are called but few are chosen, but they are seen as accepting or rejecting school on the basis of whether the teachers they meet are fair or explain things well.

One important weakness in Merton's original formulation which is certainly reflected in Wakeford's work is its individualistic emphasis. Merton constructed his theory as if people experienced their choices in a kind of social vacuum, each person having to make their own assessment of the opportunities available to them and adapting accordingly. As a result the theory is rather static and mechanistic. As Cohen (1965) comments, the theory focuses on 'initial states and deviant outcomes rather than on the processes whereby acts and complex structures of action are built, elaborated and transformed'. Cohen's own response was to retain the Mertonian focus on goals and means, but to emphasize the *social* nature of adaptations. The result was the development of the concept of 'subculture': an idea that has proved seminal in work on deviance both inside and outside schools. It is to a consideration of this second major tradition in sociological studies of school deviance that we now turn.

Subcultures at School

Status Deprivation Theory

At the same time that Merton was developing the concept of anomie, another American sociologist, Sutherland (Sutherland and Cressy, 1966), was developing his own theory of deviance entitled 'differential association'. Rather than examining the social structural conditions that promoted deviance, differential association theory focused on the social processes by which an individual became deviant. Sutherland maintained that people actually learned to become deviant through association. Crime was not a product of the lack of socialization as positivists would have it, rather it was learned in just the same way as non-criminal behaviour. The learning not only included the techniques of committing crimes, but also the rationalizations, attitudes and drives associated with it. Learning occurred through association with other people, particularly those who formed part of one's intimate personal group. The efficiency of such learning depended on the duration, primacy, intensity and frequency of contact.

Later sociologists came to see that differential association theory could complement anomie theory. Both theories accepted Durkheim's suggestion that deviance was to be accepted as a natural part of social life. As Rubington and Weinberg (1977) comment:

> Merton's theory could explain why rates of deviant behaviour are higher in some sections of society than others; it could not however explain why some persons in those sections engage in acts while others do not. Sutherland's theory, because it is essentially a theory based on social interaction, is silent on the question of rates, but can explain why some people but not others learn patterns of deviant behaviour. (p. 147)

Two important attempts to synthesize anomie theory and differential association theory were made during the 1950s. They were Cohen's (1955) theory of delinquent subcultures, and Cloward and Ohlin's (1960) theory of deviant opportunity structures. Each will be considered in turn.

Despite similarities in their theorizing, Cohen was critical of Merton. He argued that while anomie theory, and especially 'innovation', was a highly plausible explanation of adult crime it could not explain the non-utilitarian, malicious and negativistic behaviour of young working class male delinquents. Delinquents might steal, therefore appearing to appreciate money, but they also often threw away what they had stolen or concentrated on stealing items of little value. For Cohen 'the destructiveness, the versatility, the zest and wholesale negativism which characterises the delinquent subculture are beyond the purvue of this (anomie) theory' (Cohen, 1955:36). Cohen argued that the motivation for delinquent solutions was therefore not to be found in anomie but in status problems. Large groups of adolescents, particularly those from lower social class backgrounds who were unsuccessful at school were 'status deprived'.

For Cohen the school was crucial. Echoing Merton's more general theory he considered school to be one of the primary institutions designed to integrate young people into the social structure. Schools were intended to make young people care about social status and academic achievement. However, in reality they denied this opportunity to all but a minority. Because schools were essentially middle class institutions holding out middle class criteria of status it was the working class child who was most frequently excluded. Many working class children were faced with the problem of adjustment; they were status deprived in a system that emphasized status. They therefore evolved their own system of values and ways of behaving in which they could succeed; they developed a subculture that could confer status on them when they conformed to its deviant values.

Cohen's theory was different from that of Merton in two important respects. First, he saw the response to status deprivation as a social one. Groups of adolescents who found themselves with similar problems of status deprivation evolved a common solution through a process called 'reaction formation'. Cohen argued that the movement towards a deviant subculture was at first slow and tentative — 'It is a groping, advancing, backtracking sounding out process' (Cohen, 1965:9) — but what is eventually established is a *joint* solution to a jointly experienced problem. Secondly, Cohen argued that what was established was a subculture that was wedded to neither the goals nor the means of conventional society. Rather it was a subculture that celebrated the opposite values of those espoused by the respectable middle class — it was malicious, short-term, hedonistic, non-utilitarian and negativistic. It therefore had the double function of conferring status on its members for hitting back at the very system that branded them failures in the first place.

The second important attempt to integrate anomie and differential association theory was made by Cloward and Ohlin (1960). They took Cohen's contribution a stage further suggesting that not all delinquent solutions were created anew each time a group experienced status deprivation. As well as a legitimate opportunity structure there was also an illegitimate one. The presence of absence of both sorts of opportunities explained the types of delinquent subcultures that might emerge.

> Men are envisaged, therefore, as being placed in cultures which they have learned by differential association and in facing particular problems of anomie which are a function of the opportunities, legitimate and illegitimate, which such an association offers them. Out of this moral base, their culture of origin, men collectively evolve solutions to the problems of anomie which face them. (Taylor *et al.*, 1973:134)

Cloward and Ohlin defined three types of subculture which arose among young delinquents, depending on the presence or absence of stable recruitment into adult criminal activities in the local community. Where there were such patterns of recruitment into adult crime a criminal subculture would emerge — a type of gang devoted to theft, extortion and other illegal means of gaining money. Where there was no recruitment a 'conflict' subculture emerged, a type of gang in which manipulation of violence predominated as a way of winning status. Boys who failed to succeed either legally or illegally in any context would adopt a 'retreatist' subculture in which the consumption of drugs and other illicit experiences were stressed. Cloward and Ohlin therefore emphasized the role of differential association more heavily than Cohen. They also criticized Cohen for over-emphasizing the role of the school. They suggested that for most 'down town street corner' youth, school is irrelevant. Instead, like Merton, they emphasized the importance of financial success. It is failure in this regard that first leads to the frustration that propels adolescents to develop their own subculture.

The work of Cohen and Cloward and Ohlin stimulated a considerable amount of research on delinquency throughout the late 1950s and 1960s both in America and in Britain. The general conclusion within the British context was that patterns of crime and delinquency were far milder than in America and, with the possible exception of Glasgow, the notion of the gang was not applicable in any meaningful sense. Downes (1966), for example, in a study of delinquency in the East End of London in the early 1960s, reported that 'status frustration', 'alienation' and 'delinquent subcultures' were not terms that seemed to fit the boys he studied. 'Typically they were not members of structured delinquent gangs with a marked sense of territory, leadership, hierarchy and membership. Delinquency was a *fact* of life but not a *way* of life' (Downes and Rock, 1982:124).

However, if subcultural theory did not stand up to British empirical testing in terms of delinquency, it was certainly very successfully applied to school deviance. The work of Hargreaves (1967), Lacey (1970) and more recently Ball (1981) has established subcultural theory as one of the most important sociological explanations of school deviance.

Deviant Subculture in a Secondary Modern

When Hargreaves' study of pupil subcultures at Lumley Secondary Modern School was first published in 1967 it was hailed as one of the most important products of British sociology of the decade. Certainly the Lumley study, when taken together with Lacey's companion study of Hightown Grammar, marked a major turning point in the study of school deviance. Between them these two books more than any others served to establish the legitimacy of the sociological approach to school deviance.

Lumley Secondary Modern School for boys used the 11+ examination results to divide its pupils into four main streams each year and Hargreaves' study concerned the four streams during their fourth year. From the beginning, Hargreaves's approach to understanding pupil behaviour is explicitly social. He argues that within a single class friendship groups or cliques will emerge. Those who are 'in' a particular group can be distinguished from those who are 'out'. Because of their friendship, group members are more likely to interact with each other than non-members and, as a consequence, patterns of behaviour will become established. Pupils come to expect certain things from fellow members.[4] Being a member of a particular group indicates that one will behave in a way that is acceptable to other members. In other words, Hargreaves argues, groups develop norms and these norms 'control and regulate the behaviour of the group' (Hargreaves, 1967:8). Norms grow out of or are an expression of commonly held values which unite the group. 'Groups then are united by certain common values and produce norms which define the criteria of membership and expected forms of behaviour' (1967:8). However, not everyone conforms to group norms to the same degree. Some conform more closely than others, particularly those who are high on the 'informal status hierarchy'. These are the leaders. By studying the content of the norms, the processes of conformity and deviance and the development of informal status hierarchies, Hargreaves attempted to specify the distinctive subcultures of the fourth-year forms at Lumley school.

In order to carry out his research Hargreaves became a participant observer at the school, initially teaching, but increasingly taking on a more explicit research role. He employed a variety of research techniques. For example, the friendship groups or cliques in each class were plotted by the use of a sociometric questionnaire. Each class member was also asked to rank all of his class peers in terms of leadership and from this ranking Hargreaves derived an informal status hierarchy for each class. The norms of behaviour themselves were documented by a mixture of direct observation and further questionnaire work.

The picture of pupils' school life that emerged from Hargreaves' analysis was of two distinct subcultures. For boys in the A stream social status was achieved by dressing smartly, attending regularly and punctually, not copying and not fighting. For example, one boy commented: 'I don't know who's the best fighter in 4A, you know they're not interested in fighting, most of them' (Hargreaves, 1967:17). The accepted leader of the class was Adrian, who was also school captain. It was he and his close friends who embodied the class' values most explicitly; they dressed the smartest, attended most regularly and were the most academically successful. Other boys in the class such as Alf and Alan who did not conform were social outcasts; their deviant behaviour was frowned upon.

By contrast, high status boys in 4D seldom worked. For them, having a laugh was far more important:

> Derek's taking the micky out of Mr. ——— all the time. He stands for it an' all. He's a right scream Derek. (p.43)

In this class copying was rife, fighting, smoking, wearing jeans and long hair all conferred prestige; absenteeism was higher than in any of the other three classes. Among this group it was pupils who conformed to conventional academic standards who were the social outcasts.

As a result of his analysis Hargreaves suggests that the fourth year could be divided into two subcultures. The upper stream 'academic' subculture embodied in the leadership of Adrian was characterized by values that were positively oriented to the school and the teachers. The lower stream 'delinquescent' subculture was characterized by values which were negatively oriented to the school. His representation of the two subcultures is presented in Fig. 4.4.

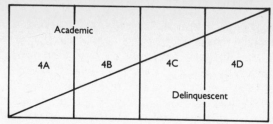

Figure 4.4. Hargreaves' representation of the two subcultures in a secondary modern school.
Source: Hargreaves (1967).

Hargreaves emphasized that subcultural polarization is a *process*. A comparative study of the second year did not reveal the same pattern of attitudes and behaviour. Polarization only became entrenched as the boys moved up the school.

What is Hargreaves' explanation for the process which he so vividly documents? Like Cohen and Merton he argues that achievement is a key value in our society and the school is a central focus and means by which an individual can achieve. At school, achievement means academic achievement. Academic achievement is therefore an embodiment of our society's values as well as a major determinant of future occupation. Perhaps most important of all it is the means by which pupils are selected and differentiated. In Britain at the time Hargreaves was writing the educational system selected and differentiated its pupils in two different ways — first through the 11+ and secondly through streaming:

> Though there may be good educational reasons for doing so . . . we can not ignore that the effect of streaming is to separate children with relatively greater academic achievement into 'high' streams; and to most of the public 'higher' is synonomous with 'better'. To succeed at school is to succeed in society. To divide our children means that we must also have children who fail by not obtaining entry into the grammar school and/or a high stream. (1967:166)

The boys in the bottom stream at Lumley School were therefore double failures — they had not entered a grammar school or the high streams of the secondary modern. The school then compounded their sense of failure by encouraging them to socialize only with each other and by assigning them the 'worst' teachers. Not surprisingly the pupils achieved very little in the eyes of the school and their occupational aspirations had to be reduced considerably in scope. In other words the boys were status deprived by the school system itself. As a consequence they rejected the values of the school which conferred prestige on the academically successful and were forced to seek a substitute. Hargreaves suggests that substitute was a subculture based on anti-academic values: 'It is through the anti-academic rejection of the schools' values that the informal status within the juvenile delinquent group is achieved. They reject the pupil role and replace it with an autonomous and independent peer culture (1967:171–2)

Delinquent Subcultures in a Grammar School

Colin Lacey's study (1970) which was published shortly after that of Hargreaves also stands in the subcultural tradition of Cohen and Coward and Ohlin. The research, undertaken in the same university as that of Hargreaves, employed similar research techniques but was concerned with a very different educational setting – a traditional boy's grammar school in the northern English town of 'Hightown'.

Grammar school provision was available for only 15–20% of pupils each year at Hightown, and Hightown Grammar was the most prestigous of all L.E.A. secondary schools for boys. It is therefore not surprising that the boys who arrived at the school at the age of 11 had been used to playing the 'best pupil' role in their junior schools. They were the top scholars, team leaders, school monitors, head boys and teacher's favourites – an experience which Lacey considers very significant in their subsequent adaptation to school.

Once they arrived at Hightown Grammar, Lacey reports that the boys were randomly assigned to four mixed-ability classes. This, together with the fact that they were recruited from 22 primary schools, meant that most of the boys were isolated from their primary school friends. As a result of their relative isolation and their history of being 'best pupils' they became highly committed to school and developed an intense rivalry. They adhered rigidly to school uniform (caps and blazers were proudly displayed), they attended school clubs and functions in disproportionate numbers. In class they were eager, cooperative and highly competitive – any question from the teacher producing a forest of waving arms with everyone eager to be chosen. The purpose of Lacey's longitudinal study was to explore how and why a substantial number of such boys changed during their school careers from commitment to rejection, from enthusiasm to disillusionment. Why was it that even among the academic élite that entered Hightown Grammar a small group each year deliberately rejected their schooling and came to be seen by their teachers as uncooperative and anti-academic? To answer these questions Lacey developed the twin concepts of 'differentiation' and 'polarization'.

Differentiation refers to the way in which a relatively homogeneous group of pupils is sorted and ranked according to criteria of academic achievement and 'good behaviour'. It is essentially a process carried out by teachers. Polarization, on the other hand, takes place among the pupils themselves as a result of differentiation — it is the process by which they produce their own subculture. It was because some boys failed (relatively) and lost their cherished 'best pupil role' that they became polarized and produced their own subculture. 'It is a process of sub-culture formation in which the school-dominated normative culture is opposed by an alternative culture which I refer to as the 'anti-group' culture' (Lacey, 1970:57). Lacey argues that the content of this anti-group culture varies depending on the school and its setting. In a minor public school it might focus on C.N.D. and folk music while in an inner-city secondary modern it might involve petty crime and delinquency. In this sense Lacey's argument is similar to that of Cloward and Ohlin's notion of deviant opportunity structures. At Hightown Grammar, Lacey reports, the anti-group culture fell between these two extremes and was influenced by the large working class and Jewish communities of Hightown.

One of the most interesting findings that Lacey reports is that although differentiation began almost as soon as the pupils started school (exams were held each term and rank ordered class lists were produced) polarization was slower to emerge. During the first year the most common response to relative academic failure was for pupils to develop symptoms of emotional upheaval and neurotic disorder. Lacey lists the following symptoms that were documented in school records during the first year of the pupils he studied.

Symptoms that occurred in the first year intake 1962

Bursting into tears when reprimanded by a teacher.
Refusal to go to school or to a particular lesson, accompanied by hysterical crying and screaming.
Sleeplessness.
Bedwetting.
Playing truant from certain lessons or from school.
Constantly feeling sick before certain lessons.
One boy rushed to the stage in assembly clutching his throat and screaming that he could not breathe.
Consistent failure to do homework.
High absence record.
Aggravation of mild epilepsy.

(Lacey, 1970:59)

The response to school failure at this stage was essentially an individual one presumably because of the relative social isolation of unsuccessful boys in mixed ability classes.

At the end of the first year the pupils were assigned to four streams and to begin with those placed in the lowest streams were again prone to individual emotional distress. However, after six months of the second year friendship choices became increasingly confined to the form group and polarization set in. After six months of streaming not only were the bottom class regarded as the least academically successful, they were also widely regarded by the staff as the worst behaved. To quote two teachers: 'They're unacademic, they can't cope with the work.' 'Give them half a chance and they'll give you the run around' (p. 61). Lacey reports that these pupils spent less time on homework, were more often late and more than three times as likely to be punished as any other second-year class. By contrast, the top class were least likely to be absent, were seldom late and had a very low rate of detentions. In other words, Lacey argues that after six months of working together, the boys in the bottom stream had developed a *social* solution (anti-group behaviour) to what had previously been experienced as an *individual* problem (relative academic failure).

Deviant Subcultures in a Comprehensive

Although they are still highly relevant today in terms of their analyses Hargreaves' and Lacey's studies are now somewhat dated in their substance. Secondary moderns and grammar schools have largely disappeared and, partly as a result of these studies, rigid streaming is no longer the dominant form of classroom organization. Today, comprehensive schools with bands, sets and mixed ability groupings predominate and Ball's (1981) more recent study of Beachside Comprehensive therefore provides a useful contemporary exposition of the subcultural thesis.[5]

Beachside School operated a system of fine streaming up until 1969. From 1969 to 1976 the dominant model of organization was banding, though from 1973 onwards mixed-ability groups were gradually introduced. As a result of the change from banding to mixed ability Ball was able to compare the two types of organization and thereby 'test' the thesis of status deprivation theory as it is applied to schools.

Under the banding system the cohorts were divided into three broad ability bands. Bands I and II had four parallel forms each and band III had two forms, one of which was designated remedial. Pupils were assigned to their band by negotiation with the primary school teachers. If too many children were recommended for a particular band then the feeder primary schools were asked to revise their recommendations until the correct number of forms in each band was filled. The primary schools were therefore in the first instance the selecting institutions and Beachside merely implemented their selections. Despite the rather arbitrary nature of the band assignment, Ball reports that comparatively few pupils were moved between bands, especially after the first term.[6]

Ball reports that one of the most important consequences of the move from streaming to banding was the emergence of discipline and control problems in Band II classes. Interestingly, Ball found that it was not the lowest status groups (Band III) that were the most difficult to control. Teachers tended to define and deal with these pupils in terms of emotional problems or maladjustment rather than belligerence. The real problem for teachers were the Band II classes who represented a 'behavioural and disciplinary blackspot' (Ball, 1981:23) for the staff.

Ball suggests that a significant factor in the differentiation and polarization of pupils was the way in which they were labelled and stereotyped by their teachers. Teachers typifications for the three bands are set out below:

The Band I child

Has academic potential...will do 'O' levels...and a good number will stay on to the sixth form...likes doing projects...knows what the teacher wants...is bright, alert and enthusiastic...can concentrate...produces neat work...interested...wants to get on...is grammar school material...you can have discussions with...friendly...rewarding...has common sense.

The Band II child

Is not interested in school work...difficult to control...rowdy and lazy...has little self control...is immature...loses and forgets books with monotonous regularity...can not take part in discussion...lacks concentration...poorly behaved...not up to much academically.

The Band III child

Is unfortunate...of low ability...maladjusted...anti-school...lacks a mature view of education...mentally retarded...emotionally unstable...a waste of time.

(Ball, 1981:38–9)

Ball argues that because band allocation was a 'given' label imposed from the outside prior to any contact with pupils, teachers were 'taking' these labels and deriving assumptions on the basis of them rather than 'making' their own evaluation of the pupils. 'Once established, the typification "Band II" or "Band II pupil" merely awaits the arrival of each new cohort in the school' (p. 36). Being labelled a Band II pupil, Ball argues, imposed certain constraints on the sort of identity that might be negotiated by a child. Teachers would jump from a small number of behavioural or academic clues to a general picture of the pupil as a whole and arrive at a stereotype. Teachers expectations therefore became a major means by which differentiation and status deprivation were communicated to pupils.

Although it was suggested to the pupils and their parents that they were placed in Band II so that they could be given work more suited to their abilities, what actually happened was that teachers simply expected them to be pupils of low or second-rate ability.

> For these children their secondary school career had begun with a decision which meant that they were to strive for rewards in a race from which they had already been disqualified. (p. 40)

It is therefore not surprising, Ball argues, that the pupils in these bands created their own deviant subcultures.

During Ball's research, the school moved from a system of banding to mixed-ability grouping. Ball argues that as far as the staff were concerned, the dominant motive for change was not directly educational. It was hoped that if difficult pupils were segregated, and those of low academic achievement spread throughout the year, it would be easier to monitor and manipulate them. For the most part this strategy seemed to work. Staff felt that pupils' behaviour was significantly improved by mixed-ability grouping and this was substantiated by Balls' own findings. Most significantly, no large anti-group culture emerged. Inevitably small groups of pupils were still disaffected from school, but unlike the anti-school groups that emerged in banded classes these groups were not alienated from all aspects of school. Sports in particular provided an important avenue for participation and several pupils who appeared in class to reject their education represented the school in sports teams. The anti-school feelings that were so total among the Band II pupils were limited to only two or three pupils in each mixed-ability group. These small deviant cliques were neither large enough or coherent enough to dominate the ethos of a whole class.

To some extent Ball's study can be taken as a test of the status deprivation thesis as it has been applied to school. If it is the institutional experience of status deprivation communicated through banding and streaming arrangements that stimulates a subcultural response, then a move to mixed-ability grouping where the process of differentiation is less clear should help to reduce deviancy. And to a certain degree it must be admitted that Ball's evidence does support this interpretation — deviance was reduced in the move to mixed-ability grouping, though it is important to note that it was not eradicated. Yet simply to change the institutional expression of pupils' differentiation (banding and streaming) does not remove the process itself. Schools still have to differentiate their pupils even when they adopt mixed-ability grouping and those who are academically unsuccessful will still be status deprived even if it is not made explicit under some organizational arrangement. In some of my own research (Furlong, 1984) it became apparent that the most liberal comprehensives can now conceal the full nature of academic differentiation from their pupils until well into the fifth year — mock C.S.E.s were the watershed in the school I studied. As in Beachside Comprehensive, the lack of explicit differentiation appeared to reduce the more extreme forms of disaffection. Only a small minority of pupils were entirely alienated from the school. However, schools cannot protect their pupils for ever. The public examination system and the (un)employment market inevitably exert their influence. It may be that, as in the school I studied, concealing the inevitable leads to even greater disappointment and hostility once the secret is out.

The legacy of Durkheim and Merton's thinking has been profound in the study of school deviance. The concepts of anomie and status deprivation have been influential from the very beginning of sociological analysis in this area and still retain an important currency in contemporary writing (see for example D. Hargreaves' (1982) recent analysis of the problems of the comprehensive school curriculum). Moreover it is clear that their potentiality is far from exhausted. For example comparatively little sociological research has been undertaken on primary school deviance. Yet it would seem that the concepts of anomie and status deprivation may have something to say about why so many children, who at the age of ten appear content with schooling, become disruptives or truants at the age of fourteen. It may be that primary schools, with their less overt emphasis upon academic differentiation, are able to incorporate children more effectively, valuing them as individuals and responding to their particular needs and talents. It is perhaps only when children grow older and experience the humiliation of academic failure in more stark terms, that those who fail find the need to reject the school. Competitive individualism may be more a hallmark of the secondary than the primary school curriculum.

This line of argument also raises important questions about the apparently greater conformity of girls at school. As will be argued in Chapter 8, it may be that girls are equally as disaffected from school as boys but simply express their rejection in a different form. They may choose forms of expression that teachers find less challenging (avoidance of confrontation, verbal rather than physical abuse (Davies, 1984)). However an alternative explanation may be derived from anomie and status deprivation theory. Girls may reject school less vehemently when they fail because their commitment to education is less straightforward than that of boys. Sharpe (1976) argues that girls are in an ambivalent or contradictory position with regard to educational achievement. On the one hand there *is* pressure to succeed academically which is rewarded by school and parents. On the other hand, particularly amongst adolescent girls, there is an awareness of the feminine role stereotype which implies that it is undesirable that girls should be as clever as boys; 'this implies that "over-achievement" involves losing an important ingredient of "feminity"'. (Sharpe 1976:135). Sharpe argues that amongst the school girls she studied there was general agreement that boys do not like girls to do better than them in school work. 'The implication is therefore — if you want to attract boys, don't start by showing how clever you are' (Sharpe 1976:136).

If girls are subject to such contradictory expectations their commitment to academic success might be less clear-cut than it is for boys; as a consequence it may be easier for them to shrug off academic failure. Committed or not it would seem that there is a strong alternative value system (romance, femininity and marriage) that can, for many girls, adequately compensate for the experience of failure. For some it is perhaps strong enough to precipitate failure in the first place. There are clearly many fruitful lines of analysis here that have yet to be systematically explored.

Difficulties with Anomie and Status Deprivation Theories

Despite their continued currency within educational circles anomie and status deprivation theories are, however, not above criticism on a wide variety of grounds. For example, both theories assume that schools have a single value system to which all pupils subscribe. It is because some pupils subscribe to the values of academic achievement but are systematically debarred from success that they adapt or form their own subculture. Yet while it may be true that society in general and schools in particular are dominated by an ideology that stresses the equal opportunities of all to succeed, it is wrong to see such values as uniformly subscribed to by all groups of children and their families. Working class families may not explicitly reject the *status quo* but they may indeed be cynical, fatalistic or detached from school. The dominant values of society are not subscribed to in a monolithic unquestioning way, but without assuming an initial conformity the logic of polarization and reaction formation fails. As will be demonstrated in the next chapter, other authors emphasize the pluralism of society, 'in which different groups and associations negotiate compromises and reach contingent accommodations that derive, if at all, only at several removes from a consensus over some ultimate values' (Downes and Rock, 1982:110).

A second and related problem is that anomie and status deprivation theorists subscribe to only a limited conception of human rationality. In contrast to positivism pupils are seen as having *some* choice in how they act but that choice is largely limited to attempts to link the predetermined goals and opportunities that confront them. If that fails, they may 'innovate' new means either individually or through a subculture to achieve the same goal and, only if all else fails, are they seen as innovating new goals and new means. Members of subcultures are doubly constrained, first by the opportunity structure of the school and then by the norms of the group. It is the group norms which 'control and regulate the behaviour of the group' (Hargreaves, 1967:8). As a result the theory 'over-predicts' the actual amount of deviance there is among the academically unsuccessful and under-predicts what we might expect from high achievers. As Young (1981) comments:

Such a position considerably underestimates the rational undermining of accepted values and legitimate procedure which constantly occurs; negotiation of values, cross-cuts in means, reinterpretation of goals, cynical conformity, distancing of commitment. In each case, human reason steps into the determining process—rebellion is rare, so too is the simple acceptance of the central values which the strain theorists describe. Normality and deviance are not separate watertight categories of behaviour, nor does normal behaviour automatically precede ventures into deviance. Rather, at times, they blend together, are mistaken for each other or are irrevocably interwoven into the actual patterns of social behaviour.

(Young, 1981:285)

A third problem is that status deprivation theory in particular has become explicitly male-oriented because of its focus on subcultures. It is no coincidence that the majority of research within this tradition has been undertaken with boys. Those studying girls have found little evidence of coherent deviant subcultures (Meyenn, 1979; Llewellyn, 1980; Davies, 1984). One of the main reasons for the popularity of subcultural theory is that it works — it fits the 'facts' as they are conventionally understood. It is working class, urban, low stream *boys* who are the most problem for their teachers. Girls apparently do not present so much difficulty but girls' deviance is hardly taken seriously. The theory has become culturally myopic, built around one cultural form of expression — overt masculine group behaviour. Boys themselves may marginalize girls with their sexist assumptions but this does not excuse researchers for doing the same.

Another consequence for accepting the conventional picture of school deviance (i.e. urban, working class, male, low stream) is that it rules out any serious consideration of the impact of teachers' responses to deviance. Ball supplements his analysis by drawing on a different tradition, that of labelling, and provides evidence to suggest that teachers' expectations and stereotypes are crucial. With difficult classes teachers may move all too quickly from one or two cues to imputations about the child as a problem. In other words, children who are not 'status deprived' may engage in a great many acts which are *intended* to be challenging, but are not interpreted as such. It may therefore be that the conventional picture which portrays deviance as mainly confined to the educationally unsuccessful is misleading. The way teachers teach and respond to deviants is crucially important yet these theories in themselves cannot cope with such subtleties. As Woods (1979) notes, teachers employ a wide variety of different strategies to achieve their own goals and these goals may relate to a greater or lesser extent to those of the school. They also respond to deviance in a variety of different ways and that response may be critical in determining whether or not a pupil is disruptive or plays truant again. Anomie and status deprivation theories may explain why some pupils reject school in the first place but they tell us little about what happens to them afterwards. The complex process of the creation of a deviant 'career' is obscured.

Finally, a more structurally informed critique of both theories would question the reformist principles on which they are based. It is really possible to lessen the strain of anomie without challenging the educational system as a whole? Ball's (1981) study would suggest that although it may be possible to produce a form of school organization that at least does not exacerbate feelings of status deprivation it cannot in the end eliminate them. Many would argue that the process of pupil differentiation has its origins beyond the boundaries of the school and at best teachers can provide lacunae to protect pupils from the inevitable. The ideology of opportunity for all may serve to legitimate what is presented as an open and meritocratic system, yet as Hargreaves, Lacey and Ball all demonstrate, the reality is that it is mainly working class pupils who adopt deviant adaptations and subcultures. In this way the existing class structure is preserved. Anomie and status deprivation theories provide us with little in the way of clues to analyse this contradiction. As Taylor (1971) has put it in an often quoted passage:

> It is as though individuals in society are playing a gigantic fruit machine, but the machine is rigged and only some players are consistently rewarded. The deprived ones then either resort to using foreign coins or magnets to increase their chances of winning (innovation), or play on mindlessly (ritualism), give up the game (retreatism), or propose a new game altogether (rebellion). But in this analysis nobody appears to ask who put the machine there in the first place and who takes the profits. Criticism of the game is confined to changing the pay-out sequences so that the deprived can get a better deal (increasing educational opportunities, poverty programmes). What at first sight looks like a major critique of society ends up taking the existing society for granted. The necessity of standing outside the present structural/cultural configurations is not just the job for those categorised in the rebellion mode of adaptation — it is also the task of the sociologist. (p. 148)

Notes

1. The term 'strain theory' is often used to describe this approach to deviance.
2. Later in his book, Woods (1979) explores teacher adaptations in more detail.
3. More recently Woods (Woods 1980a, Measor and Woods 1984) has employed a more interactionist view of deviance and replaced the concept of 'adaptation' with that of 'strategy'. See Chapter Five, below.
4. In this notion of reciprocal expectations and obligations there are echoes of Homans' (1951) exchange theory of group processes.
5. Ball's study is in fact not exclusively in the subcultural tradition. He also utilizes 'labelling' theory (see Chapter 6). However, the major thrust of his analysis follows a subculture line of argument.
6. Only 8% of Band II pupils were reallocated. Ball suggests that this represented a discovered error of placement smaller than the 10% error found in the 11 + exam!

CHAPTER FIVE

The Pupil's View – Interactionism

The theory of anomie which has been so influential in research on school deviance is essentially functionalist in origin. Whether the focus of the research is on society as a whole or a particular school, each 'social system' is seen as an organic whole. It is because every pupil understands and at least initially subscribes to the value of education that those who are systematically excluded from success feel status deprived. The notion of adaptation, whether at an individual or subcultural level, is premised on a consensual view of schooling and society.

The theories of deviance to be considered in the next two chapters start from a rather different premise. Where functionalism assumes consensus, interactionism sees pluralism; where functionalism examines social systems, interactionism focuses on the individual. As an approach to sociology, interactionism reached the height of its popularity in the 1960s and early 1970s. It was influential not only in the field of deviance but also in the sociology of education generally, as well as in other fields such as anti-psychiatry and feminism. As Young (1981) comments:

> The approach had a close relationship with libertarian currents widespread in western capitalism at that period and can be seen as a radical attempt to recover the "meaning" of behaviour denied by the determinism of the earlier perspectives of functionalism and positivism (p. 286).

Within the field of deviance, the most significant contribution of interactionism has been the development of labelling theory. However, labelling itself is not a theory, but is derived from interactionism, which therefore needs to be outlined first. It is

also important to recognize that labelling is not the only interactionist contribution to the study of deviance. For example,
the emphasis on naturalism has stimulated a number of
'appreciative' studies in which the subjective world of different
groups of deviant pupils has been systematically documented.
Other studies have focaused on the way in which pupils use
deviant and conformist *strategies* in the establishment of their
own identities. Yet others have examined the dynamics of
classroom interaction. In this chapter the central tenets of interactionism will be outlined and a number of different types of
interactionist study will be considered. Labelling theory, in its
interactionist and other forms, is presented in Chapter 6.

Symbolic Interactionism — Its Central Tenets

The symbolic interactionist conception of society is a particular
interpretation of the work of G. H. Mead and is based on the
premise that people are *active* agents in their social world. From
this perspective pupils are not driven to be disruptive becuse of
some inner psychological need, nor are they determined in their
behaviour because they are status deprived. Rather, pupils are
seen as purposively *choosing* their behaviour as a result of the
way they interpret their world.

For interactionists, the concept of interpretation is central.
They do not see the world as made up of 'things' or 'events' with
fixed meanings, rather it is made up of symbols, and symbols
demand interpretation. Teachers have to interpret certain forms
of behaviour as difficult or challenging and what one teacher
finds a problem another will not. Pupils also have to interpret
their teacher's actions; forms of punishment can be fair or
unfair, lessons can be interesting or boring. For the interactionist, none of these things are objective facts, for we all live
in a 'symbolic environment' (Rose, 1962:5), the meaning of
which is something to be achieved not given. As Blumer, one of
the foremost exponents of interactionist theory says:

> In any of his countless acts... the individual is designating different
> objects to himself giving them meaning, judging their suitability to his
> action and making decisions on the basis of the judgement. This is what
> is meant by interpretation or acting on the basis of symbols. (Blumer,
> 1962:182)

If it is accepted that there is this vital process of interpretation going on all of the time then it is essential to postulate
the existence of some internal mechanism to engage in this pro-

cess. For symbolic interactionists this is the 'self'. In the hands of different authors this self has been seen either as a structure, where the individual brings into play certain set perspectives to interpret the situations that are met, or as a process — a continually changing dialogue. Meltzer and Petras (1967) say of the latter, more sensitive approach, that the self is seen as:

> A process of internal conversation in the course of which the actor can come to view himself in a new way, thereby bringing about changes in himself. Moreover in his transactions with others there occurs a flowing sequence of interpretation of the conduct of others during which the actor may subject his attributes to highly variable use — or disuse. (p. 52)

In other words, the self is involved in a continuing dialogue with the external world — it is a moving communication process, in which we continually notice things, assess them, give them meaning and consequently decide how to act.

For the interactionist the most important thing that the self interprets is the meaning of other people's behaviour. If each of us is locked in our own subjective world then 'joint action' is something of an achievement. Everybody who is engaged in social interaction has to continually take others into account in deciding how to act.

> Taking another person into account means being aware of him, identifying him in some way, making some judgement or appraisal of him, identifying the meaning of his action, trying to find out what he has on his mind and trying to figure out what he intends to do. (Blumer, 1953:194)

Joint action, whether it is a classroom discussion or a group of pupils playing together, is always a fragile affair — it is only possible because each of the participants agrees to define the situation in the same way. Different participants may have different roles. The rules governing the behaviour of the teacher are different from those of the pupil, but each must know what the appropriate rules in any particular context are, and actively support them. Precisely what rules of behaviour are appropriate will depend on how the participants subjectively define the situation. For example, a pupil's definition that a group of people in a room constitutes a Maths lesson will help him or her make sense of what other pupils and the teacher are doing. If the lesson is English, then different rules will be in play. Appropriate rules of behaviour will also vary depending on the 'phase' of the lesson. What is expected of pupils in the opening phases is different from what is expected at the end.

In any of the countless situations that pupils and teachers meet during the day, the interactionist sees them as defining situations and mutually negotiating the appropriate rules of behaviour. Teachers obviously have more power in the negotiative process but pupils still have to participate and actively conform. What becomes of interest from our point of view is when pupils as individuals, or as a group, define the situation differently from that of their teachers; when, for some reason, they interpret the lesson as boring, as irrelevant or as a resource for 'having a laugh'. On these occasions pupils establish a different definition of the situation and order breaks down.

For the interactionist, therefore, social life is an enormously complex affair. In any classroom situation there are literally thousands of contextual rules which pupils have to understand and interpret in order to make social life happen. They can either interpret these in the ways intended by their teachers and classroom life will flow smoothly, or they can deliberately challenge them, along with their teacher's authority.

In summary we can point to two distinctive features of inter-actionist theory that have been highly influential in the study of school deviance. The first and most fundamental principle is the emphasis that is placed on the concept of the self. It is the self that is at the centre of the universe and the self that is consequently at the centre of interactionist theory. It is the individual who consistently interprets the world, noting its significance and in the light of this deciding what to do. Every action has to be defined and interpreted and its significance for the present course of action assessed. As Blumer says:

> What a person takes into account are the things he indicates to himself. They cover such matters as his wants, his feelings, his goals, the actions of others, the rules of his group, his situation, his conception of himself, his recollections and his image of prospective lines of conduct. (Blumer, 1965:17)

As we will see, interactionist studies of school deviance emphasize the subjective world of teachers and pupils. Inter-actionists believe that the first task of any researcher is to document the meaning that school and classroom events have for the participants. Without an understanding of the participants' phenomenal world, interpretation is considered inappropriate because it is *imposed* from the outside.

The quotation above from Blumer helps to establish the second distinctive feature of interactionist work. All of his examples of things the self takes into account are rooted in the social, spacial and temporal present. Whether the self is inter-acting with the physical world or with the social world, symbolic interactionists understand that process primarily in the present tense. From this perspective, social interaction is understood only as a process of interpretation and definition. Participants involved in face-to-face interaction (and it nearly always is face-to-face interaction that is studied), are pictured as fitting their lines of individual action together in an active way with each participant constantly defining the other's action and guiding them in how to act. Social interaction, even when it is recurrent and 'cultural', is seen as a fragile affair that constantly has to be remade by the participants.

Most of the interactionist studies to be considered below are rooted very much in the temporal and spacial present. Deviance has been studied as it has happened or as it has been responded to in the classroom or in the school. Social structure, history and biography are only seen as relevant to the extent that they are explicitly recognized by participants in their day-to-day practice of school life.

The Four Basic Assumptions

Before turning to some of the substantive research on school deviance that has been undertaken in an interactionist framework, it might be useful to consider this theory in relation to the four paradigmatic questions addressed in previous chapters. These were: questions concerning ontology, or the nature of reality; human nature; epistemology, or the nature of knowledge; and research methods.

In terms of ontology, it is clear that interactionism focuses almost exclusively on people's subjective views of the world. Indeed, for the interactionist, there is no such thing as an objective social world apart from that which is understood and experienced by people in their day-to-day lives. As a result, the theory leads to a very non-determinist view of human nature. In contrast to both positivism and anomie theory, people are seen as profoundly, almost radically free; they are free to create their own subjective view of the world.

Interactionists are essentially sociological relativists. They suggest that subjective views of deviance vary across social groups and across time. For example, truancy may be seen as a serious misdemeanour by some pupils and their families, while for others it may be a routine occurrence to be accepted if not actually condoned. Even more significant for the study of deviance is the recognition that non-attendance would not have been considered a formal offence at all before the passing of the Mundella Act in 1880. To borrow a phrase from Young, people live in 'overlapping normative ghettoes' (1981:287), and the first task of the interactionist is to document these subjectively constructed worlds.

The injunction to study people's subjective lives obviously has important methodological implications for it is not possible to document them by the use of questionnaires or by simply sitting in an armchair. If researchers are to understand the complex subjective worlds of their subjects then they must get as close to them as possible, working with them and to some extent sharing their lives. Interactionism has therefore established the importance of participant observation work, with researchers spending long periods of time working in schools. Those who adopt this approach use a variety of different anthropological techniques to record their data — observation, semi-structured interviews, or documentary analysis. Only by such intensive 'thick description' is it considered possible to document something of the subjective world of the participants — only then is it considered possible to plot the connections between communication, meaning, symbolism and action.[1]

Interactionists therefore hold an idealist view of society, freedom and subjectivity are paramount; the first purpose of empirical work is to document the subjective worlds people create. As a consequence, 'knowledge' for the interactionist is appreciating the subjective views of other groups, and the 'appreciative' studies discussed below attempt to do precisely this. They try to record pupils' views of school and their explanations for their difficult behaviour. However, this approach to research is epistemologically limited; all it can do is record a series of discrete case studies of how different groups of pupils view school, and hope they fall into a variety of 'ideal types'. This knowledge is seldom cumulative. As a consequence interactionists often emphasise the way in which such subjective knowledge is *used* by pupils at the school. Some researchers, concentrating on *pupil strategies*, have examined the way in which pupils use deviance and conformity in the establishment of their own identities. Others have examined the process of *classroom interaction*. They describe the negotiations that take place between teachers and pupils through which order is maintained or challenged. All three types of interactionist study — appreciative studies, studies of pupil strategies and classroom interaction studies — will be examined in turn.

'Appreciating' Deviant Pupils

One major strand of interactionist work on indiscipline at

school has been to explore the subjective world of deviant pupils. The approach is essentially 'appreciative', interpretative judgements being witheld in the interests of exploring the subjective nature of the pupil's world. In some senses such studies are necessarily limited, dwelling as they do on the character of a particular set of events. However, taken as a whole, they have significantly increased our knowledge of selective aspects of the 'underworld' of pupils' school lives and have alerted us to the complexities of their judgements. Three major studies will serve to illustrate the approach and some of the insights that can be gained by this method of analysis.

Disorderly Rules

One of the studies most explicitly devoted to exposing the subjective logic of much misunderstood and piloried groups is Marsh *et al.*'s (1978) *The Rules of Disorder*. This study focuses on football hooligans as well as disruptive pupils. The authors begin by suggesting that most people think of schools or football terraces where violence breaks out as 'settings of anarchy and disorder' (1978:1). Yet they argue, in reality, life as it is lived in the classroom and on the terraces has nothing of the characteristics of anarchy and impulsiveness that are so often attributed to it; it is rule governed and organized. 'Football hooligans' and disruptive pupils are not 'sick' or 'mindless' as they are often presented in the media. In reality, Marsh *et al.* argue, they are knowledgeable about their situation and the meaning of their actions, and quite capable of displaying a high standard of theorizing about their activities. 'In short they have an explanatory rhetoric at their command. But it is different from that of the media' (p. 6).

For Marsh *et al.* it is this 'explanatory rhetoric' which is all important, for they see it as the key to understanding the rules that underlie disorderly behaviour. In one important sense the rhetoric 'explains' deviant behaviour. Like other authors in this tradition Marsh *et al.* search pupils' accounts of their behaviour in order to expose its internal logic. From talking with pupils about disruptive events they suggest that they are able to identify specific 'offences' committed by teachers, as well as 'principles of retribution'. These offences are the precipitating causes of disruption from the pupils' point of view. The principles of retribution guide their response. For example, one offence is that of 'contempt', when teachers are distant or straight-laced; another is anonymity, where teachers do not know pupils' names. A third is the offence of 'softness'. In each case the offence is based on a contrast. For example, 'softness' contrasts with expected strength:

> As we read our participant's accounts, the severity of retribution is to be understood against the background of the degree to which they feel let down in relation to their expectations. (p. 38)

The authors suggest that the peer group are the arbiters of appropriate retribution. Whenever an offence is committed, particularly when it is taken to be demeaning, then some form of retribution is expected. For example, in describing his response to a soft teacher, one pupil said:

> I remember once we knocked one out. Miss Wright. Nobody liked her and, well, we used to play on her because we knew she was soft. She was always crying and storming out of the classroom. And it was a French lesson I think. Nobody liked French I don't think. Anyway she went out to get some textbooks, so there was a few of us who thought we'd have a bit of a laugh, something to catch her out. So we got a pair of football boots and some books and we wedged this on the door thinking she'd naturally see them. She walked straight in...they knocked her clean out...there was a big line of us outside the headmaster's office. (p. 38)

This teacher was thought to be demeaning because of her evident inability to control the class. Retribution was therefore legitimate.

Marsh *et al.* conclude that what the pupils they studied appeared to want were 'good teachers' who could establish a balance between freedom and complete rigidity. A control based on interpersonal respect: 'Someone who can take a joke but will make us work and get the work done' (p. 53).

Many of Marsh *et al.*'s findings are similar to those of Werthman (1963, 1970) in his classic American study of a gang at school. The gang members he described also made systematic judgements about their teachers — they objected to teachers who were weak, who were unfair and who did not know their names. As in Marsh *et al.*'s work, Werthman decribes how the pupils withdrew their support and challenged the authority of those teachers who committed such 'offences'.

Marsh *et al.*'s study provides us with a great many interesting and sensational accounts of violence and disruption in school and on the football terraces. However, it is essential to ask if the analysis actually gives any *real* insights into pupil's motivations. Does a pupil's explanatory rhetoric really explain his or her behaviour or is it merely an excuse? Tattum (1982), another researcher in the 'appreciative' tradition, also takes up this question.

Explanations as Neutralizing Techniques

Tattum (1982) made a study of 29 disruptive pupils in a special unit, in other words they had been removed from main stream schooling. He reports that the children he studied made no attempt to deny that they had behaved very badly at school, nor did they see themselves as out of control. They always described their past behaviour as deliberately chosen and justifiable. For example, more than half of the pupils he spoke to admitted physical attacks on teachers, yet they all claimed provocation — usually they said the teacher hit them first. Tattum suggests that 'teacher provocation' is an example of a 'technique of neutralization' used by pupils. It is a partisan view of the 'truth' used as a way of accounting for one's behaviour and attributing to it more or less honourable motives. As Sykes and Matza (1957) note, one of the skills necessary for becoming a successful deviant is to learn how to master one's guilt. Neutralizing techniques allow the selective, retrospective interpretation of events that help this process. The accounts may well be true from the pupils' point of view but teachers, one need hardly add, would probably give a quite different description of the same event.

From his work with disruptive pupils, Tattum documents five common techniques of neutralization used by pupils. Most experienced teachers will have come across them in one form or another during their careers.

1. 'It was the teacher's fault'
Tattum suggests that from the profession's point of view the most important quality of a good teacher is being able to control a class — this is more important than imparting knowledge. Yet he argues for the pupils the reverse is true. The effective teacher is someone who can interest or occupy the class, for it is boredom that leads to indiscipline.[2] Many of the pupils he spoke to were of average or below average ability and were highly critical of inappropriate work set by teachers and the lack of assistance. As in Werthman's (1963) study, if pupils decided their teachers were effective at their work, and the quality of their relationship with the teacher was good, they would accept discipline. Disruptive behaviour emerged when that relationship broke down, when teachers 'showed them up' in front of their friends[3] when they shouted[4] and when they set them inappropriate work.

. . .it depends on the teacher sometimes. If I think I haven't done much wrong but it's a nice teacher it's no point getting into trouble with her right...er...I'll take it like you know. But if it's a teacher I can't stand and starts coming funny...I'll start arguing with him. (Tattum, 1982:95)

2. 'Being treated with respect'

What the pupils wanted, Tattum reports, was to be 'treated proper' — to be granted respect and treated with politeness. However, given that they were known to be violent and aggressive they often found themselves being treated with less than respect by their teachers. When this happened they would return such abuse in like measure. To be passive in the face of disrespect would be demeaning. It would involve a loss of face in front of those whose esteem they cherished more than that of their teachers.

> Talk to us like a dog...they're terrible — can't talk to you nice — some can, but some talk to you like you're blinking dogs. And that's what makes me go mad then you see. If someone shouts at me I got to shout back at them. If a teacher hits me I got to hit them back. (Tattum, 1982:98)

3. 'Inconsistency of rule application'.

This was the most frequent explanation for disruptive behaviour offered to Tattum. Pupils emphasized again and again that teachers must be scrupulously fair in their dealings with them, they must have no favourites and above all they must not use scape goats. Although the pupils did not claim innocence, what they did claim was justification for misbehaviour. Once a teacher had broken the rules of fair play their own disruption was legitimate.

4. 'Everybody messes about — only having a laugh'

The joke and the 'laugh' at school is an inherently social affair. Much of it is inoffensive and arises naturally out of group friendships. As Woods (1979) argues, it is an important antidote to the boredom of schooling. However, it can also be used as a reaction against authority. Pupils can deliberately make teachers feel uncomfortable and excluded, or use a 'laugh' to create disorder. Alternatively, pupils' jokes can be directed at their friends. If you cannot gain esteem through officially approved behaviour one alternative is to gain it through the approval of peers — to be a joker is to be accepted by the group. In any form of disruption that is based on humour pupils can and do protest their innocence at least in terms of intent — 'I was only joking'.

5. 'It's the fault of the school system'
In these forms of accounts children expressed feelings of frustration and hostility at simply having to come to school. Like many of their teachers they said that they were tired at the end of the day:

> If I've had a hard day I really feel down in the dumps — got to take it out on someone. (Tattum, 1982:107)

In these circumstances pupils appeared to feel that disruptive behaviour may not be right but it was at least understandable.

Tattum argues that the pupils he spoke to all justified their behaviour by appealing to one or other of these five neutralizing techniques. For the pupils they provided 'true' accounts of events leading up to a disruptive incident and gave them a way of legitimizing their misbehaviour to themselves and to outsiders.

In both of the appreciative studies outlined above the explanations provided by pupils focus on their lives at school. Pupils seem to argue that they are disruptive or violent because teachers are unfair and treat them inappropriately or because the lessons are boring. However, pupils' explanations for their behaviour do not always focus explicitly on school factors as is shown in another 'appreciative' study by Bird *et al.* (1981).

A Conflict of Values

Bird *et al.* (1981) made a study of 115 'disaffected' pupils in six outer London comprehensive schools over a period of four terms. The research team documented both pupils' explanations for their behaviour and the way that the schools responded to them. Following a broadly interactionist line of argument, Bird *et al.* suggest that most disaffected behaviour can be understood as an implied if inarticulate critique of schooling. When pupils feel critical of school they have comparatively few means of expressing their criticism. They can only stay away, be disruptive or withdraw and not participate.

The majority of Bird *et al.*'s work was with older pupils. Until the age of 13 or 14, they argue, school is often taken as a fact of life by pupils. Certain parts of it may appear irritating or annoying but comparatively few of the younger pupils they met had constructed well organized opinions about why they objected to it. However, as they grew older many pupils managed to 'find a voice' to express their dissatisfactions. Bird *et al.* identified four areas of concern which, older pupils particularly, used to explain their difficult behaviour. As in Tattum's study, some

of these complaints focused on institutional aspects of schooling — the curriculum, their sense of academic failure. However,
other explanations had a broader logic, often rooted in a conflict
of values between the home or community and school.

In some cases the conflict of values was muted, but it could
still be used by pupils to justify their behaviour. Sandra was a
case in point, she justified her truancy by saying: 'Me Dad says
school don't learn me anything ... he didn't have much learning when he was at school' (Bird *et al.*, 1981:30).

Others pupils studied seemed to come from families which
rejected more explicitly the values of education. Bird *et al.* use
the case of Jack to illustrate the point:

> Jack hated school from the first year and had nothing good to say about
> it when he was interviewed in his third year. Staff regarded his
> behaviour as atrocious. His academic ability was apparently low,
> although this was difficult to assess as he seemed unwilling to display
> such talents as he had. He was highly disruptive, drawing other children
> into his rebellious activities, and thinking nothing, it seemed, of insult-
> ing any member of staff who tried to restrain him. Jack rejected school
> totally on the grounds that it offered him nothing that he needed. His
> future in the family trade was assured so the teachers' opinions of him
> did not matter. The school's attempts to enlist Jack's parents' support
> to modify his attitudes failed repeatedly. Jack's behaviour was not a
> problem at home, and they argued if he was difficult at school it was the
> school's job to solve its own problems with him. They would have no
> part in it. Jack would emerge triumphant from such encounters and the
> teachers would be left outraged and despairing. In effect Jack's parents
> were giving him licence to rebel in school as he thought fit. (p. 23)

Once again, this pupil was able to use his parents' hostility to
school as a way of justifying his disruptive behaviour.

All pupils are exposed to a variety of educational values which
vary in the extent to which they are compatible with those of
school. A major source of educational values is the pupil's
family. If family attitudes encourage or imply anti-school
values pupils are able to justify questioning the aims and
organization of schooling.

A second justification for rejecting school documented by
Bird *et al.* concerned the clash between the child's role as a pupil
(in which there is often a subservient relationship with those in
authority) and the alternative identities pupils may have begun
to construct outside school. Many of these alternative identities
(as part-time employee, girl friend or boy friend, responsible
elder brother or sister), bring with them different freedoms and
responsibilities. Most important of all they often bring a
different relationship with authority. As a consequence many

pupils find their continued subordinate child-like role a constant irritant:

> **Elaine:** Well it's the way they treat us as children when we're really adults.
> **Elizabeth:** And it's the way they call us kids, I really can't stand that!
> **Elaine:** Yes that's right. Everyone's labelled as a kid whatever year they're in.
> **Elizabeth:** 'Cos in every other way we're adults aren't we? 'Cos we do everything else that adults do. Nobody treats us as a kid when we're outside school, they treat us like one of them. We go into pubs, we have boy friends, we go to discos. Why is it we have to be treated like kids in school? (p. 30)

Bird *et al.* argue that such complaints are not merely trivial but point to deeper conflicts. Many of the fourth- and fifth-year pupils they worked with did lead independent lives with considerable freedom and responsibility outside of school time. For some the contrast with being a pupil was too great. The response of Elaine and Elizabeth was to truant.

A final explanation for rejecting school offered by pupils to Bird *et al.* concerned their perceptions of their future lives. In one sense all schooling is preparation for future life but pupils often do not start to look at it in this way until they are older. Making decisions about options to be studied in the fourth and fifth year is a watershed for many pupils. Bird *et al.* note that at the same time as the pupils begin to think about their future lives, the school curriculum begins to change and becomes oriented toward examinations. For example, they report that in the six schools that they studied all fourth and fifth-year pupils spent 80% of their time working on examination syllabuses. Examination success is obviously significant for the future of many pupils but a minority clearly challenge its relevance. Some of the boys interviewed claimed they already had jobs lined up for them — if they did not have to compete in the job market, examinations were felt to be irrelevant. Others, particularly girls, aspired to occupations that did not demand qualifications.

Bird *et al.*'s work is not straightforwardly interactionist. Although there is a clear concern with pupils' subjective meanings (which are illustrated through many varied case studies), there is also an implicit recognition of the impact of wider factors on pupils' views of the school. The labour market, gender relations and working class culture all cast their shadow on the views espoused by pupils. In this sense the study has much in common with more recent neo-Marxist analyses considered in Chapter 8. However, unlike writers such as Willis

(1977), McRobbie (1978) or Fuller (1980) there is no explicit attempt to locate pupils' views within these wider structural factors. We are simply left to speculate on why, for example, so many girls opt out of their education or why some working class parents are so hostile towards school.

Pupil Strategies

Although the appreciative studies described above give some insight into how pupils view school, the picture they paint is a rather static one. We are given no insight into how pupils *use* their subjective perceptions in their day to day lives at school; in this section we concentrate on that process. Here the concept of 'strategy' is central. The focus is on the way in which pupils actually use deviance and conformity in the achievement of their own ends. This perspective is best exemplified by Measor and Woods (1984) in their recent study of a single class of pupils during their transition from a middle to a secondary school (age twelve).

For Measor and Woods, the concept of strategy is central. In an earlier work, Woods (1980b) defines strategies as 'identifiable packages of action linked to broad general aims' (Woods 1980b:18). As in the adaptational and sub-cultural model, the model implies that pupils have different general orientations to school (conformist, deviant etc.) but for these authors the main interest is in the way in which pupils develop a *range* of different strategies during their first year at secondary school in order to express their own particular orientations. For Measor and Woods therefore, strategies are individually chosen. Certain forms of action may be repeated and therefore become 'cultural' but they suggest that pupils self-consciously assess their situation at school and deliberately choose to act in a way that will achieve their own ends. Particularly important in this process is 'impression management'; pupils, they argue, try to manage the impressions others have on them. To this end pupils present themselves as conformist, deviant, or those in between, the 'knifedgers'.

Measor and Woods report that when the group of pupils they studied first arrived at their new secondary school they were almost all conformist and keen to demonstrate to each other and their teachers their commitment to school. This, the authors describe as a honeymoon period; for some it was short-lived. By the second or third week of the new term, the pupils began to re-establish their old identities developed in their previous schools. Some publically displayed their strengths and weaknesses in particular subjects and others (firstly the boys but then the girls) experimented with minor forms of deviance. For example, both deviant boys and girls challenged the expected rules of school dress in minor ways and started to adorn their pencil cases and rulers with graffiti. Deviant boys began to experiment with minor forms of subversive humour.

Initially, Measor and Woods suggest, friendship groups were built around any existing relationship pupils had outside the school — neighbourhood friendships, membership of the same middle school. However, during the second term, friendship patterns began to change. Pupils started to build new friendships that were supportive of their own sense of identity. Central to this growing differentiation amongst friendship groups were pupils' attitudes to school. By the beginning of the third term, pupils had developed into three identifiable camps — the conformists, the deviants and the 'knifedgers'.

Conformists, they argue, were highly competitive and keen to show their teachers and classmates how hard they worked. As a consequence they were looked down on by their peers. Amongst the deviants there were clear distinctions in the strategies used by boys and girls. Deviant boys, for example, became more explicit in their challenge to the school rules of dress throughout the year and developed more and more sophisticated skills of repartee. To begin with these jokes were only amongst themselves but later in the year they became more 'centre stage' and publically disruptive. The boys also elaborated many different ways of 'making space' within the classroom — arriving late, taking time over going to the lavatory, etc. Some, at the end of the year, even took to 'bunking off' specific lessons.

With each of these strategies, Measor and Woods report that the deviant boys first experimented with low status teachers and in low status subjects. Home economics and needlework were prime targets for messing around as were lessons taken by supply teachers and students. As the year wore on, the deviant boys became more explicit in their challenge to teachers' authority sometimes challenging higher status subjects and moving their challenges more in the public eye.

Deviant girls also developed the strategies of 'display' by the clothes they wore (which increasingly took on a more fashionable look) and the hours they spent adorning rough books and pencil cases with graffiti and pop star stickers. However, their approach to winning space inside the classroom was more one of avoidance and passivity than any direct challenge. For example by the Summer term the girls would quite often dream away the lessons apparently undetected by their teachers. They would undertake the minimum of work necessary to avoid trouble but very often even this could be 'passively' achieved by getting their teachers to do the work for them.

> The passive nature of much of this work avoidance was complemented by the display of a quality of shy quietness. In a German class, for example, Mr. Brandt asked Amy and Valerie a question, based on their homework. Neither of the girls had done the homework, so could not answer the question. They sat, silent and looking shy and demure. The teacher sighed and asked someone else. The girls had 'got away' with it. This was the teacher who had caned another pupil, Bob, for not knowing the answer, and for having not done his homework. Shy embarassment is signalled as an acceptable quality for girls, to such an extent that it is obscured as deviance, at least with male teachers. (Measor and Woods 1984:116)

Teachers, Measor and Woods suggest, did little to check the girls' avoidance strategies because in comparison with the boys their deviance was invisible.

Just like the boys, the girls too had developed these strategies throughout the year. Firstly experimenting in what they saw as low status subjects (metalwork and woodwork) and then increasingly challenging the rules elsewhere.

The third group Measor and Woods described are the 'knifedgers'. These were pupils who were highly committed to school and wanted to achieve but who apparently did not want to attract the social stigma directed at the conformists. While both boy and girl knifedgers would work hard, they would all try to conceal the amount of work that they did. While they quite often used deviant strategies in class, they did so in places and at times that involved minimal risk of being caught. They were deviant 'in spaces that had already been mined by the ace deviants' (Measor and Woods 1984:136). By this means they established the reputation as acceptable members of the class but maintained their teachers' positive view of them.

Studies of Classroom Interaction

One final sort of interactionist study to be considered in this chapter focuses on classroom interaction itself. In both the appreciative studies and that of Measor and Woods there is a somewhat individualistic view of pupils' decision making. Lessons are either relevant or irrelevant, teachers fair or unfair;

pupils decide for themselves how they wish to respond. As a model of decision making this is clearly very crude and other interactionist work has been more explicitly concerned with the dynamic process by which patterns of definition get established. This sort of research has focused on classroom interaction and in particular the process of *negotiation* between pupils and teachers and among pupils and themselves. It is as a result of negotiation, it is argued, that pupils and teachers come to interpret classroom events in particular ways. It is through negotiation that scenes of order or disruption become established in the classroom.

It was precisely the social nature of the decision making process in the classroom that I sought to capture in some of my own earlier work on 'interaction sets'. (Furlong 1976).

'Interaction Sets' in the Classroom

The purpose of my study was to describe the way in which pupils *collectively* establish their subjective views of classroom events. My focus was therefore explicitly on the process of interaction amongst the pupils themselves. Drawing on interactionist theory I defined interaction as situations where individuals come to a common 'definition of the situation' by using similar common sense knowledge and by making common assessments of appropriate ways to behave. By this I did not mean that pupils who interact behave in the same way, rather that they behave in ways that can be interpreted by others as showing a similar view of what is going on in the classroom. It is also unnecessary for pupils to 'tell' each other how they see things for their actions symbolically communicate this to the whole class. In this way running out of a class or shouting out an answer to a teacher can be examples of interaction when the pupils take into account that they are being given support by the smiles and laughter from the others present. They 'know' by their support that others see the classroom situation in the same way; they share the same common sense knowledge of it. In these circumstances I argued that it is not enough to look at the individual alone, for pupils will be aware that their behaviour is 'joint action' and others are taking part.

The following example of interaction comes from my observation notes. The incident occurred after Carol (one of the pupils in the class I studied) had been told to leave the room because she had been rude to a teacher.

She [Carol] wanders out slowly, laughing and looking round at Valerie

and Diane who laugh as well. She stands outside the door looking
through the window for a few minutes ... trying to catch the eyes of
the people inside the room. (Furlong, 1976:27)

While she was walking out of the room, Carol was obviously
aware of Valerie and Diane and was making continual non-
verbal contact with them. Even when she was outside the door
she maintained this contact for a few minutes but after a while
she gave up and wandered off out of sight.

In this example Carol was communicating with two other
girls in the room each of whom appeared to interpret what was
happening in the same way. They symbolically communicated
this to her by the way they acted (laughing and looking at her)
and therefore communicated their support. I therefore argued
that these girls were choosing their behaviour together. They
formed part of a group or a set and in order to distinguish this
from any other sort of group I adopted the phrase 'interaction
set'. The interaction set at any one time was a group of pupils
who perceived what was happening in the same way, communicated this to each other and defined appropriate action together.

At other times Carol would interact with a much larger group
of girls. Participants would move in and out of interaction sets
as the classroom context changed. With different teachers and
different sorts of work, specific groups of pupils would come
together to establish their own particular definition of the
situation.

While this social model of how pupils' establish deviant
classroom definitions is more subtle than that implied by, for
example, Marsh *et al.*, this is also its weakness; the variability
of the behaviour I observed led me to a sort of cultural nihilism.
Because the pupils I observed seemed to move in and out of
interaction sets so frequently as subjective definitions changed,
I concluded:

> Consistent groups do not exist in reality and observation has shown
> that there is no consistent culture for a group of pupils. Norms and
> values relate to specific definitions of the situation and particular inter-
> action sets rather than to particular groups of pupils. (p. 30)

In retrospect, this now seems wrong; my view was the result of
observing behaviour too close up. In searching for subtlety I
had thrown out any sense of pattern or order except that which
might be established for a fleeting moment by a random group
of pupils who happened to define a situation in the same way.[5]
Relativism and subjectivity had gone too far.

More recently the balance in interactionist work has been
redressed somewhat by Turner (1983) in his attempt to inte-

grate interactionist and adaptational approaches to analyse how pupils establish deviant and conformist definitions.

A Hybrid Model — Interactionism and Adaptation

The central questions Turner pursues in his research are 'How do pupils come to develop particular orientations to school and how are common definitions of the situation established?' Like other interactionists, he explicitly rejects the static 'subcultural model' which presents pupils as either pro- or anti-school. Instead he tries to develop the earlier 'adaptational' approach[6] along interactionist lines. The result is an interesting hybrid with many of the strengths of both approaches. He acknowledges the complexity and variability of pupil action while at the same time trying to develop generalizations about pupil orientations to school.

> Unlike some authors, I do not reject the level at which the subculture and adaptational models are pitched — that of generalisation about types of pupil orientation to schools. Indeed my account is designed to provide a sounder foundation for this kind of generalised analysis. (Turner, 1983:147)

Turners's objective is to describe the way in which order is *negotiated* in the classroom. He emphasizes that whatever teachers may pretend, all the demands that they make are in fact negotiable. What he tries to explore is the way in which the negotiation game is played out. To this end he identifies a range of different strategies that are available to pupils — compliance, distanced compliance, withdrawal, sabotage, refusal. However, unlike the adaptational model, he argues that these strategies are not confined to particular pupils — everyone uses them at some time or another. Teachers recognize these strategies and use their own (persistence, threats and promises). Both sides are constantly engaged in attempts to out-manoeuvre the other to establish their own definition of the situation.

For both teachers and pupils the most important strategy is the mobilization of support. A teacher's definition, or that of the deviant pupil, is more likely to succeed if others can be encouraged to support it. But this, Turner argues, is highly problematic and demands a great deal of skill on the part of teachers or deviant pupils.

Turner criticizes the concept of the interaction set because it takes for granted that pupils who interact see a classroom situation in the same way. The difficulty for pupils engaged in deviant classroom behaviour, Turner asserts, is precisely that they *do not know* if others see things in the same way. Therefore, rather than documenting deviant or conformist interaction sets, Turner suggests that it is more productive to concentrate on how pupils *try* to mobilize support for certain courses of action in lessons: 'This would involve considering what Furlong altogether ignores, why some attempts to gain support are successful and others are not', (Turner, 1983:76).

Turner suggests that the ability of a pupil to mobilize support for a deviant definition is a significant form of power. A class will be made up of 30 different individuals each with their own subjective judgements of the teacher and the lesson. Being able to mobilize them to conform to one alternative definition demands a great deal of tactical skill. The problem is compounded by the fact that most teachers are highly experienced at countering pupils' deviant initiatives before others have a chance to respond. However, as Turner demonstrates, some pupils are successful in establishing deviant definitions though not usually with the whole class. Far more frequent are collaborations between small groups of pupils especially when major acts of deviance are under way. It is on the basis of these forms of classroom collaboration, Turner suggests, that established ways of behaving or subcultures are built.

Negotiating a Working Consensus

This concern with the way in which deviant definitions are established in the classroom is taken a stage further by Pollard (1979) in his work on deviance in primary and middle schools. Pollard begins by emphasizing that teachers and pupils have different interests but in order to survive in the classroom they must establish a 'working consensus'. His study highlights the way that working consensus is established.

Pollard suggests that teachers in fact do not expect perfect conformity in their classroom; everyone expects pupils to 'have a laugh' sometimes. Pupils also accept that teachers will censure them when they break the rules in this way. However, not all acts of deviance or censure are legitimate. From the pupil's point of view teachers can be unreasonable in their censures and from the teacher's point of view pupils can engage in non-legitimate disorder. In either case the other party considers the behaviour a unilateral challenge to the working consensus.

According to Pollard both teachers and pupils see each other's unilateral acts as semi-mindless or uncontrolled — the teachers 'go mad' and the children 'act daft'. Yet they each see their own unilateral acts as recouping dignity. The teacher 'shows who's boss' while the pupils 'prove they're tough'. Pollard argues that within the classroom pupils can have considerable impact on the working consensus that becomes established. Like Turner, he argues that power lies in their ability to mobilize support.

By using sociometric questionnaires, playground observation and attitude questionnaires, Pollard documented 12 different friendship groups in a middle school which he studied. Many of the groups had overlapping and contradictory attitudes towards schooling but they could be broadly classified as 'good' groups, 'joker' groups and 'gangs'. The critical factor in distinguishing between different groups was the degree to which they supported teachers when they censured the class. The 'good' groups supported teachers censures even when they were unilateral, while the gang members saw almost every act of censure as unfair. The majority of pupils were in between — they were 'jokers'. They wanted to have a laugh, but also wanted to do well. They therefore confined their deviance to having a bit of fun, which they did mainly for intrinsic rather than subversive reasons. On the crucial issue of whether they granted legitimacy to teachers' censures, they argued 'It all depends'.

Pollard argues that in the classrooms he observed and taught in it was the negotiation between the jokers and the teachers that was crucial in the establishment of a working consensus. 'These children neither passively conform nor actively rebel — they negotiate a viable *"modus vivendi"*. They participate in routine deviance to provide laughs and a relief from boredom and routine but in general they do not participate in unilateral acts of disorder' (Pollard, 1979:89). Gangs, Pollard says, have no such inhibitions and make situational choices of action from a 'less structured range of possibilities' (p. 89), while the good groups tended to act in conformity with whatever they thought the teacher wanted. For the working consensus to succeed from the teacher's point of view it was therefore essential to secure the support of the intermediate joker groups.

Criticisms of Interactionist Studies

The studies oulined above illustrate the scope of contemporary interactionist work on school deviance. 'Appreciative' studies attempt to document the subjective definitions of school held by different groups of pupils and as a result of these sorts of studies we have gained some significant insights into the pupils' world (for example, their views of the way teachers treat them, their views of the curriculum, their views of the relationship between school and their lives outside). The idea of pupil strategies highlights the way in which pupils use deviance and conformity in the construction of their own identities. Classroom interaction studies have concentrated on the subtle process of negotiation in the classroom whereby pupils and teachers establish a particular view of events. It is these socially established definitions that give rise to scenes of order or disruption in the classroom.

Despite the productivity of the approach interactionism has been criticized on a great many counts and from a wide variety of different perspectives. For example, positivists are frequently exasperated by the interactionists' stubborn refusal to adopt a more scientific approach to their research. Rather than logically scanning a problem, deriving an hypothesis and rigorously assessing the data to support or refute it, the interactionist is hesitant, tentative and shies away from elaborate hypothesis development. Interactionists argue that hypotheses should be developed from the field of research itself. The purpose of research is to learn; the world of the deviant is unknown and complex and to impose hypotheses on it from the outside would be quite illegitimate. As Downes and Rock (1982) note, interactionism fails on the Popperian notion of science for it does not produce propositions that can be logically falsified.[7] Interactionists continue to shrug their shoulders arguing that life is indeterminate, subtle and contradictory. 'Proof' of any propositions that they might develop is therefore by definition an impossibility.

If positivists criticize interactionists for being unwilling to impose a little scientific rigour on their research, phenomenologists criticize them for not being sensitive enough to the meanings and understandings of the pupils and teachers they study. As will be seen in the next chapter, this criticism has been most frequently levelled at interactionist versions of labelling theory but it could equally be applied to all interactionist work. Phenomenologists argue that many of the concepts that interactionists use to describe their pupils' lives are of their own making and not of the actors themselves. Notions like the 'interaction set' or even 'deviance' itself are essentially sociologists' concepts and have a problematic and essentially unknown relationship to how pupils and teachers see their classroom lives. Despite all their protestations to the contrary, phenomenologists accuse interactionists of 'forcing' members' accounts into sociological categories.[8]

Perhaps the most significant criticism of interactionism is that it is not a theory at all. It says nothing of causation or of response. It tells us nothing of the structural and wider social antecedents of deviance as does anomie and status deprivation theory. It tells us nothing of how deviance is reacted to as does labelling theory. The cumulative picture that appreciative and classroom interaction studies present is a series of isolated worlds each with their own teeming complexity and ambiguity. Deviant pupils are neither entirely constrained nor entirely free. Each group struggles to come to terms with the constraints of their own world in their own particular way. One delinquent group differs from the rest in unknown ways and any commonalities in their ways of responding to school are to be sought in empirical fact, not theory. These studies suggest no theory of social structure. Any structure there is in society will be highly complex and contradictory and can only be discovered slowly and painstakingly through empirical research.

In conclusion it can be said that interactionist studies have contributed considerably to our knowledge of the lives of deviant pupils. They have given us some interesting insights into the complex and highly differentiated worlds that pupils inhabit. Whether these studies do more than this is open to debate. Plummer (1979), himself an interactionist, provides a fitting and contradictory conclusion:

> Its [interactionism's] view of the world may be quirky and its contradictions may be intellectually unsatisfying; it may find few sympathizers willing to stay with it for long — it is a phase one may pass through on the way to loftier enterprises. But — even in the face of all that — the interactionist does continue to provide an alternative vision of the world. It is a necessary and radical, though modest, counter balance to most traditions of thought. Its final irony is that whilst it is consistently rejected as a valid approach to the world in academic writing, it is consistently acknowledged, most of the time in our daily lives. (p. 94)

Notes

1. For a more detailed exposition of the methods and procedures involved in participant observation, see Hammersley and Atkinson (1983).

2. Gannaway (1976), takes a different line. He argues that the ability to control the class is the most important criteria on which pupils evaluate their teachers.

3. See Woods (1979) for a more detailed discussion of 'showing us up'.

4. Davies (1979) documents other forms of degradation, such as sexual degradation, used by teachers.

5. More recently a rather different (and equally plausible) explanation has been advanced by Davies (1984) for the variability in behaviour that I saw. Like others

(McRobbie, 1978; Meyenn, 1980) she suggests that coherent subcultures are essentially male cultural forms. The reason that the girls did not appear to conform to a consistent value system was precisely because they were girls and not boys.

6. See Chapter 4 for an exposition of 'subcultural' and 'adaptational' approaches to school deviance.

7. See Downes and Rock (1982:58).

8. Downes and Rock (1982) specifically refute this charge arguing that concepts such as deviance are merely 'sensitizing concepts' which are developed and changed once research begins.

CHAPTER SIX

A Question of Labelling?

One of the most important contributions to the study of deviance made by interactionists has been the development of labelling theory. Indeed so significant has their contribution to this approach been that interactionism as a whole has often (inappropriately) been termed 'labelling theory'.

Labelling theorists argue that people break the rules of society in minor ways all of the time. As adults we may often exceed the speed limit in our car or take an extra long lunch hour when the boss is away. As pupils we may have sometimes complained of feeling ill in order to be allowed an afternoon off school, or borrowed a friend's homework to copy so as to meet a deadline. These acts, labelling theorists would argue, are common events; they are seen as an essentially normal part of everyday life. We may all commit these 'crimes' at some stage, but we do not necessarily come to look upon ourselves *as criminals*. Most of us successfully normalize our misdemeanours. As a consequence they make very little impact on our view of ourselves as law abiding and moral citizens.

However, labelling theorists argue that deviant behaviour takes on a qualitatively different form when it is discovered; when it is labelled as deviant, particularly by those in authority. Once rule breaking becomes a public affair, we can no longer normalize it so easily. If we are caught speeding and convicted of reckless driving we must somehow come to terms with this officially sanctioned label. Are we or are we not a reckless driver? If a child is caught playing truant and is called up in front of the head teacher then that child has to come to terms with the label 'truant'. Being officially and publically labelled as a deviant can have a profound effect on the way we view ourselves; it can also influence whether or not we commit the same misdemeanour again. While the intention of those in authority is to stop us breaking the rules again, labelling theorists argue that in some circumstances public labelling can have the reverse effect. It can encourage some people to increase rather than decrease their deviant behaviour. After all, if you are a truant, then why not try and live up to that reputation?

The labelling perspective is in many ways different from other approaches to school deviance. Most other perspectives focus on the initial causes of deviant behaviour; such causes are variously sought in the individual, the school or society at large. By contrast, labelling theorists focus on the way in which indiscipline is *reacted* to by those in authority. They argue that the reaction to deviant behaviour has a profound effect on its future development; it is in this sense more important than initial causes.

In fact, as will be shown in this chapter, labelling does not constitute a coherent theoretical perspective in itself. What researchers in this tradition are pointing to is a process — the process of 'social reaction' to deviance. A range of different questions have been asked about this process. Plummer (1979) suggests that the following four questions are central:

1. What are the characteristics of labels, their varieties and forms?
2. What are the sources of labels, both societally and interpersonally?
3. How and under what conditions do labels get applied?
4. What are the consequences of labelling?

(Plummer, 1979:88)

Most writers and researchers in this tradition have attempted to answer these questions from an interactionist perspective. They have been primarily concerned with the social psychology of deviant labelling in school, most particularly the effect of labelling on pupils' views of themselves. However, such questions do not have to be addressed from this point of view. In more recent times, interactionists generally and labelling theorists in particular have entered into a series of debates with other strands of sociological thought with some important consequences for their study of labelling. Writers such as Cicourel and Kitsuse (1963) and Hargreaves *et al.* (1975) have attempted to develop a more phenomenologically informed approach to labelling. This work focuses in much greater detail than does interactionism on the way in which teachers *interpret* behaviour; how they come to see certain sorts of acts and certain sorts of pupils as deviant. They argue that the process of interpretation is far more complicated and important than interactionists would allow. At the same time, another group of contemporary researchers such as Sharp and Green (1975) and Chessum (1980) have attempted to take seriously some of the more structurally informed criticisms of labelling theory. These authors have focused on the sources of teacher's labels; they ask what is it in the political and material context of the teacher's world that encourages them to label pupils in certain ways. All of these writers are still concerned with the same process. They are all interested in labelling, but they ask very different questions about that process. These contemporary developments in labelling theory will be considered more systematically at the end of the chapter. First, it is necessary to set out the interactionist approach in more detail.

The Interactionist Theory of Labelling

Labelling theory was initially constructed entirely within an interactionist framework. Its emergence in the early 1960s had a profound effect on the understanding of deviance both inside and outside school. It has not generated a great deal of substantive research in schools, certainly not as much as in other areas of deviance, but its intellectual impact on our understanding has been significant. It has also entered popular thought; teachers now discuss the dangers of labelling pupils too early and pupils themselves use the fact that 'they've labelled us!' as a 'neutralizing technique' to account for their behaviour.[1] Perhaps part of the appeal of labelling theory is that it involves a deliberate (and somewhat romantic) attempt to turn upside down many common sense ideas about deviance. From this point of view it is not the delinquents who are at fault — rather they are the victims. Those responsible for social control — the teachers, the police and the magistrates — are the victimizers. It is they who single out certain sorts of pupils and certain sorts of behaviour as deviant in the first place. As Becker (1963) puts it:

> Social groups create deviance by making the rules whose infraction constitutes deviance, and by applying those rules to particular people and labelling them as outsiders. From this point of view deviance is *not* a quality of the act the person commits, but rather a consequence of the application by others of rules and sanctions to an 'offender'. The deviant is one to whom that label has been successfully applied; deviant behaviour is behaviour that people so label. (p. 9)

Becker is suggesting that in one important sense there is no such thing as a deviant pupil or a deviant act, pupils only become deviant when others perceive them in this way.

Deviance is seen as a relative phenomena; appropriate behaviour varies from place to place. It may be considered quite appropriate to call a teacher by his or her first name when on the playing field or on a school trip but inappropriate to do so in the classroom. Deviance also varies over time. Only 20 years ago, girls from a single-sex grammar school might have been reported to their head teacher if they were caught 'fraternizing' with boys on their way home from school. Today in mixed comprehensives friendly relations between boys and girls are considered natural and something to be encouraged. Deviance then is not static, *it is not a product of the act itself*, but is much more the product of how others, and particularly powerful others, react to it.

The focus of interest for the labelling theorist is therefore not the pupils themselves. Since all pupils break rules to some degree, what is of interest to the labelling theorist is the way in which some types of behaviour and some types of pupils are picked out by those in authority for special treatment. As Kitsuse (1962) puts it:

> I propose to shift the focus of theory and research from the forms of deviant behaviour to the *processes by which persons come to be defined by others*. (p. 248)

The original causes of truancy and disruption are many and varied but in any real sense they are ultimately unknowable because they are so personal. What a group of pupils who are labelled 'truants' have in common is not a common *cause* of their behaviour but a common *reaction* to it — the only experience they share is that of being labelled truants. It is this, labelling theorists argue, that should be the focus of study.

Why is it that publicly labelled behaviour is considered so significant? The answer is to be found in the interactionist notion of the self. Because pupils break rules all of the time and for a wide variety of different motives it is assumed that rule breaking as such has only very marginal implications for the individual pupil, especially when it is undetected. As was noted above, if rule breaking is unnoticed it can be easily 'normalized'. This is what Lemert (1951,1967) calls 'primary deviance'. However, if the same act of truancy is noticed and is taken up by those in authority the child has to respond in some way. As the self is socially constructed the opinions and actions of others have to be taken into account.

Hargreaves (1976) suggests three possible consequences of

pupil labelling. The first possibility is that the pupil does not play truant again. In this case the child accepts the school's labelling of the act as wrong and agrees to conform in future; the labelling is effective as a form of social control. A second possibility is that the pupil might utilize one of the 'techniques of neutralization' discussed earlier to justify the behaviour ('Well Miss X is hopeless anyway' or 'It's not worth bothering with French, I'll never use it in the job I'm going to do'). In this way it is possible for the pupil to avoid accepting the teacher's definition of them as a deviant. A third possibility arises when the labelling does not deter and cannot be normalized. Instead the label is accepted by the child as part of his or her identity. Instead of rejecting the label the self is redefined to include it, the pupil deliberately embraces the identity and plays up to it by committing more deviant acts instead of less. This is called 'secondary deviance'.

> The reactions of the labeller, his indignation and his punitive orientation generates further deviance in the sense that labelling fails in its intended purpose (to deter, to punish etc.) but creates problems for the labelled person which are paradoxically, partly solved by further deviance. (Hargreaves, 1976:203)

In the case of secondary deviance the pupil responds to public labelling by building a personal identity around the facts of deviance. If they are treated by their teachers as truants and disruptives they accept that definition as part of their self-identity and deliberately try to live up to it — they embark on a deviant 'career'.

It is the impact of labelling on the creation of secondary deviance that labelling theorists have been most interested in. As Becker (1963) comments:

> We are not so much interested in the person who commits a deviant act once as in the person who sustains a pattern of deviance over a long time, who makes deviance a way of life, who organises his identity around a pattern of deviant behaviour ... One of the most crucial steps in the process of building a stable pattern of deviant behaviour is likely to be the experience of being caught and publicly labelled as a deviant. (Becker, 1963:3)

In a very useful article called 'Reactions to labelling' Hargreaves (1976) lays out four conditions which will effect whether or not a child will accept a deviant label, take it as a part of his or her identity and embark on a deviant career.

1. The frequency of labelling
If a child is called a troublemaker or a disruptive influence on

the class once or twice then it is likely to have little or no effect on his or her self-identity — we are all 'called names' by many different people without it having any long-term effect on us. However, if one particular label is repeatedly applied by a variety of teachers in a wide variety of situations then, as Hargreaves notes, at the very least the pupil will be under no illusions about what the teachers think and part of the groundwork for the acceptance of the label will have been laid.

2. The extent to which the pupil sees the teacher as a 'significant other' whose opinion counts
If we care about people and think they are important we are more likely to accept their opinion of us. Pupils who value their teacher's opinions are therefore likely to accept labels more readily. This, as Hargreaves notes, can have long and short-term implications. One child (middle class?) who values the teacher might, at an early stage, accept the teacher's imputation that he or she is a disruptive influence and start to conform. Another child (working class?) who places less importance on the teacher might reject such a label when it is first applied by neutralizing it in some way. The pupil may still therefore carry on being disruptive. However, this pupil may be forced to accept the label at a much later stage when it is routinely and consistently applied by a variety of different teachers. While it may be possible for such pupils to neutralize labels in the short term, that may become less possible in the longer term.

3. The extent to which others support the label
In a study of 'disaffected pupils' in which I participated (Bird *et al.*, 1981) one of the early observations the team made was that not all teachers shared the same opinion of the pupils. If we asked one teacher to produce a list of the pupils they thought were the most difficult, another teacher would produce a quite different list. When we brought teachers together to discuss their 'nominations' there was frequently a great deal of debate. In only a small number of cases was there any general agreement about who was and who was not a problem. As Hargreaves notes, pupils who are a problem for only one or two teachers tend to remain hidden. Teachers may not even talk about them very much because not being able to handle them may reflect on their personal competence. When this happens it is unlikely that the pupils will accept the label. However, there are a minority of pupils who do develop a public reputation among staff as being difficult. In discussing these pupils it is not considered a personal reflection on one's teaching ability to

admit that they are a problem and very often teachers develop opinions and expectations of such children even before they have met them. Hargreaves suggests that once labels become public and widely supported by teachers in a school then they are more difficult for pupils to reject.

4. The public nature of labelling

When a pupil is labelled in a public way, for example in front of a large class or school assembly, then he or she is more likely to internalize the label than if it takes place in a more personalized setting. Woods (1979) and others have shown children resent being 'shown up' in front of their friends. As Hargreaves comments:

> Public labelling humiliates and it also disseminates. The larger the audience who witness the labelling the greater the number of people to whom the label is communicated and the greater the chance that some of the audience will use the label and treat the pupils in accordance with it. (pp. 202–3)

Hargreaves argues that if these four conditions are met and the label sticks then a number of consequences will follow which are likely to have an even greater impact on the pupil making it more difficult for the deviant identity to be avoided.

The most important consequence of effective labelling is the drastic change in the pupil's public identity. No longer are they considered ordinary or normal, instead they are 'troublemakers', 'truants' or 'thugs'. They are no longer children who have caused some disruption or who have truanted, they are *a* disruptive or *a* truant. 'Instead of the act being just part of the person, the deviant act comes to engulf the person' (Hargreaves, 1976:204). The chances of resisting the label become more and more remote.

A second consequence is that teachers and others inadvertently start to treat the pupils with suspicion. The pupil is no longer innocent until proved guilty but is constantly surveyed and the slightest deviance taken as evidence of a challenge to authority. Pupils who are publicly labelled often complain of being picked on by their teachers for the slightest offence that would be overlooked if committed by another child. As this is often true it is not surprising that such pupils react to surveillance with hostility and frustration and consequently confirm everyone's expectations. Given the increasing difficulty of sustaining a non-deviant identity pupils turn to others who have been stigmatized in the same way for social support; they develop a deviant subculture.

Once a deviant subculture is developed some theorists (Marsh *et al.*, 1978; Young, 1971) suggest that a further process of 'deviance amplification' can set in. If teachers operate with stereotyped views of groups of pupils they may expect a certain reaction ('they are disruptive and aggressive'). The pupils themselves are likely to develop their own expectations of teachers ('they are intolerant and always picking on us'). In these circumstances it is predicted that some classroom situations become settings where these stereotypes are tested out. Not surprisingly when such stereotypes are tested in this way teachers and pupils confirm their theories about each other and the result is deviance amplification. At the next public testing the teacher's expectations are even worse, so they are more vigilant, and the pupils are even more sensitive to being picked on. As a consequence they react in an even more hostile manner.

As will be clear from what has been outlined above, the interactionist version of labelling theory has been developed in a quite elaborate way in relation to schools. But what empirical evidence is there to support the theory? In a direct sense the evidence is comparatively thin. There are plenty of studies that show that teachers do indeed label pupils[2] but very few studies have systematically documented the impact of these labels on pupils' deviant careers.[3]

Teachers' Labels

One of the best known studies of teachers' labels is by Keddie (1971) who has shown that teachers often label pupils in terms of their ability. In her study of a humanities department of a London comprehensive she reports that teachers made clear differentiations between different 'types' of pupil depending on whether they were in an 'A' stream, a 'B' stream or a 'C' stream. In other words these were explicit labels applied to pupils which, as Hargreaves (1976) suggests, influenced the teachers in their expectations even before they had met individual pupils. Keddie argues that these differences in the way the teachers thought about their pupils were significant for their teaching. It was considered that 'A' stream pupils did not need illustrations or examples when they were being taught, while 'C' stream pupils could only grasp issues in a concrete way. More significant from our point of view, 'C' stream pupils were considered potentially more disruptive than 'A' stream pupils. As a result, a question such as 'Why are we doing this lesson?' was likely to be interpreted as a challenge to authority if it arose in a 'C' stream class, whereas the same question would be interpreted as a genuine enquiry to be answered seriously if it was asked in an 'A' stream lesson. As a result, Keddie argues, pupils who were considered 'bright' were not necessarily those with the greatest capacity for abstraction and generalization, but those who were the most conformist and willing to accept on trust the teachers' definitions of 'important' knowledge.

School pupils then can be labelled by teachers in terms of their 'ability' and this can have important consequences for the way they are treated. Another obvious way in which they are labelled is by their sex. Davies (1984) has recently demonstrated that teachers have different expectations of girls and boys at school and treat deviant boys in different ways from deviant girls.

Davies administered a sex role stereotyping questionnaire to teachers in a mixed secondary school in order to highlight their expectations about 'ideal pupils'. For most of the items on the questionnaire, 'good boy' and 'good girl' pupils were seen to have similar qualities but some important differences were noted. For example:

> The successful well adjusted girl would be gentler, more interested in her own appearance, cry more easily, be less active, dislike maths and science more, and interestingly, be more competitive than either boys or pupils in general. The successful boy on the other hand would be less emotional than girls, more ambitious, enjoy art and literature less and be more inclined to think himself superior to girls. (Davies, 1984:67)

Davies concludes that, whereas 'good girl' pupils tended to be valued because of their good behaviour in class, 'good boy' pupils were more valued because of their commitment to work. When she asked teachers which sex they would choose to teach if they had to make a choice most teachers opted for boys. It would seem that boys were seen as more difficult to control, but they were more easily understood — they were seen as having a greater commitment to work and their deviance was overt.

> What worried the teachers was not being made aware of what pupils were thinking until perhaps it was too late. "The girls are inhibited, I don't know them, the boys seem to make you feel more at ease", "I feel more comfortable dealing with a lad." (p. 72)

Teachers in the school Davies studied clearly held different expectations of the two sexes — pupils were to some extent labelled by their sex. She also shows that boys and girls were likely to be treated differently when they played truant or when they were disruptive in class. In the classroom teachers would more frequently use verbal means of admonition with girls, whereas with boys the 'informal clout' was more common. Female teachers would sometimes hit boys in class but male teachers never hit girls ('for obvious reasons'). At the school level, these differences were sustained. Boys were often caned for serious offences whereas with girls it was more common to use verbal means of discipline and to bring in parents. Girls were thought by senior staff to be particularly susceptible to these more public forms of degradation. Davies suggests that girls may therefore have found them harsher than the short sharp shock of a cane administered to boys in the privacy of a senior teacher's office.

Both Keddie and Davies demonstrate that teachers do label pupils in different ways and this has important consequences for how they treat their pupils. But to what extent does this differential labelling and treatment have an effect on the child's subsequent 'career' as labelling theory predicts? At a common sense level the differences that, for example, Davies documents, would seem to be highly significant. However, there is comparatively little direct evidence to support (or refute) the theory. Fortunately there is however a great deal of 'secondary' evidence where data collected within a rather different theoretical tradition has been reinterpreted to support the labelling approach.

The Impact of Labelling on Pupils

One of the few pieces of research which has explicitly explored the impact of teachers' labels on pupils is that of Bird (1980). Bird's study was part of a larger research project (Bird *et al.*, 1981) on disaffected pupils in six outer London comprehensives. The pupils she studied were a 'difficult' group of fifth-year girls. Many of her conclusions challenge the predictions made by labelling theorists. Bird worked with both teachers and pupils. Her work with teachers suggested that the impact of labels on pupils in a large comprehensive is likely to be minimal. In the first place, she argues that in her case-study school where there were 1500 pupils a teacher might see 150–300 pupils a week and a pupil may be taught by up to 15 different teachers. The likelihood of one particular label being repeatedly applied by such a large number of teachers was therefore small. Labelling therefore often remained individualized rather than consensual. This individualization of teacher's perspectives was increased by the size of the staffroom. With a staff of 70–80 the chances of everyone having the opportunity to swap opinions about a particular pupil were minimized.

The impact of labelling was further reduced by the variety of different contexts available for dealing with pupils in a large comprehensive. In a classroom crisis a teacher may have used fairly crude categories calling a pupil a 'troublemaker' or a 'disruptive'. Such crude labelling may be necessary if the teacher is to get some action or support from senior staff. But in the more relaxed atmosphere of the head of year's office or at a 'case conference'[4] the possibility of a more sophisticated understanding of pupils was encouraged which was also likely to reduce the impact of deviant labelling on pupils.

Bird's work with the pupils she studied corroborate her view that behavioural labels had little lasting impact. In the first place pupils individualized teachers' responses to them. Rarely did girls think that all teachers considered them a problem all of the time. They would behave consistently badly in specific lessons or locations and would recognize that they were labelled a nuisance in that context. However, they also recognized that they were seen as hard working and conformist in other contexts. Bird also suggests that over the one and a half years she monitored this group, teachers' labels changed in relation to any one pupil. Crises came and went and pupils' infamy in the eyes of teachers rose and fell. This fluidity and change meant that many pupils were never fully aware of the labels that might be attached to them by certain teachers.

A final factor that minimized the impact of labelling was that the school was comparatively unimportant for these girls. By this stage in their deviant careers they were happy to play truant two or three times a week. School was more important to them as a place to socialize with their friends than to work. As Bird concludes:

> To these pupils, school appeared to form only a small part of their every-day experience taking its place with part-time jobs, socialising and home activities. Even when they were in lessons they were faced with a new teacher and a new class every hour or so. It [therefore] seems realistic to suggest that as far as these girls were concerned any form of teacher labelling was of little consequence. (Bird, 1980:102)

Bird's study is very small-scale and clearly needs replicating in other contexts before any firm conclusions can be claimed. However, the girls she studied had apparently not internalized the deviant labels attributed to them by some of their teachers and it seems reasonable to suggest that this was in part a product of the size and organization of the contemporary comprehensive school. This would tend to suggest that labels might be more potent either for social control or in the encouragement of secondary deviance in smaller and especially primary schools. However, as yet no research on the impact of deviant labelling in primary schools has been undertaken.

Although Bird's study challenges many of the predictions of labelling theory in relation to behavioural labels it fails to provide an alternative explanation. If these girls rejected or did not know that they were called troublemakers or disruptives then why were they so difficult? It may be that they were in fact reacting to labels — but to academic and not behavioural ones. All of the girls understood the way the school typed them academically and had to a significant extent internalized these academic labels. When they were asked how they thought teachers saw them and whether teachers put pupils into groups in their own minds, they immediately suggested academic forms of classifications.

> P: Well, they do. Bright ones over there, dim ones there and medium ones in the middle, things like that.
> CB: Where do you see yourself fitting into that?
> P: Oh, I'm one of the thick, stupid ones at the bottom.
> P: She sort of separates out those who can do it and those who can't do it. If you're stuck with those who can't do it . . . you never get any further.
> P: . . . Yes they're always helping the brainy ones and they're the ones who don't really need help. It's the stupid ones who need more help isn't it?
> P: I mean, I'm in the pink band, that means I'm not very bright. The teachers tell you that. It's the same in all my lessons. You get split up into groups in the lesson, I'm always with the bottom ones.
>
> (Bird, 1980:103–4)

Academic labels may in fact be far more potent than behavioural ones because they are so frequently enshrined in the organizational structure of the school (streams, bands, etc.). It may be that the girls that Bird studied had accepted their low-status academic labels long ago and by the fifth year had developed an alternative life for themselves outside the school.

Perhaps the most important study to provide evidence in support of labelling theory is that of Ball (1981). As was noted in Chapter 4, Ball provides extensive evidence about the importance of teacher's academic labels in his study of Beachside Comprehensive. It is perhaps worth looking again at the way teachers stereotyped the three bands at Beachside. While the bands were a formal expression of academic stratification and labelling it is significant how teachers consistently conflated academic and behavioural stereotypes.

The Band I child

> Has academic potential . . . will do O-levels . . . and a good number will stay on to the sixth form . . . likes doing projects . . . knows what the teacher wants . . . is bright, alert and enthusiastic . . . can concentrate

... produces neat work ... is interested ... wants to get friendly ... rewarding ... has common sense.

The Band II child

Is not interested in school work ... difficult to control ... rowdy and lazy ... has little self control ... is immature ... loses and forgets books with monotonous regularity ... cannot take part in discussions ... is moody ... of low standard ... technical inability ... lacks concentration ... is poorly behaved ... not up to much academically.

The Band III child

Is unfortunate ... is low ability ... maladjusted ... anti-school ... lacks a mature view of education ... mentally retarded ... emotionally unstable and ... a waste of time. (Ball, 1981:38-9)

As was noted in Chapter 4, the pupils at Beachside certainly lived up to their teachers' expectations both behaviourally and academically.

If we accept that the clearest and most significant labelling of pupils in schools is not that which goes on in staffroom gossip but that which finds expression in the formal structure of the school, in streaming, banding and setting, then any of the status deprivation studies outlined in Chapter 4 (Hargreaves, 1967; Lacey, 1970; Ball 1981) can be interpreted as providing support for the labelling thesis. From this point of view pupils do not set up a deviant subculture because they are status deprived; instead, labelling theorists would argue that the prime cause of deviant subcultures is the fact that some pupils are constantly labelled as educational failures and potentially difficult. As a consequence of teachers' preconceptions, their behaviour is closely monitored and selectively interpreted as evidence of lack of ability, disruption and subversion. Over-zealous attempts at control on the part of teachers confirm all of the pupils' worst suspicions about their teachers picking on them and they therefore become more disruptive. This in its turn simply confirms the teacher's worst prejudices.

Labelling and Phenomenology

Symbolic interactionists see themselves as very much concerned with subjective meanings. The 'appreciative' studies examined in the last chapter represent the most explicit expression of this concern. The objective of these studies has been to document the way pupils look at many aspects of school life — their teachers, their curriculum, their role as pupils. The same concern with subjectivity is expressed in interactionist studies of labelling too. Researchers have tried to document how teachers subjectively label pupils as well as how pupils respond. However, another group of sociologists, known as phenomenologists, have criticized interactionists for not being sensitive enough to teachers' and pupils' subjective meanings. They argue that many of the categories that interactionists use to describe events, such as 'disruptive' or 'truant', are very crude. They are sociological categories and not those of the participants themselves. Interactionists, it is argued, do not take enough care in specifying how they 'know' when a child is being difficult in class. On the surface such an interpretation may seem straightforward; phenomenologists beg to differ. They suggest that a great deal of 'work' goes on among teachers and between pupils in *interpreting* behaviour as instances of disruption or truancy. This subtle and all important process of interpretation, through which certain actions come to be defined as 'deviant' and others as 'normal', is overlooked by the interactionist. They still utilize the same common sense understanding that they themselves criticized positivists for holding; they assume that they know deviance when they see it, rather than asking how the participants themselves interpret it.

For the phenomenologists the major focus of concern is precisely this relationship between the meanings assigned to events by the participants themselves (these they call first-order constructs) and their own more general concepts (second-order constructs). Both are treated as problematic. They want to ask how teachers and pupils come to interpret some behaviour as rule breaking and other behaviour as 'normal', and they are also concerned with the relationship between these sorts of meanings and their own social scientific knowledge. For the phenomenologist all sociological explanations must grow from and be translatable back into members' own common sense meanings. This is the final criteria for assessing the validity of any research — anything else is mere interpretation; it is of no greater or lesser significance than anyone else's pet theory.

Phenomenology had an important impact on theories of school process during the mid 1970s.[5] However, comparatively little substantial research was undertaken within this framework. One major exception was Hargreaves *et al.*'s (1975) *Deviance in Classrooms*. This study is therefore both important in itself and as one of the most fully developed British examples of phenomenological work in schools.

Hargreaves *et al.*'s study is clearly located within the labelling perspective. Their phenomenological perspective does not encourage them to challenge the basic thrust of labelling theory. What they question is the methodology of interactionist research, arguing that it is not based on a sensitive and systematic study of the way in which teachers and pupils come to interpret and understand rule breaking at school. Hargreaves *et al.* emphasize their scepticism most clearly when they say: 'The dominant, symbolic interactionist, version of labelling theory rests on unexamined and inexplicited foundations. They may be sand' (p. 16). For them the purpose of their study was to provide some much needed underpinning for labelling theory.

Out of the many steps involved in labelling theory Hargreaves *et al.* subject only two to phenomenological analysis. First, they ask how does a teacher come to describe a given pupil *act* as deviant and, secondly, how does a teacher come to define a given *pupil* as deviant. In other words, they try to explain 'some of the common sense knowledge and inter-pretative work whereby teachers are able to define acts and actors as deviant' (p. 217). The focus of their study is further narrowed by concentrating exclusively on classrooms rather than the wider arena of the school as a whole. The impact of labelling on the pupil and the pupil's subsequent career is not systematically examined though presumably they would be equally susceptible to the same kind of phenomenological analysis.

Hargreaves *et al.* suggest that in order to understand how teachers and pupils look at classroom deviance it is first necessary to understand the rules of classroom behaviour. By this they do not mean the school rules that might get written down and posted on a notice board but the highly complex inter-related sets of institutional rules, situational rules and personal rules that teachers have to enforce within their classrooms. As the researchers suggest, they could not understand the way the teachers they studied defined deviance until they knew what rules were in operation in a particular context. As a consequence one of their major tasks was to describe the rules in play in particular classroom contexts. By detailed observation and discussion with teachers they identified five typical phases within each lesson. Different behavioural rules would be in play in each of these phases. They were:

(1)   the 'entry' phase,
(2)   the 'settling down' or preparation phase,
(3)   the 'lesson proper' phase,
(4)   the 'clearing up' phase,
(5)   the 'exit' phase.

Within the 'lesson proper' phase they identified a number of sub-phases. For example, in one common sub-phase the teacher was usually highly active, working examples on the board or giving a verbal explanation while the pupils were relatively inactive. Hargreaves *et al.* comment:

> In all these [types of] sub-phase the dominant rule in play is the pay attention rule, i.e. pupils must sit quietly and listen to the teacher. Any pupil's activity which conflicts with conformity to this rule is defined as deviant, especially talk, movement and auto-involvements. (Hargreaves *et al.*, 1975:75)

They argue that every phase or sub-phase brings into play a distinctive combination of rules. Pupils know which rules are in play because they know which phase they are in. The rules form part of the common sense knowledge of classrooms that teachers and pupils all develop and it is on the basis of this knowledge that teachers and pupils can understand deviance imputations even when no explicit reference is made to the rule in play (see Edwards and Furlong (1978) for a more 'socio-linguistic' analysis of the same process).

After identifying these key phases and the rules associated with them Hargreaves *et al.* then move on to ask how it is that teachers know that a given act is deviant. What interpretative procedures and rules do they have to follow in order to classify certain sorts of behaviour as deviant? The authors describe teachers acting like detectives searching for evidence. One of their most important forms of evidence is their knowledge of pupils. The second major focus in their study was therefore to develop a phenomenological theory of how teachers 'type' their pupils — the way in which teachers move from typing deviant *acts* to typing deviant *persons*. By this they do not mean that they are interested in crude labelling. Most teachers know their pupils as unique individuals. Even so pupils have to be understood; they have to be 'formulated' in some way.

By following a group of first-year pupils when they entered a school and documenting the perceptions of their teachers, the researchers identified three phases in the development of teachers' perceptions. These were (a) speculation, (b) elaboration, and (c) stabilization. They suggest that from the very first days of contact in the secondary school, teachers have a lot of 'pre'-information about their pupils. They know a great deal about the catchment area and the primary schools that the pupils come from, and they also remember classes from previous years. They are therefore able to make comparisons and form judgements about each individual child in relation to what might be expected. Teachers also look at appearance, conformity, likeability, etc. All of these factors are involved in the first 'speculative' phase.

Once a teacher has an initial hypothesis about a child they suggest that he or she will move into the second phase of 'elaboration', where they will be especially sensitive to the repetition of acts which confirm their developing view. Elder siblings are particularly important in this early stage; they are a yardstick with which to evaluate pupils. A child with a good sibling who is naughty is 'just settling down', whereas a child who is good but with a bad sibling will 'reveal their true nature later'. However, during this elaboration stage definitions are not fixed and can be changed in the face of substantial evidence. At the last stage teachers' perceptions become stabilized, pupils are seen as unique individuals yet at the same time they are seen as particular sorts of pupils — conformists, helpful, trouble-makers, truants, etc. The authors argue that once this stage has been reached a redefinition of the child by the teacher seldom occurs. A similar process of the categorization of pupils has been identified in nursery schools by Rist (1970) using an inter-actionist perspective. He too points to the importance of 'pre'-information in the formulation of teachers' opinions and how they become stabilized and confirmed over time by the actions of teachers themselves towards pupils of different types.

By this sort of detailed analysis Hargreaves *et al.* try to provide firmer, phenomenologically based foundations for labelling theory. It is certainly true that their research is much more systematic and thorough than some of the cruder versions of teacher labelling described by some interactionists. Their work highlights the complexity of interpretative judgements involved in understanding deviance as well as the subtle way in which teachers type their pupils. It may be that if, for example, Bird (1980) had undertaken a more detailed analysis of how teachers labelled their pupils she may have found more evidence of their impact. It may be that interactionist versions of labelling theory are simply too crude a representation of this subtle interpersonal process.

However, the phenomenological perspective is itself not above serious criticism both internally and externally. An important internal criticism of phenomenological work on deviance is that in its own terms its objectives are unachievable. The task of describing and understanding pupils' and teachers' first-order constructs cannot in fact be achieved, for any piece of written analysis must change and distort what has been studied. True, the work of Hargreaves *et al.* is more complex and subtle in its documentation of actors' meanings than that of, say, Bird, but is it of a fundamentally different order? Have they achieved utter fidelity to the way the teachers themselves saw deviance? It seems unlikely. One of the tests of validity that phenomenologists erect for their own work is whether the subjects themselves would recognize the account that is given. Hargreaves *et al.* do not say whether they took their accounts back to the teachers they studied. If they had, the teachers may have found it a plausible analysis but, as teachers so seldom have time to stop and analyse their own daily lives in such detail, they would hardly be in a strong position to challenge the veracity of the record. As Downes and Rock (1982) comment:

> What (the teachers) would be offered could thus be 'correct' but still almost wholly foreign. And the subject could as readily be converted by a description as recognise himself in it. Descriptions work on people and change them. In all this the gap between constructs of the first and second degree remains unbridged. (p. 179)

Phenomenologists set themselves high ideals — it may be that they are too high to be really achievable.

In addition to these internal criticisms of phenomenology there are many external criticisms that can be made as well, particularly concerning the relationship between deviance, labelling and social structure. These criticisms have given rise to other forms of research within the labelling perspective.

Deviant Labelling and Social Structure

Both interactionist and phenomenological approaches to labelling have been subject to more structurally informed critiques, most particularly for their neglect of power. The second of Plummer's (1979) questions outlined at the beginning of this chapter suggested that labelling should focus on the sources of labels both societally and personally. Interactionism and phenomenology both address the personal sources of labels but pay scant regard to their broader origins. As Sharp and Green (1975) comment, these approaches are concerned with social psychology; a social psychology of labelling is essential but 'does not enable us to pose the question of why it is that certain stable institutionalised meanings (e.g. labels) emerge from practice rather than others' (p. 24). Why do teachers find certain sorts of behaviour so problematic? Why do they label certain sorts of pupils as troublemakers and others as psychologically disturbed? Interactionists and phenomenologists allow detailed analyses of the subtle, personal way in which teachers define pupils as certain sorts of problems, but they tell us little or nothing about the broader social origins of these labels.

Some attempt to examine the broader origins of labelling has been made by Sharp and Green themselves in their case study of a primary school and by Chessum (1980) in her study of two comprehensive schools. The work of these authors remains within the labelling perspective; they are concerned with the same process as interactionists and phenomenologists but they ask rather different questions about it. However, as will be seen, both studies fail to go beyond the boundaries of the school. They take only the first step towards a broader analysis by locating teachers' labelling of pupils in the ideological, political and material context of particular institutions.[6]

Teacher Theories as a Source of Labels

From a study of two comprehensive schools, Chessum (1980) identified two ideologies or theories that were particularly strong among teachers in explaining disaffected pupils' behaviour. The two ideologies she identified were 'personal and family pathology' and the 'hard core' theory of deviance; it was these theories that were the main source of teachers' labels. The purpose of Chessum's research was to try to explain why it was that these two particular ways of understanding school deviance were so popular among teachers. Many teachers in the schools she studied were aware of different sorts of explanations; indeed in their more reflective moments (in the staff room or in the pub) they would sometimes speculate on alternative explanations of pupil deviance (the impact of unemployment, the problems associated with academic failure). However, in the day-to-day life of school it was 'family pathology' and 'hard core' theories that were the most dominant.

Out of the two theories, Chessum suggests that 'family pathology' or 'home background' explanations were the most significant. As was documented in Chapter 2 there is plenty of psychological literature to support the view that certain kinds of home-based factors, such as family relationship abnormalities or particular styles of child rearing, are associated with emotional difficulties and intellectual handicaps among children. Chessum reports that in her two case-study schools teachers dealt daily with problems which appeared to be a direct overspill of disturbance and difficulties at home. Teachers' own contacts with pupils and their wider reflections on society and school often yielded insights into very different explanations for disaffection, but in individual cases teachers almost invariably invoked notions of family and personal pathology as a way of labelling pupils. Indeed this overall theoretical perspective was often tenaciously preserved despite teachers' contradictory experiences.

> Some teachers expressed astonishment when pupils were exceptionally resistant to teacher influence despite an apparently supportive home background. They were equally surprised if model pupils were inadvertently revealed to live under adverse home circumstances. Faced with a rebellious or uncooperative pupil, teachers were often prepared to assume that there *must* be something wrong at home even if no evidence was immediately available. (Chessum, 1980:123)

Chessum reports that although theories of personal and family pathology were very popular among teachers in explaining individual cases of disruption and truancy teachers also found it necessary to invoke explanations which explained collective behaviour. Pathological explanations were not much help when teachers were faced with a large group of pupils who were neither notoriously difficult nor exceptionally unenthusiastic about school but who were nevertheless occasionally challenging. Chessum suggests that it could be argued that the more overtly troublesome children were the tip of an iceberg — a symbol of a more fundamental malaise in the school as a whole. Teachers were more likely, however, to describe a 'hard core' of offenders as the real source of the problem. As in the case of personal and family pathology theory, Chessum reports that the 'hard core' theory was espoused despite flaws in the analysis and the existence of counter arguments.

For example, teachers were often reluctant to describe *particular* pupils as members of the 'hard core'. Their understanding of the complexity of pupil motivation made it easier to portray pupils as *under the influence* of ill-intentioned characters rather than being such themselves. Moreover, teachers could not always agree on which pupils comprised the essential hard core. It seemed to vary significantly over time and between teachers.

Chessum suggests that these two ideologies were enormously powerful in the schools she studied; they were a major influence on policy and practice with regard to disaffected pupils. These ideologies were the source of the labels applied by teachers to difficult pupils.

Why was it that these particular ideologies were so popular? Chessum argues that their main attraction was that in the specific context of the school they appeared to work — they were helpful to teachers in a variety of ways. First, they were *readily available* and were *uncontentious*, both theories being widely supported in the literature and by the 'welfare network'[7] or other state agencies that surrounded the school. It was therefore possible to hold a conversation with social workers, educational psychologists and educational welfare officers and 'talk the same language'. These theories also helped by making the problem of pupil disaffection *accessible* to teacher influence. By developing understandings in terms of personal and family pathology teachers could go on to devise solutions in terms of individually administered counselling or therapy. The 'hard core' theory allowed them to identify and split up difficult groups and distinguish named pupils who could be dealt with by established pastoral and disciplinary procedures. As Chessum comments, an alternative conceptualization of the problem which, for example, located the difficulty and solution in a political sphere or implied major changes in the structure of school, might find sympathy among some teachers as they reflected on education, but would offer little in terms of a course of action in dealing with their day-to-day problems.

To render a problem accessible to teachers was therefore important. These particular ideologies had a further advantage in that they also provided teachers with some degree of *professional* and *personal idealism*. Many teachers would spend long hours guiding and counselling a few individuals partly as a necessary containment strategy but also as an opportunity to achieve high professional ideals. A final advantage of these theories was that they both made allowances for acceptable teacher failure. None of the solutions applied to difficult pupils seemed to work entirely. Disciplinarians attributed pupil disobedience to a relaxation in rules and punishment, but when this failed pastorally-minded teachers argued that the alternatives to discipline were tactically necessary and more ethically defensible. Yet when more liberal methods also failed these teachers in turn often had to resort to a firm disciplinary stand. As a consequence, Chessum argues, the theories of personal and family pathology and the hard core theory had a major explanatory, even *consolatory* role to play, in that while giving scope for teacher intervention they also provided an ultimate justification if all the interventions failed.

Chessum's analysis is useful in that it highlights the fact that forms of explanation and ways of labelling children are not freely chosen but have to serve certain ends for teachers. If they do not conform to the criteria she suggests then teachers are unlikely to find them satisfactory. However, the two theories of disaffection she describes are not the only ones sponsored by schools. As Bird *et al.* (1981) demonstrate other schools sponsor different explanations.[8] For example, in some, 'social' explanations which blame the influence of the neighbourhood are frequently espoused. Another popular explanation is in terms of socio-biology — adolescents all go through a period of rebellion, it is a natural phase. Presumably each of these theories needs to conform to the points Chessum mentions. To be effective any theory must allow the prescription of certain sorts of practical action; it must allow for a degree of professional idealism and it must help to explain failure. But one must also ask why some forms of explanation are taken up and sponsored in particular institutional contexts. There is a political as well as a material dimension to the way teachers label pupils. It is this added dimension that is addressed by Sharp and Green (1975) in their study of a progressive primary school.

The Political and Material Context of Teachers' Labels

Sharp and Green (1975) set out to explore a major contradiction apparent in the work of three infant teachers in one primary school. The contradictions were between the theory and practice of progressive education. The school espoused a strong child-centred ideology. Teachers would argue that it was important to know their pupils in a unique and individual way; they would discuss the dangers of premature labelling and would congratulate themselves on their ability to retain open minds about pupils' potentialities and capabilities. This was the theory. The reality, Sharp and Green argue, was that some pupils did develop reified identities. Some pupils were seen as 'really thick', others were 'peculiar' and yet others were 'different'. In other words they were labelled. Moreover, Sharp and Green noted that the labelling had important consequences in terms of the amount and kinds of interaction pupils had with their teachers. Those who were regarded as more successful at school were given far greater attention than the others. As a consequence such pupils were more likely to be known in an individually unique way and less likely to be stereotypically labelled.

Sharp and Green suggest that the paradox between the theory and practice of the school could not and should not be explained entirely in terms of teachers' consciousness. The teachers did not simply *choose* to label their pupils in this way for their own reasons. These ambiguities were themselves reflections of the structure of material and social constraints external to the classroom which impinged upon the teachers and structured their activities.

> In our analysis we shall suggest that teachers are encapsulated within a context which produced the necessity for some hierarchical differentiation of the pupils in order that the teacher may solve the problems she is confronted with and provide some legitimation for the allocation of her time and energies. (Sharp and Green, 1975:116)

Sharp and Green suggest that the teachers they studied were subject to a range of constraints on their practice, both political and material. On the political level there were strong expectations communicated to teachers from their senior colleagues about developing good pedagogical practices compatible with the child-centred philosophy of the school. The teacher most warmly favoured by the head was the one who most clearly articulated this approach. However, there were also expectations communicated from parents and governors concerning levels of achievement that had to be maintained. Whatever the liberal philosophy of the school the parents wanted tangible evidence of progress displayed through achievement in basic skills.

In addition, pupils imposed their own constraints. As other writers have noted (Pollard, 1979), pupils are not merely passive objects but exert their own significant influence on the teacher. Other constraints were of a more material and physical nature. The teacher–pupil ratio is obviously a factor as is the architecture and layout of the classroom. All of these factors influenced teachers when faced with the problem of 'what to do in the classroom'. As in Chessum's study, teachers had to choose strategies and ways of dealing with pupils that 'worked' on a pragmatic basis and in this particular context, but which also articulated with the school's espoused child-centred ideology.

In line with its philosophy the school pursued a policy of an integrated day — pupils were allowed to freely choose from a range of activities provided by their teacher. This policy presented the teacher with an important practical problem — what to do with 25–30 freely choosing children. Their particular solution was 'busyness', where children were urged to choose an activity that did not require the constant attention of the teacher. The teachers constantly urged their pupils to 'be busy', to 'get on on your own' or 'find yourself something to do'. Sharp and Green argue that this strategy was not freely chosen by the teachers themselves, rather it was essential in their attempt to implement a particular educational ideology (the one espoused by the head and senior staff) in that particular context. It also had the advantage of freeing the teachers to work individually with pupils on literacy and numeracy so that they could 'deliver the traditional goods' in terms of progress on these basic and very visible skills.

It was the teacher's chosen strategy of 'busyness' that defined the nature of deviance, for a key problem associated with abnormal children was that the teacher's approach manifestly did not work with them. Pupils who were 'difficult to get through to', who 'dribbed and drabbed' or who 'would not show an interest in anything' became a problem for their teachers. They subverted the strategy of 'busyness' that was so essential if the teacher was to carry out her work.

As Sharp and Green point out, these pupils were not *inherently* problematic. If a teacher had time to work with them on a one-to-one basis over a long period they may have regarded them differently. In a more traditional context these particular children may have been less problematic and others would have been singled out. The children were labelled as a problem for their teachers in this particular social context. Thus rather than seeing labelling as a situation where the social controller (in this case the teacher) applies some hard label to the pupils, Sharp and Green instead suggest that we should see it as a far more subtle process, where the rigidity or the variability of the labels is as much related to the state of social control within the organization as to the rigidity of the teachers' thought processes:

> The social structure throws up problems [for the teacher] and allows her, given her projects and the field of constraints, only certain solutions or structures of opportunity to solve them. This process is dynamic and open ended but points to the way in which social structure, meaning and behaviour, are related together. (Sharp and Green, 1975:127)

The studies of Chessum and Sharp and Green represent a first and important attempt to develop a broader theoretical perspective on the process of labelling. By focusing on the social reaction to deviance, interactionist work has pointed to an important dimension in the process of delinquent development. However, a more fully social theory of labelling must, as do these authors, ask why it is that teachers label pupils as they do. Yet these studies take only the first step in that process. They seek the sources of teachers' labels entirely within the institutional context of the school itself. The material and political context of particular schools are held to be paramount in influencing the teachers' perspective. Other studies, as we will see in the next chapter, have attempted to take the analysis somewhat further by locating school deviance in a more explicitly class context. Before turning to these alternative approaches it is necessary to consider criticisms of labelling in more detail.

Criticisms of Labelling Theory

Whatever theoretical perspective is taken to labelling, interactionist, phenomenological, or neo-Marxist, a number of important criticisms remain unanswered. Most of the difficulties derive from the fact that labelling does not explain why pupils are deviant in the first place. The emphasis on secondary deviance provides a plausible explanation of how *some* pupils might respond to being publicly labelled. The notion of a deviant career is a significant contribution to our theorizing, but only the most crude formulations of labelling theory would suggest that it is the label that creates the deviance in the first place. Two possible explanations of primary deviance are implicit in the theory but both of them are unsatisfactory. Either rule breaking is seen as ubiquitous — everybody does it all of the time but only some deviance gets publicly labelled — or the reasons for initial deviance are so personal and idiosyncratic that they cannot be explained systematically. In either case the initial cause is considered far less important than the reaction to it. While social reaction is important it is hardly the whole story and is manifestly unimportant in some cases. (Presumably school phobics are entirely unbothered how teachers define them — however they were labelled they would rarely come to school.)

A further problem arising from this lack of concern with initial causes is that labelling theory implies that there is nothing wrong with schooling. Pupils are not seen as choosing to reject their school because of the inequalities they feel they face. They are not seen as even choosing to reject school because they are bored and want some excitement. Instead they are seen as free and spontaneous, simply acting on the whim of the moment until the intervention of a teacher, the police or a magistrate. Despite labelling theory's interactionist heart, deviance is not seen as a meaningful act. Pupils do not choose certain sorts of behaviour because they *know* they will be challenging or anarchic. For the labelling theorist it is the teacher who bestows meaning on behaviour when he or she labels it. Deviance only gains meaning when pupils attempt to respond to labels forced on them by unjust teachers.

The lack of concern with aetiology also leads to another

problem. By insisting that rule breaking is equally distributed among all types of pupils, but only certain sorts of behaviour are defined as deviant, labelling theorists rule out the possibility of asking why it is that certain groups of pupils (for example, urban working class boys) are so frequently in trouble with their teachers. While it is true that teachers may be more vigilant with these pupils and official figures therefore need to be treated with caution, it is simply wrong to suggest for example that academically successful middle class girls are equally involved in breaking the rules of school. By challenging the entire validity of the official record the opportunity to raise broader questions is lost.

As we will see in Chapter 7, a more fully developed 'radical' theory of school deviance is precisely concerned with the structural and cultural location of pupils who most frequently engage in acts of disruption and truancy. Pupils are seen as choosing certain sorts of behaviour *knowing* that it will be interpreted as deviant — they deliberately choose to violate the moral code of the school. If we believe that pupils know how their behaviour will be interpreted then this fundamentally alters our understanding of the choices they appear to be making.

Notes

1. See Chapter 5 for a discussion of 'neutralizing techniques'.
2. See, for example, Cicourel and Kitsuse (1963) and Rist (1970).
3. Perhaps one of the reasons for this neglect is that it is much easier to research teachers' ways of labelling pupils than it is to work with pupils and explore their subjective perceptions of labels.
4. In the school Bird studied, regular 'case conferences' were called to discuss particularly problematic pupils. Teachers, the School Counsellor and, if appropriate, a representative from the social services would participate in these meetings, attempting to diagnose difficulties and devise appropriate strategies for intervention.
5. See, for example, Dale (1974) and the Open University Course E202.
6. By contrast Taylor *et al.* (1973) emphasize the importance of exploring the 'wider origins' of social reaction.

> One of the important formal requirements for a fully social theory of deviance, that is almost totally absent in the existing literature, is an effective model of the political and economic imperatives that underpin on the one hand the "lay ideologies" and on the other the "crusades" and initiatives that emerge periodically either to control the amount and level of deviance . . . or else . . . to remove certain behaviours from the category of "illegal" behaviours. We are lacking a *political economy of social reaction*. (p. 274)

7. See, for example, the workings of the 'welfare network' surrounding schools as described by Johnson *et al.* (1980).
8. See also Furlong and Bird (1981).

CHAPTER SEVEN

Class Theories of School Deviance: Working Class Heroes

One of the most consistent findings to emerge from sociological research on indiscipline at school is that as a phenomenon it is far more common among working class than middle class children. As was noted in Chapter 2, positivists have demonstrated time and again that it is the children of social classes 4 and 5 (those from semi-skilled and unskilled families) who most frequently challenge the moral authority of their teachers by playing truant or being disruptive in the classroom.

The same observation has been made by researchers working in other intellectual traditions. For example, writers employing the adaptational and subcultural perspectives outlined in Chapter 4 have nearly all noted that it is working class children who most frequently adopt intransigent or rebellious strategies; it is working class children who most frequently develop deviant subcultures. Yet despite noting these correlations, authors such as Hargreaves (1967), Lacey (1970), Woods (1979) and Ball (1981) have not systematically studied the phenomenon in itself. As was argued in Chapter 4, studies in the adaptational and subcultural traditions have concentrated on the organization of schools rather than on the workings of society in general. Pupils are seen as rejecting school because they are in the bottom stream or band, not because they are working class. The fact that the majority of the pupils in these bottom streams or bands are mainly working class has remained a recognized but unexplored side issue.[1]

The factor that unites the studies to be considered in this chapter is that they all take the relationship between school deviance and social class as their starting point; it is this constant relationship which their research endeavours to explain. The most significant body of theory and research to address this topic is derived from neo-Marxist work in which education is seen in the context of the 'social and cultural reproduction' of society. Reproduction theorists argue that education is fundamentally implicated in the maintenance of an unequal society which is structured in terms of social class. From this point of view, school deviance, or 'resistance' as it is termed, is seen as a form of 'mediated class conflict'. Disruption and truancy are the ways in which working class children consciously or unconsciously respond to their domination.

In this chapter a number of different theories of reproduction will be briefly outlined and some of the early attempts at empirical research in this tradition will be discussed. In Chapter 8 the scope of the argument is broadened and the relationship between deviance, race and gender as well as class is considered. Before turning to reproduction theories, however, it will first be useful to consider a rather different approach to explaining working class indiscipline at school — cultural conflict. This approach is important for it explores different dimensions of class culture and in this way anticipates many themes which have been taken up more recently.

Cultural Conflict

The idea that indiscipline at school is at least in part a product of cultural conflict is one that often receives support among teachers.[2] From this perspective, it is argued that there is sometimes a conflict between the values of the working class home and community and those of the school. Working class children, it is suggested, subscribe to different values from those of their teachers and it is the pursuit of these alternative values that brings them into conflict with the school.

It was Miller (1958) who first and most explicitly developed a cultural conflict model to explain delinquent behaviour among working class youth. His work was intended to challenge the interpretations of the early subcultural theorists (e.g. Cohen, 1955) who argued that delinquent subcultures are established by a status-deprived group turning the values of bourgeois society upside down. Instead, Miller suggested that there is a substantial segment of society 'whose way of life, values and characteristic patterns of behaviour are the product of a distinctive cultural system which may be termed "lower class" (Miller,

1958:6). From this point of view young people get into trouble because they pursue these working class values which inevitably bring them into conflict with those in authority.

After a period of three years fieldwork, in which seven trained social workers kept contact with 21 groups of adolescents for between 10 and 30 months, Miller felt that he was able to define a number of distinctive 'focal concerns' of lower class culture, the pursuit of which contributed to greater deviance among working class youth. He defined the key features of this culture as follows:

Trouble: Getting into trouble is not valued in itself, but is frequently a means to achieve other covertly and overtly valued states. For example, the pursuit of excitement and risk often involves the possibility of getting into trouble. Being cared for and subject to external constraint is often covertly valued by working class youth — this too can be achieved through trouble.

Toughness: This involves a complex of interrelated factors which are valued, such as physical prowess, masculinity (symbolized by a lack of sentimentality and a lack of concern with art and literature), and bravery in the face of physical threat.

Smartness: There is an emphasis on 'non-intellectual' cleverness; the capacity to outsmart and outwit others and the capacity to achieve status and goods by wits rather than physical effort is admired.

Excitement: There is a constant search for a 'thrill'. With adults it might come through betting or a night on the town in sexual adventures, for younger people of school age it may involve running the gauntlet with the police, angry neighbours or teachers.

Fate: Many working class people feel their lives are subject to forces over which they have relatively little control — either you are clever or lucky or not. Hence the need for other things in life such as excitement.

Autonomy: Here there is an important distinction between what is overtly and covertly valued. On the overt level there is a strong and frequently expressed resentment at any external control. However, at the same time there is an idea that to be subject to authoritative control implies that one is being taken care of. There is a discrepancy, Miller argues, between what is overtly called for and what is actually done. Many working class people actively seek out situations where external controls are maintained. For example, working class children often report that they like teachers who are strict and tough.

According to Miller the main reason that so many working class adolescents get into trouble is not because they are status deprived or suffer from anomie but because they are pursuing these particular cultural goals. Young people may appear negative and rebellious from the point of view of those in authority but, Miller argues, any degree of rebelliousness is unimportant compared to the *positive* attempts by adolescents to pursue the values held most closely by their own reference group, other working class adolescents.

Despite the importance of Miller's work in the study of youth, comparatively little notice has been taken of his argument in the study of school deviance.[3] However, one possible exception is Lacey's (1970) study of Hightown Grammar. Lacey argues that pupils who are status deprived by the school develop an anti-school culture. Unlike Hargreaves (1967) and Cohen (1955) he recognizes that the subculture that is formed is not merely the reverse of the school values but is informed by the cultural milieu that pupils inhabit outside the school. In his study Lacey suggests that the anti-school culture at Hightown Grammar was informed by working class and Jewish culture within the school's local community. However, Lacey does not develop this aspect of his work fully and unlike Miller he sees working class culture as a resource to be exploited by pupils *after* they have been rejected by the school. It is not a prime cause of disaffection in the first place.

A study which has more affinity with that of Miller is the research by Bird *et al.* (1981) outlined in Chapter 5. This study of disaffection in six outer London schools examined both pupils' and teachers' perspectives on school deviance. Although the work with pupils is centrally influenced by interactionist thinking there is clear evidence of a broader understanding of why pupils become disaffected from schools. In the tradition of interactionist work, the authors point to factors concerned with the institutional life of school that pupils reject. In addition, however, they also explore a number of other cultural factors which from the pupils' point of view are highly influential in their rejection of schooling. In much of the analysis there is an implicit, if underdeveloped, notion of class cultural differences in pupils' values and attitudes and these values are seen as originating primarily from outside the school.

Although these studies are clearly important in recognizing the significance of a class-based culture in relation to school deviance, they have a major weakness from the point of view of attempting a more thoroughgoing class analysis. There is no serious attempt to locate the class culture which is described in any structural or historical context in the work of Miller, Lacey or Bird *et al.* Miller does not attempt to explain why 'lower class culture' should embrace the values of excitement, toughness and autonomy, and Bird *et al.* do not explain the reasons why, for example, girls should be more concerned with marriage than a career. *Class* cultural conflict is thereby reduced to *cultural* conflict — a war of attrition between two opposed but unexplained cultures.

More recently writers in both criminology and education have attempted to explore the class basis of deviance and crime in more systematic ways by the importation of various strands of neo-Marxist thought. It is this work which forms the focus of the remainder of this and the subsequent chapter.

Reproduction and Resistance

Within the field of criminology the impetus for a Marxist theory of crime and deviance came from a rather different tradition from that outlined above. It came from a critique of labelling theory. Most significant in this movement were Taylor *et al.* (1973) with the development of what they called 'critical criminology'.

In their work on critical criminology, Taylor *et al.* attempt to retain many of the insights of labelling theory but relocate them within a structural context. They argue that it is possible to use a Marxist framework to show how in contemporary and historical periods there have been attempts by the dominant class to order society in specific ways. For them the capitalist economic system is the central framework for analysing crime; deviance is inseparably bound up with questions of political economy. The potential radicalism of labelling theory is inhibited because it does not produce a macro-societal analysis of capitalist power structures and most particularly a theory of the state.

The attraction of Marx's work for criminologists is that it at least potentially offers a way out of many of the old dualisms that have so haunted earlier writing. The notion that men and women make their own history, but not just as they please but under conditions inherited and transmitted from the past, challenges, at least at the level of rhetoric, distinctions between structure and process, determinism and freedom, the macro and the micro. However, many of the early attempts at Marxist analyses retain a fairly crude determinism.

Intellectual developments seldom occur in water-tight compartments and at the same time that critical criminologists were 'rediscovering' Marxist categories, sociologists of education were doing the same. They were doing so in a way that would eventually place school deviance, or 'resistance' as it was renamed, at the centre of the research agenda. Resistance has become a central concept in the analysis of 'social and cultural reproduction' within education for it is seen as a way of rescuing early formulations of such theories from charges of functionalism and determinism.

Theories of Social and Cultural Reproduction

Theories of reproduction are essentially concerned with the way in which the economic mode of production of a society is reproduced; the way in which individuals are equipped with suitable skills and qualifications for a stratified occupational structure and the way they are socialized into the existing political and moral order. Given that in Western capitalism societies are unequal, and structured by class relations, the question for neo-Marxist reproduction theorists is how that inequality is reproduced. Willis (1977) poses the question most succinctly when he asks: 'How do working class kids get working class jobs?' One could also ask why do middle class kids get middle class jobs and why do working class kids let them.

For many reproduction theorists education is seen to be central to such a process. It is schools, more than any other institution in modern society, that are implicated in the reproduction of the same class divisions in society from generation to generation. As Willis (1981) comments, the reproduction perspective poses

> almost a timeless ahistorical question as if the generations were stopped; how is the *new* generation placed in relation to capital? Clearly education becomes an important site for this if only because this is where the kids are. Also it becomes a privileged site because, as the conventional sociology of education recognises, there are clear class inequalities in educational outcomes even, or perhaps especially where ... schooling promises the opposite — namely equality and humanistic self advance. The real social relations of domination are achieved under the rubric of an ideal social relationship. This offers fertile ground for the reproductive interest. (p. 51)

Schools then are heavily implicated in the reproduction of an unequal society because, as has been demonstrated by sociologists so often, educational achievements are heavily structured by class. The central question for reproduction theorists is how that process is achieved. If, in the words of Giroux (1981), there is a 'deep structure and grammar of class domination and inequality' in school then what precisely is its nature and how is this class domination realized in the day-to-day practices of schools?

Different theorists have formulated the 'deep structure' and 'grammar' of domination in different ways. Althusser (1971), for example, argues that ideology is central. It is through ideology that people acquire not only the skills needed for the labour market but more importantly the 'ideological predispositions', the attitudes, values and norms, so essential for the maintenance of the existing class relations of production. According to Althusser, schools communicate ideologies which impose sets of ideas on pupils, socializing them into class-specific roles. These ideologies then become constitutive of the subjects themselves. Subjectivity is created through ideologies which have a single purpose — to reproduce the conditions of capitalist relations.

Bowles and Gintis (1976) place less emphasis on ideology for the achievement of social reproduction. For them the structural features of the school itself are central. They argue that there is a 'correspondence' between the social relations of school and those of production. Schools are bureaucratic, based on hierarchical authority and on various forms of stratification ('ability', age and sex). They are also predicated on a system of external incentives, exam success and the threat of failure. By participating in contemporary schooling pupils are subject to a 'hidden curriculum' which inculcates the values and attitudes appropriate to a class society.

Althusser and Bowles and Gintis focus on *social* reproduction. Theorists of *cultural* reproduction (for example, Bourdieu, 1977; Bourdieu and Passeron, 1977), are also concerned with how class societies reproduce themselves. However, for them, the main emphasis is on the role of culture in that process. The economy plays a less direct role than in theories of social reproduction. Institutions like schools have a 'relative autonomy' from the economy. Nevertheless, they still serve its interests, if more indirectly.

Bourdieu argues that schools help to produce and distribute a dominant culture that is compatible with the needs and interests of the ruling class. Power in our society, he argues, is not achieved by crude economic control, but by the more subtle process of 'symbolic violence', whereby one class is able to impose a definition of the social world on another. Schools are fundamentally implicated in the process by defining what it means to be educated in terms of the dominant culture or 'habitus' which equips the educationally successful to understand and work within it. In this way one particular class culture is apparently neutralized and comes to act as a source of social integration. At the same time by selectively valuing different sorts of 'cultural capital' schools implicitly disadvantage those children who have not grown up with the 'right' linguistic and cultural competencies. Because of the apparent neutrality of school knowledge social differences between classes become reproduced and legitimized.

The questions that these theorists have been pursuing are highly complex and sophisticated and no full account or critique can be entered into here. However, one important common problem that each of them share is that the domination they describe seems too complete. Despite notions of 'relative autonomy' and some lipservice to the issues of subjectivity and consciousness there is little or no concern with the role of the dominated; there is no room for any form of response. The reproduction of the existing order is just too neat. As Giroux (1981) comments:

> The notion of domination at the heart of these two sets of theories (social and cultural reproduction) is onesided and undialectical. Power is seen as purely negative. Whether it is located in the state, the mode of production (or) the cultural sphere ... power emerges in these accounts as a form of imposition. Power as a form of production, invention and resistance is not considered. (pp. 11–12)

Willis (1983) makes an essentially similar point. Of Althusser he says: '"Reproduction" becomes a mechanical inevitability. A *pre-given* and *pre-empting* structure of class relations is simply replaced' (p. 116). Similarly, according to Willis, Bowles' and Gintis' notion of 'correspondence' 'Omits the independent effort of the working class and its relationship with the dominant class, thus overlooking consciousness and culture as moments of social process' (p. 117). Willis sees Bourdieu's concern with bourgeois culture as a clear advance on social reproduction theories but argues that there is in Bordieu's work still no account of why the 'powerless' accept their unequal lot. 'How *do* the 'powerless' understand and accept their position? What is *their* role in reproduction?' (p. 120). It is in the light of such criticisms that the notion of resistance has achieved such significance for contemporary reproduction theorists.

The existence of disruption and truancy demonstrates that working class children *do* respond to the forms of class control they experience at school. They do challenge the dominant ideologies of individualism and competition that are fostered at school; they do challenge the social relations of school that confine them to rule-governed subordinate positions; they do challenge dominant notions of culture that marginalize and devalue their own cultural experiences. These, it is argued, are evidence of the *response* of pupils to the domination they experience at school. But this implies a more dynamic and less stable view of reproduction than that implied by the theorists outlined above — it implies a notion of 'hegemony'.

Hegemony and Resistance

Since the mid-1970s the notion of 'resistance' has become a central concept in the sociology of youth, both in and out of school. The change in term is significant. Disruption and truancy are no longer interpreted as evidence of maladjustment or even deviance. The term resistance unequivocally places these activities within the broader framework of class relations. Researchers using the concept of resistance may draw only indirectly on the work of writers such as Althusser, Bowles and Gintis or Bourdieu, yet it is clear that they are all pursuing the same questions of how a class society reproduces itself. Where they differ from these analysts is in the belief that social reproduction is never complete but is always faced with partially realized elements of *opposition*. They argue that there are gaps and tensions in institutions like schools which allow the 'deep structure' and 'grammar' of class domination to be continually challenged. In the move to this more dialectical notion of class relations the work of Gramsci (1973) and particularly his concept of hegemony has been central.

Gramsci used the term hegemony to denote the way in which certain ruling groups in our society achieve ascendency not just in the economic sphere, but in the social, political and ideological spheres as well. While such ruling groups can and do sometimes use force to maintain their ascendency a more important form of control is achieved by the establishment of social authority. They attempt to win the hearts and minds of subordinate groups by presenting their own philosophy as the 'official' view of the world, apparently representing the interests of all. Such social authority cannot be achieved by force, it demands the consent of the subordinate classes, yet once achieved it is far more potent as a form of social control.

Gramsci does not see consent emerging naturally, rather it is something that has to be created and worked for, particularly in the institutions of 'civil society' such as the churches and the schools. What distinguishes Gramsci's analysis from other theories of reproduction is that he does not see hegemonic control as static. Rather it is inherently unstable, challenged and changing. It is a 'moving equilibrium'. Hegemony is unstable for two reasons: first, because power is never exercised permanently by the same alliance of 'class factions' — new alliances have to be formed and compromises reached to deal with new situations. Secondly, it is unstable because as rational beings we all have the capacity to think our way round these dominant ideas. All men and women have the capacity for conscious criticism. We are all to some degree intellectuals. Consequently there is a possibility of people bringing into being new modes of thought.

Hegemonic control may be pervasive, but it is never complete. Gramsci believes that the dominated groups can still hold their own unofficial views of the world grounded in their own life experience. Hegemony cannot incorporate all cultural forms or destroy the class conflict inherent in capitalism. The problem for those wishing to maintain their supremacy is to cause people to 'think right things', to consent to ruling ideologies by accepting them as common sense. Resistance is thinking yourself out of these ideas and logically bypassing them. Such resistance is rational, purposive and conscious though seldom revolutionary. Far more frequently resistance takes the form of a spontaneous cultural reponse where one aspect of domination is challenged while others remain accepted as common sense.

Working class resistance takes many forms in our society. Trade union activity and strikes are obvious examples — so too is the creation of the working class neighbourhood.[4] Schools are particularly important for they are major sites for the achievement of hegemonic control. For Gramsci they also offer the possibility of achieving a new revolutionary counter-hegemony. More importantly for our purposes they are seen as the site of a great deal of working class resistance to dominant ideologies, expressed in the form of violence, disruption and truancy.

The Four Basic Assumptions

Where do theories of reproduction stand in relation to the four paradigmatic assumptions outlined in previous chapters (ontology, human nature, epistemology, and research methods)? Unfortunately it is not possible to provide a straightforward answer for there is no coherent view on at least one central issue, that of human nature. For example, writers such as Althusser take a very deterministic view of human nature —

consciousness is constructed through participation in dominant ideologies. For researchers working in this tradition, the prime focus of research is to explore these dominant ideologies; the ways they are created and maintained, the ways they function in particular institutions and the relationship between them and the economic base of society. Subjective reality is constituted through ideology and research methods must be developed that will 'fracture' that closed circle of meanings to reveal the 'deep structure' of economic relations on which they are predicated.[5]

In sharp contrast the work of Gramsci and his followers implies a much more active view of human nature — people are presented as seeing through, questioning and challenging features which dominate their lives. The focus of concern from this perspective is both with the material and ideological factors which structure peoples lives *and* with the spontaneous and 'profane' cultures developed by people in response. Subjectivity, even if it is only constructed in conditions of subordination, is an important topic for research.

The issue of subjectivity or consciousness is critical in distinguishing between the empirical studies of working class resistance to school to be considered below. The three studies to be discussed in the remainder of this chapter (Corrigan, 1979; Humphries, 1981; Anyon, 1981a,b) adopt what Young (1979) has termed a 'left idealist' approach to deviance. They assume that working class pupils are conscious of their domination at school and therefore explicitly and consciously rebel. Disruption and truancy are seen as forms of conscious class conflict. By contrast, writers such as Willis (1977), to be discussed in the next chapter, adopt a more subtle and sophisticated notion of consciousness. For him, pupils develop cultural practices, such as disruption and truancy, which may be based on a consciousness of subordination, but are far more often valued because of their 'resonance' with the *experience* of subordination. Such 'resonances' need not be raised to the level of consciousness. Certain ways of behaving 'feel right' and 'make sense' so they are repeated. In this way cultural forms of resistance are established.

Working Class Heroes

A number of important studies of deviant pupils have been undertaken in recent years using the concept of resistance, though they have varied considerably in the subtlety and sophistication of their argument. One of the clearest and most straightforward presentations of a neo-Marxist theory of resistance is presented by Corrigan (1979) in his study of approximately 100 14-year-old boys in two working class Sunderland schools. In his book Corrigan illustrates the way he moved from his initial hypothesis about why the boys rejected school to a class conflict approach. He had expected to find a delinquent subculture on the lines of that described by Hargreaves (1967) and Lacey (1970). He assumed that the boys he studied had initially supported school, were rejected by it and so developed their own oppositional group. When he came to talk to the boys about truancy, for example, he expected them to value it as a 'good thing'; he assumed it would be part of their 'delinquent' culture. However, what he discovered was something rather different. When he asked the boys why they came to school half of them said that they only came because they *had* to: '50 of the boys perceive school as a place you only come to because you *have* to: and it provides us with answers not at all in terms of value, but in terms of *power* (Corrigan, 1979:22).

Corrigan argues that studies of working class culture suggest that working class children learn a number of strategies in dealing with oppressive authority. First, ignore it, it may well go away; secondly, try to remove yourself from it as much as possible; thirdly, recognize it only in so far as it can enforce recognition. For Corrigan truancy is part of a cultural response to the imposition of compulsory schooling. It is an attempt by pupils to remove themselves from it as much as possible. He argues that such a response is clearly built in terms of class culture. If, for example, a group of middle class students were *made* to attend lectures which they found boring and irrelevant, they might use a variety of strategies to improve the situation — arguing with the teacher, getting together to apply collective pressure through petitions, etc. Corrigan argues that these forms of opposition are not available to working class children at school for they do not form part of their class cultural experience. For them truancy is a more natural form of expressing opposition to authority.

Corrigan reports that the realization that the boys he studied were using truancy as a response to the power of schools and teachers led him to change the whole direction of his study. He was still interested in working class education, truancy and disruption, but he became much more concerned to ask why pupils were made to go to school in the first place.

This meant that the focus of the research changed from simply being

about the boys' perceptions of their situations to seeing their perceptions as the *starting point* of the research and therefore looking at the
relationship between school refusal and the power of the state to make
boys go to school. (Corrigan, 1979:29)

For Corrigan the question of why pupils play truant cannot be
answered without asking first why they have to go to school; the
answer to this prior question is to be found in the study of
history. Echoing many of the arguments outlined in Chapter 1
he argues that nineteenth century education was established as
a form of cultural domination. The working class family was
widely condemned as a 'source of evil' and education was
specifically designed to change their lives and attitudes. By
reference to historical materials he illustrates a number of
themes of working class education as it was established in the
nineteenth century. Schools were established to:

(1)   Provide bourgeois facts and theories to counter 'revolu-
      tionary' facts and theories being put about by the work-
      ing class themselves.
(2)   To provide a bourgeois moral and religious code which,
      once it had been taught to the working class, would
      change their behaviour.
(3)   To create a disciplined and punctual work force.
(4)   To create a national hierarchy based on education which
      would recreate and *legitimate* class differences.

The critical point for the analysis of contemporary resistance to
school, Corrigan argues, is that education is still conceived in
broadly similar terms. It is still about changing working class
culture. The arguments that raged in the nineteenth century
about the form popular education should take set the
parameters for contemporary schooling.

In order to support this historical leap of faith Corrigan
quotes Butler's presentation of his 1944 Education Act, suggesting that it echoes the same ideology:

> Here I want to make it clear that it is no part of the government's policy
> to supplant the home; I should like to indignantly repudiate any sugges-
> tion that this is our policy. But unfortunately, the experience of evacua-
> tion and other war time experiences has shown how many homes need
> helping. (Corrigan, 1979:42)

In the Newsom Report of 1963 he argues, the relationship
between the school and the area it served was still seen as one
of challenge and attempted change:

> The picture which the headmasters have so movingly drawn for us make
> it clear that the social challenge they have to meet comes from the whole

neighbourhood in which they work and not from a handful of difficult families. (pp. 42–43)

Corrigan argues that whether or not we feel that the attempts at intervention are for the good or not, it is clear that a significant minority of children experience this undoubted intervention as a form of attack. Education, says Corrigan, is not entirely about imposition, but this is an important strand within it and it is for this reason that it was resisted by the boys he studied using their own cultural resources. Conflict arises because there is a concerted and sustained attempt by those in authority to change the values and behaviour of the working class for their own ends. It is because of this cultural imposition that working class pupils rebel in the only ways they know how. They play truant and muck about. They find their own freedom in areas outside the school such as football matches and pop concerts.

A very similar argument to that of Corrigan is put forward in another empirical study by Humphries (1981) in his book *Hooligans or Rebels*? However, rather than examining the experience of contemporary pupils, Humphries uses oral histories elicited from old people reflecting on their school experience in the early part of this century.

Like Corrigan, Humphries argues that education was conceived of as an imposition on the working class. It was not designed to implant literacy skills and knowledge as ends in themselves — instead it was conceived as a means to an end. It was 'potentially the most powerful instrument to inculcate in successive generations of working class children, values and attitudes that were thought necessary for the reproduction and reinvigoration of an industrial capitalist society' (Humphries, 1981:31).

Humphries' list of the objectives of education at the turn of the century is similar to that described by Corrigan. Among other things education was intended to ameliorate certain social problems: crime, violence, disease and drunkenness. It was also intended to elevate the child to a middle class morality and to provide an educational ladder whereby talented working class children could achieve success and provide the skilled manpower that was increasingly in demand for industry and commerce. These he regards as education's more liberal objectives. There were also other more conservative objectives, such as the concern to create an orderly and disciplined work force. However, whatever the formulation, conservative or liberal, he argues that there was a consensus that schooling should seek to train young minds to fit the existing social structure.

Humphries argues that in order to study the way in which these forms of imposition were resisted it is essential to use oral histories because the official records so frequently distort the evidence. It was not, he argues, in the interests of head teachers to record the full measure of resistance to school and even where disruption and truancy were recorded the meanings of the behaviour were frequently distorted. They were interpreted in a value-laden way as 'insubordination', 'defiance', 'ill manners', 'ignorance' or 'foul language'. To redress the balance of the official record, 'We must listen to the testimony of those old working class people who stand accused in the official records of acts of resistance against rational state instruction' (Humphries, 1981:29)

As we saw in Chapter 1, Humphries uses his evidence to argue that in the period he studied, pupils' opposition to school was extensive and purposeful. Pupils, supported covertly and overtly by their parents, frequently engaged in truancy, larking about, violence and even school strikes as a way of resisting the form, content and structure of state education. According to Humphries, the authoritarian and bureaucratic state school system was an instrument designed to perpetuate, reproduce and legitimate capitalist relations; pupil deviance was a challenge to this process.

> When viewed from this perspective, the occasional or persistent truant, the children who disrupted lessons and protected class mates from punishment, the parents who threatened or assaulted teachers must be seen to have been involved in a fierce class-cultural struggle over the form of social relations that were to prevail in schools. (p. 89)

A final study in this tradition is Anyon's research in a group of elementary schools in America (Anyon, 1981a,b). Anyon's study is rather different from that of either Corrigan or Humphries. Not only does she concentrate on younger pupils but her main focus is on forms of 'cultural reproduction'. Her research poses two questions: first, are there observable differences in the sorts of 'knowledge' communicated to different social class groups within a specific community, and secondly, if there are such differences, how do the pupils respond? In order to explore these questions, Anyon made a participant observation study of five elementary schools in two school districts. She argues that the schools served relatively homogeneous class communities and she therefore classifies the schools in the following way: two 'working class', one 'middle class', one 'affluent professional' and one 'executive élite'.

As a result of observation and analysis in these five schools, Anyon suggests that despite the similarities in curricula *topics* and *materials*, there were some subtle and some dramatic differences in the curricula taught and in the 'curricula-in-use'. Most significant for the study of school deviance were the two working class schools. Anyon reports that in these two schools, teachers tended to speak of knowledge in terms of facts and simple skills. Mathematical knowledge was often restricted to the procedures or steps to be followed, the purposes of which were seldom explained to the children. Social studies instruction commonly involved carrying out tasks such as copying teachers' notes, answering text book questions or colouring and assembling paper cut outs. When she asked the pupils what they thought of when she said the word 'knowledge', most of them replied in the same mechanical terms. They spoke of 'skills', 'doing work sheets', 'doing pages out of our books and things'.

All of this was in marked contrast to the form of curriculum received by pupils in other social class districts. For example, in the 'affluent professional' school the emphasis was on individual discovery and creativity, while in the 'executive élite' school, the emphasis was on intellectual processes such as reasoning and problem solving.

Anyon argues that these differences in what was actually taught were highly significant in the way the children responded. For example, in the 'executive élite' school there was an acceptance by the teachers and the pupils that 'excellence' was an important goal. In the working class schools, however, the dominant theme was 'resistance'. Although some resistance appeared in all of the schools in the study, Anyon reports that in the working class schools it was a dominant characteristic of pupil-teacher interaction. This resistance was sometimes active, for example 'someone put a bug in one student's desk, boys fell out of chairs; they misplaced books or forgot them' (Anyon, 1981a:10). At other times resistance was passive; pupils would withhold enthusiasm or refuse to answer questions: 'On occasions when teachers finally explode with impatience because nobody "knows" the answer, one can see fleeting smiles flicker across some students faces, they are pleased to see the teacher get angry, upset' (1981a:10).

Anyon argues that the practices of the working class schools were 'reproductive' in two significant ways. First, these pupils were given little or no conceptual or critical understanding of the world or of their situation in it. Secondly, there was an emphasis on mechanical behaviours which would ensure their subordinate position in future employment. 'These working class children were not offered what for them would be *cultural capital* — knowledge and skill at manipulating ideas and symbols in their own interest' (1981a:31). Interestingly, however, Anyon argues that there was little attempt to win the hearts and minds of these working class pupils. Control was almost entirely physical — hence their continued resistance. Anyon therefore places her hope for future social (and socialist) change in this disaffected group.

> The absence of traditional bodies of knowledge and ideology may make these children vulnerable to alternative ideas, the children may be more open to ideas that support fundamental social change. Indeed, some of the children were already engaged in struggle against what was to them an exploitative group — the school teachers and administrators. They were struggling against the imposition of a foreign curriculum. They had "seen through" the system. (1981a:32)

Left Idealism

The rather simplistic approach to the issue of reproduction and resistance implicit in the work of Corrigan, Humphries and Anyon was closely paralleled in the middle and late 1970s by other work in sociology and history. For example, Donajgrodski (1977) uses similar arguments in the analysis of a wide variety of elements of everyday life in the nineteenth century. Whether it is the sermons of the clergy, the philanthropy of the middle class, the police or the emergence of the juvenile court system, the 'real' purpose behind these initiatives was the single-minded repression of the working class. For such authors the 'state' (and it is always a reified coherent and sinister state) was and is engaged in a massive and concerted attempt to repress the working population in order to serve the interests of capital. Any act which challenges the law or, in the school, the rules of expected behaviour, is not deviance but resistance.

In an important article of self-criticism, Young (1979) labels this approach 'left idealism'. Young defines its key characteristics as including voluntarism, a coercive conception of order and functionalism:

> A voluntaristic conception of human nature coupled with a notion that social order is essentially maintained by a series of coercive institutions structured together in a functionalist fashion. (p. 13)

Society apparently hangs together by the *voluntary* consent of individuals. Humphries' children at the turn of the century and

Corrigan's boys in Sunderland are real, live, free individuals. They are not determined by the unseen forces of their biology or their personality but are free rational human beings. If people are free to choose, how is our unfair social order maintained? The distinctive answer of the left idealists is that it is maintained by coercion, though not in a direct way. Our society is totalitarian and mystifying at the same time. Some institutions like the police and the prisons are the directly repressive wings of the state, others use more subtle means. These ideological state apparatuses depend on consent and that consent is won through mystification. This mystification involves two elements. First, the degree of consensus and support for the institution is greatly exaggerated — there is a great deal of dissent within schools but this is rarely reported. Secondly, institutions like schools try to convince their pupils that what is on offer is in their interests. The left idealists argue that schools and similar institutions are constantly engaged in this mystification process, attempting to convince the mass of the people of their neutrality and fairness, whereas in fact what they are doing is reproducing and shoring up a very unequal society.

Naturally, even in institutions like schools, coercion is never far from the surface — the iron fist in the velvet glove. The real point of disciplinary procedures at school is not to correct that minority of pupils who resist school (attempts at punishment seldom achieve their purpose), but to maintain the conformity of the majority and establish the legitimacy and authority of those in power. By disciplining those who resist, teachers present themselves as doing no more than putting down antisocial behaviour. The implication is that such behaviour is against everybody's interest. Being a disciplinarian, therefore, helps to establish and maintain the existing order as seeming fair and equal.

The 'functionalist' ideas within this model of society should now be clear. Each institution within society, whether it is a school, the police or the welfare state, is explained in terms of its relationship to the whole. The function of education is simply to produce young workers with the right skills and attitudes to fit into the existing order. But despite this massive effort at control, human will breaks through all the time. Pupils challenge their teachers, the working class commit crimes. 'Crime and deviance are the visible signs of the triumph of the human spirit over conditioning.' 'Crime (or school deviance) is the first flicker of consciousness, a proto-revolutionary event which challenges property relationships, reappropriates value or counter poses a violent definition against the power of the state' (Young, 1979:15). The disruptive and the truant are transformed at a stroke into working class heroes.

There are a number of criticisms that can be made of this approach, only some of which have been overcome in more recent work. For example, the functionalist tendencies of much recent neo-Marxist theory has frequently been commented on. For example, Giddens (1979) notes:

> Much writing in contemporary Marxism centres about the analysis of reproduction and the dominant tone is a functionalist one. Marx's analysis of simple and expanded reproduction quite readily lend themselves to functionalist readings and have often been interpreted in such a fashion by those who have looked to them as a source of insight into the relations of capital and labour in capitalist development. (p. 112)

It is quite inadequate, Giddens suggests, to define the functions of the state or indeed any section of it, such as education, in terms of how it contributes to the 'needs of the system':

> Not even the most deeply sedimented institutional features of society come about because those societies need them to do so. They come about *historically* as a result of concrete conditions that have in every case to be directly analysed; the same holds for their persistence. (p. 113)

Such a criticism goes to the very heart of the argument for it challenges the idea that the 'real purpose' of schooling is to reproduce an unequal society. If this is so then it also raises questions about the 'real purposes' of indiscipline — is it really a form of class conflict or resistance?

This leads to a second criticism of left idealist accounts of deviance — they are predicated on a very crude historicism. Despite their interest in history, many left idealist analyses are in a sense ahistorical, assuming that the same political and economic conditions obtained in the 1860s, the 1920s and the 1980s. No attempt is made to examine the specific economic and political factors that structure class relationships at any one time or for any one particular community. Popular education is not the same now as it was in the nineteenth century, and if children are rejecting schools today they are rejecting them as they are now and not as they were 150 or even 50 years ago.

There are also institutional differences between schools that need to be taken into account. Corrigan's study was undertaken in two different schools, yet in his analysis we get no sense of them. The explanations offered are entirely in terms of generalized class conflict. Schools differ considerably in terms of their organization and practice. Some urban sink schools of the type he studied may be oppressive and see their task as simply keeping their pupils off the street. However, others pursue genuinely liberal educational objectives in which valuable and personally rewarding activities are available for children. Schools are not uniformly oppressive. They may in the last resort have to segregate and classify children but this is neither their only function nor is it always done in the same way.

A further problem is that these studies betray a simplistic and often romantic notion of working class culture. Corrigan argues that the reason the boys he studied played truant was that this was part of their cultural repertoire. When faced with an oppressive authority a common working class response, he argues, is to try to avoid it. Their response was therefore a cultural one. Humphries develops similar arguments in his interpretation of the behaviour of parents and children in their response to school at the turn of the century. While it may make some sense to see behaviour such as truancy as having this wider class logic, it is hardly a subtle analysis compared to that of say Miller (1958).

As will be seen in the next chapter, some contemporary analysts have taken the issue of cultural resources and their relationship to forms of resistance a great deal further, opening up the issue of the specific ways in which different groups of pupils (e.g. blacks, whites, boys, girls) respond to school. The issues raised by such analyses are enormously complex. It is also important to recognize that the forms of resistance used by young people are not always progressive or even heroic. As Giroux (1981) comments:

> The concept of resistance and the form it takes is sometimes over romanticised, and the 'dark side' is not readily acknowledged — anti-capitalist values do not lead inexorably towards socialism or to the dead end of alienating labour; they also contain a logic that links them to the fascism of the Klu Klux Klan and other such movements. (pp. 13–14)

A final difficulty concerns consciousness. Corrigan, Anyon and particularly Humphries seem to see deviance at school as a fully conscious class resistance. As Young (1979) comments, the model of such an analysis is of young people conscious of their own class oppression and deliberately and consciously using disruption and truancy as a means of defending themselves (Corrigan) or fighting back (Humphries). Although some of today's young people, particularly urban blacks, are overtly politically conscious, such groups are very much a minority. As the interactionists have shown, when the majority of young people are asked why they reject education they provide accounts in terms of the day-to-day realities of schooling; they talk about the way they are treated by their teachers, the lack of utility in the curriculum. The issue of consciousness therefore needs a more careful analysis. If it is to be maintained that there is a class logic to school deviance then we must ask how it is articulated if it is not fully conscious. We must also be aware that whatever authors such as Humphries may imply, not all deviance can or should be interpreted in a class context; it may be directed, consciously or not, at a wide variety of other issues as well as, or instead of, class relations. As E. P. Thompson comments:

> The historian may tend to be a bit too generous because a historian has to learn to attend and listen to very disparate groups of people and try to understand their value systems and consciousness. Obviously in a very committed situation you can't always afford that kind of generosity. But if you afford it too little then you are impelled into a kind of sectarian position in which you are repeatedly making errors of judgement in your relations with people.[6]

It may be that as A. Hargreaves (1982) has suggested, some left idealists are a little too committed in their interpretations of school deviance.

Notes

1. A similar lack of concern with the issue of class can be seen in studies of youth culture too. Murdoch and McCron (1976) go so far as to suggest that in America in the 1950s there was a deliberate attempt to exclude the issue of class from research findings.
2. See for example Bird *et al.* (1981) and Furlong and Bird (1981).
3. However, as will become clear in the next chapter, many contemporary analysts have become more sensitive to class culture.
4. See Clarke *et al.* (1976) for a discussion of contemporary forms of resistance.
5. See Hebdige (1979) for an introductory discussion of the role of *semiotics* in the study of contemporary cultural forms.
6. Quoted in the preface to Anderson, P. (1980). *Arguments Within English Marxism*, Verso.

CHAPTER EIGHT

Resistance as Cultural Production – Race, Class and Gender

The relationship between school deviance and social class has become a central topic for research and intellectual debate in the sociology of education during the last ten years. Despite the inadequacies of the 'left idealist' accounts of reproduction and resistance outlined in the last chapter, the question they pose remains to be answered. Why is it that it is overwhelmingly children from lower working class homes who most persistently and forcefully reject their schooling? If it is inadequate (as it surely is) to see deviant pupils as involved in self-conscious acts of class conflict with their teachers (the agents of an oppressive and manipulative state) then we must ask what alternative explanations can be offered. The researchers to be considered in this chapter all attempt to provide that alternative by developing a more subtle and sophisticated analysis of the relationship between reproduction and resistance.

In this move to a more sophisticated analysis of deviance and social class the work emanating from the Birmingham Centre for Contemporary Cultural Studies during the middle and late 1970s has been seminal. The focus of that work has not always been centred exclusively on the school; far more attention has been paid to analysing the role of various flamboyant youth cultures — the mods, rockers and skinheads — that so dominated the world of youth during the 1960s and 1970s (Hall and Jefferson, 1970; Mungham and Pearson, 1976; Hebdige, 1979). However, many of the themes and issues in this research have been utilized and developed much further in the study of school deviance by Willis (1977) in his book *Learning to Labour*. Willis'

work has been of profound significance both inside and outside
education. Not only has he examined the response of a group of
working class boys to schooling, but his way of conceptualizing
that response as 'cultural production' has opened up the issue
of different cultural responses to school. Issues of race and
gender have become legitimate and urgent topics for analysis
within the sociology of school deviance for the first time.

In the first part of this chapter Willis' work will be introduced.
This will be followed by an examination of work employing
broadly similar concepts within the field of deviance, race and
gender. To conclude, some of the remaining difficulties in this
body of work will be considered.

'Learning to Labour'

Willis' book (1977) is divided into two parts, ethnography and
analysis. In the ethnography Willis describes in vivid terms the
vibrant counter school culture of a group of boys self-styled 'the
lads'. He describes how these lads lived out their lives at school,
how they distinguished themselves from other groups (the
'ear 'oles' and the 'semi-ear 'oles') and how they struggled to
achieve some autonomy by differentiating themselves from the
authority of their teachers. Style was of fundamental importance in this process; the boys not only smoked, they were seen
to smoke, they not only drank, they arrived at school drunk.
Through an elaborate 'lexicography' of style they created
meaning and enjoyment in an institution which at a formal level
they found oppressive and irrelevant. What Willis therefore
describes is a group of boys who found no purpose in education
as it was presented to them but far from being defeated were
positive and creative in their response.

In many of its features the culture developed by these boys
was similar to those documented by ethnographers before. The
first question that must be asked about Willis' study is, is it any
different from any other subcultural studies such as those of
Hargreaves (1967) Lacey (1970) and Ball (1981), that claim a
different theoretical heritage? These studies too have described
how pupils who are herded together by the school into low
bands or streams and deprived of any status turn the values of
the school upside down and form their own 'delinquescent'
subculture. Is Willis really saying any more than this? The
answer is an unequivocal *yes*, for he attempts to demonstrate
that the culture of this group of boys had both an institutional

and a wider class logic at the same time — he sees the two as inextricably linked.

The institutional side of the counter school culture is familiar enough; the boys played truant, mucked about, wore inappropriate clothes, smoked and did as much as possible to undermine the authority of their teachers. Yet, Willis argues, the specific ways in which the boys chose to impose 'meaning' on their school lives were neither pure invention nor the simple reversal of the values held by their teachers. Rather they were creatively developed and reworked from a wide range of cultural resources available to them in their families and the working class community from which they came. For example, through a series of interviews with the fathers of 'the lads' Willis illustrates how the boys' informal lives at school were concerned with many similar themes to those of their fathers at work. Their fathers showed the same chauvanism, toughness and machismo as exhibited by their sons. In school, just as at work, there was a distinctive form of language, a highly developed intimidatory sense of humour and a celebration of the practical joke.

Willis argues that the counter school culture created by the boys in many ways mirrored the wider pattern of working class culture. Yet is was not simply reproduced in an automatic fashion. 'Class cultures are created specifically, concretely in determinate conditions and in particular oppositions' (Willis, 1977:59). What was shared were common themes. Ideas were borrowed, regenerated and then returned.

The aggressive masculine culture that 'the lads' developed at school had a profound impact on their transition to the world of work. In a sense their counter culture was a form of cultural preparation for a particular form of work. What they wanted out of work was a masculine situation where they would not be surrounded by 'cissies' or 'ear 'oles' doing 'pen-pushing'. They wanted a job where they would be 'really doing things', where the money was good and they could have 'a laff'. As a consequence of these demands the boys rejected the notion of a career tailored to their own particular talents and interests. Most significant for their life at school, they rejected the relevance of 'qualifications'. With what they thought of as superior insight they saw all work as hard labour — difficult, arduous and unpleasant — and what made the possibility of work bearable was good money and a 'laff'.

The sub-title of Willis' book is 'Why Working Class Kids Get Working Class Jobs'. The final irony of the book is that in finding a resource with which to resist school these boys turned to an aggressive masculine culture with its celebration of manual labour. On leaving school they therefore voluntarily opted for low status work. Their geographical location, the local opportunity structure and their educational attainments may have influenced and to some extent determined their occupational choice — they probably had very little other option but to accept low status manual work. However, Willis argues, at the point of transition they positively made decisions to willingly embrace the restricted opportunities available to them. For a brief fleeting moment — as they left school — they had a *sense* of being positively able to choose the conditions of their own existence and they chose hard manual labour.

At a general level Willis shares the same interests as the 'reproduction theorists' outlined in the last chapter. Like Althusser, Bowles and Gintis and Bourdieu he is concerned with the way in which our unequal class society is reproduced and the role of education in that process. However, in one important sense *Learning to Labour* goes beyond earlier formulations of the reproduction theses, for it challenges their functionalist lines of argument. Willis criticizes Althusser, Bowles and Gintis and Bourdieu for moving too quickly from the traditional *social democratic* view of schooling to a position where the sole purpose of education is to serve the needs of capital. It may be that it is convenient that some people such as 'the lads' reject their education and openly embrace manual labour but that can hardly be considered the formal purpose of their education. The paradox is that at the formal level a great deal of time and money is spent in trying to convince such pupils otherwise.[1] If resistance to school has reproductive consequences then that is something that is achieved through the experience and agency of the pupils themselves. It arises through their *response* to school.

Willis' objection to functionalist formulations of the reproduction argument is that they reduce the complex and creative field of human consciousness to dry abstractions. 'Capital requires it therefore schools do it. Humans become dummies, dupes or zombies ... but for all we are told about how this actually happens schools may as well be black boxes' (1983:111).

By contrast Willis is interested in that creative 'moment' in the reproductive process in which people struggle to make sense of the structured worlds they find themselves inserted into. He calls this creative response 'cultural production':

Cultural production is the *process* of collective creative uses of discourses, meanings, materials, practices and group processes to explore, understand and creatively occupy particular positions, relations and sets of material possibilities. For oppressed groups this is likely to include oppositional forms and ... cultural 'penetrations' of particular concrete sites, ideologies or regimes. (1983:114)

The subculture created by 'the lads' is an example of cultural production. The boys used the cultural resources available to them to explore their experience of school. The aggressive, masculine counter culture they created was a challenge to school in more than one way. It was not only that the boys were difficult to contain, more important was the fact that their culture 'worried at' the heart of the educational paradigm itself. It challenged the idea that pupils should be obedient in order to obtain something worthwhile — knowledge and qualifications. That idea, Willis argues, is premised on the myth that it is in everyone's best interest to struggle to succeed at school — everyone can succeed and success brings social and occupational reward. While such a view may have validity at an individual level, Willis argues its logic fails collectively — not everyone can succeed. In a fundamental sense, therefore, these boys' counter culture had 'penetrated' this important contradiction of contemporary schooling.

The notion of 'penetrations' necessarily brings us back to the issue of consciousness: to what extent did 'the lads' see the full implications of their resistance to school? For example, was their challenge to school based on an explicit understanding of the contradictions between individual and collective achievement? On this point Willis differs from the left idealists such as Humphries (1981), Corrigan (1979) and Anyon (1981) discussed in the last chapter, for he does not assume that the pupils are necessarily aware of the full import of their actions. 'The lads' were conscious of social divisions in society of 'them' and 'us' and a general deep down feeling that 'it ain't right', but only a minority would have been more explicit than this. Their opposition was primarily explored and expressed in terms of style. They selected and 'reworked' patterns of behaviour and consumer goods such as clothes, cigarettes and alcohol in order to express their own meanings. Arriving late for class or getting drunk on the last day of term became symbols of resistance used by the boys to differentiate themselves from school and demonstrate their group identity. But Willis argues that these actions, which at another level implied some limited penetration of the school system, spoke more than they knew. The boys did not engage in symbolic behaviour because they were explicitly conscious of the full implications, yet their actions were consciously chosen. They were chosen because they 'felt right' and 'made sense' of the boys' day-to-day lives at home and at school. Willis is therefore arguing that certain forms of group behaviour, certain types of music and certain styles of dress, had a 'resonance' with life as these boys experienced it and it was this 'resonance' which encouraged their particular forms of cultural production. Forms of behaviour which 'felt right' were repeated, shared and elaborated and a deviant subculture was produced.

What is important, Willis argues, is not whether the boys were fully conscious of the implications of their own rejection of school, but that they *were* right. Each year and every year in working class schools up and down the country a significant minority of pupils 'discover' the same truths about school. They may use different cultural resources to explore and express their resistance but many pupils reveal the same fundamental truths about themselves — that education, or at least schooling, is not for them.

Willis' work has had a profound impact on the theory of school deviance; it has also directly and indirectly stimulated a great deal of other research. Few authors have achieved the subtlety and sophistication of Willis' argument but the idea that specific forms of resistance to school draw upon pupils' own cultural resources and 'worry at' fundamental issues that structure pupils' lives has profound implications. His research shows how one particular cultural group (white working class boys) creatively respond to school. It has therefore opened up the possibility of examining the way in which other cultural groups do the same. Different groups — boys, girls, blacks, whites — not only inhabit different structural locations, they also have at their command different cultural resources. Their forms of cultural production will therefore be different. It is to a consideration of some of this other research that we now turn.

Resisting Babylon

Theorizing Black Resistance

The argument that deviance both in and out of school can be interpreted as a form of 'cultural production' has received significant support in the analysis of black youth in recent years. Garrison (1979), Rex (1982), Cashmore and Troyna (1983) and Fisher (1983) all argue that the Rastafarian movement with its associated styles of music, dress and language has been taken up and elaborated as a direct response to forms of racial, economic and educational disadvantage that blacks experience in contemporary Britain. The lives of black youths are structured by racial disadvantage and discrimination and it is argued that the Rastafarian movement is a creative and cultural response. It is a form of cultural production.

Rastafarianism originally arose in Jamaica in the 1930s and followed Marcus Garvey's slogan of 'Africa for the Africans'. Haile Selassie, the one black leader who seemed to have resisted colonial domination is considered divine. In short, the movement is based on a reassertion of black pride and black culture. During the mid-1970s the Rastafarian movement appeared in Britain.

> Black youths adorned themselves with the national colours of Ethiopia, coiled their hair into long dreadlocks, cultivated an esoteric language, and generally attempted to detach themselves from a society they regarded as inherently evil and exploitative of black people (Cashmore and Troyna, 1983:175).

That society is 'Babylon' in which for 450 years blacks have been repressed. As one black youth put it

> Dis Babylon is against I and I
> Fah 450 years injustice ah goan
> It ah time tings change
> We want fi get respeck as man.

> (Fisher, 1983:126)

In the propagation of this new political consciousness the role of reggae has been central (Troyna, 1978). It is through the words of reggae that many black youths have come to understand their own position as one of oppression. Reggae has also helped them glimpse the solution of their problems — the acceptance of the divinity of Haile Selassie.

How do these ideas relate to school deviance? It is certainly true that for many years Afro-Caribbean children have been seen as a 'problem' by many teachers. Evidence put forward by Rutter *et al.* (1974) discussed in Chapter 2 suggests that teachers interpret black pupils' (particularly boys) classroom behaviour as considerably more challenging than 'indigenous' pupils. There is also evidence that disproportionate numbers of black pupils are removed from mainstream schools to E.S.N. schools (Coard, 1971) and sin bins on grounds of behaviour. It is therefore not surprising that some commentators have predicted a 'black explosion' in schools (Dhondy 1974).

Afro-Caribbean pupils, and particularly boys, are therefore often seen as more challenging than their white counterparts.

One explanation advanced by a number of authors recently (Troyna, 1978; Rex, 1982; Cashmore and Troyna, 1982a) is that this challenge is directly or indirectly related to their involvement in the Rastafarian movement. For example, Rex (1982) argues that participation in the Rastafarian movement begins as a response to educational underachievement and racist employment practices anticipated by school leavers. The educational underachievement of Afro-Caribbean youth is now widely documented[2] and an almost bewildering variety of theories have been advanced as explanations.[3] Whatever the initial explanations for the failure of black children, Rex suggests that they all too often find themselves in remedial and disciplinary situations which only serves to confirm their teachers' stereotypes of them; such stereotypes help to perpetuate underachievement. Furthermore, black pupils are only too well aware that once they leave they are likely to suffer considerable discrimination in their search for work. It is in this context, Rex argues, that the message of Rastafarianism is particularly significant for it informs and structures their school resistance:

> For many West Indian children, therefore, it appears that the system is loaded against them and they take refuge in a culture which urges them to take pride in their own black culture while treating school as a time to be filled in, as a trial which one has to bear. Rasta, amongst other things, helps to restore the self esteem of the low streamers just as working class youth culture offers self justification to the "non-academic 60%". (Rex, 1982:68)

From this perspective, then, school is resisted because it is a part of white society which helps to oppress the black community — it is Babylon.

Despite the growing currency of this explanation for the challenging behaviour of black youth at school, comparatively little research has been undertaken in schools themselves. Most commentators are content to speculate from the sidelines, as does Rex, arguing that because older black youths in the Rastafarian movement appear to have totally rejected white society then so too must their younger brothers and sisters at school. It is assumed that the forms of cultural production developed by older, predominantly male, black youth are simply transferred by younger boys and girls to the school. Such evidence as is available would suggest that matters are not that straightforward. In some research of my own (Furlong, 1984) I have argued that Afro-Caribbean boys, however hostile they may appear to their teachers, do not simply reject their education but take up a contradictory attitude towards it. Fuller

(1982, 1983), whose work is considered in the next section of this chapter, presents evidence to suggest that the response of girls may be different yet again. Both of us argue that the reasons for these differential responses are to be found in the different institutional, cultural and structural positions of specific groups of pupils within the black population. Their forms of cultural production are, therefore, specific to them. Rastafarianism is simply one of a range of cultural resources to be drawn upon and adapted as specific groups of pupils feel appropriate.

Black Masculine Style

My own research was undertaken with a group of seven Afro-Caribbean boys during their fourth and fifth years at school in an outer London comprehensive.[4] These boys were nominated by their teachers as being among the most difficult pupils in the school and an examination of their school records confirmed this view. They had each had a turbulent school career involving regular confrontations, both verbal and physical, with their teachers, and by the fourth and fifth year they were involved in almost daily skirmishes with senior staff, which resulted in suspensions and or parents being brought in. From the outside it looked as though these boys, like those in Willis' study, were engaged in a constant war of attrition with their teachers, constantly sniping at those who showed any signs of weakness but never managing to finally defeat the enemy. Yet during interviews it emerged that, despite everything, they were highly committed to education. They recognized its relevance to their future careers and were keen to achieve. They appreciated teachers who were strict and made them work and reported a considerable sense of satisfaction in those occasional lessons when they did do some work. Clearly their response was different to Willis' 'lads', for their approach was riven with contradictions. In order to explore these apparent contradictions I examined the culture that these boys produced at school in more detail.

As in Willis' study, it was apparent that the culture the boys created at school drew on a variety of different resources; popular culture, parental culture and aspects of their own institutional life. I examined both the 'theme' and the 'form' of their life together which in many ways was quite different from that culture developed by disaffected white working class boys. Both black and white male cultures of resistance are often concerned with masculinity and both talk of 'hardness' as an essential feature of masculinity, but the word 'hard' is used in different ways. Among white working class youth, hardness has predominant overtones of physicality and strength. Although being able to 'handle yourself' was important for these Afro-Caribbean boys too, the way they used the word hardness was also closely associated with 'style' and maturity. It was the concern to establish a reputation as a 'man' through style that informed how they dealt with all the central aspects of their lives — their music, their dress, their girlfriends and their relationships with the school in general.

In this sense the theme of masculinity parallels the argument put forward by Wilson (1969) who, in a review of anthropological literature from throughout the Caribbean, argues that it is the need to establish and maintain a reputation that underpins the social organization of all male life there. Traditionally, he argues, West Indian society has been seen as entirely matriarchal with women dominating the family and taking precedence in any formal community life such as the church or the school. Wilson argues that women's concern to pursue the more universalistic values of 'respectability' makes them more visible in their community involvement to western anthropologists and most researchers have overlooked the far more localized and more informal peer groups that make up male social life. Unlike the universal values of 'respectability', the particular concerns of male groups vary considerably. For example, some may centre on drinking, others on gambling, and in this sense establishing a reputation for masculinity is created through intense verbal interaction by small groups.

Wilson's description of Caribbean male peer groups parallels the form of social life developed by this group of boys. They too engaged in an intensive form of social interaction. Being at school was predominantly about being with friends, and being with friends involved a continual dialogue. It was the fact that their social life was so dependent on social support that brought them into continual conflict with their teachers. They almost never truanted, but they would often arrive late for lessons, leave early and even walk into other teacher's classes to see their friends. Much of their social life at school was focused on achieving private time and space in order to engage in this intensive form of verbal association.

The theme of 'reputation' for masculinity and the form of intensive association that characterized this group's life were therefore essentially traditional to male Caribbean society. The interests of the boys were modern, they were concerned with aspects of contemporary culture — Dub music and Rasta — but on another level they had rediscovered and reworked traditional forms and themes of social behaviour in developing their own particular culture of resistance to school.

As Cashmore and Troyna (1982a) predict, popular culture in the form of music was central to the lives of these boys and many of the songs they liked related to Rasta texts. It was therefore not surprising that they were interested in and knew about the Rastafarian movement. But they did not adopt the Rasta creed wholesale. Rather they appropriated specific aspects of it. They were interested in Rasta dress and hairstyles, but not in the less stylistic aspects of its philosophy. They appropriated aspects of the Rasta movement that were in line with their own needs. They were interested in its possibilities for establishing a reputation as a man — hence their concern with style — but at this stage of their development they were less concerned with its theology and its fundamental break with white society. Why was this? What is different in their position as pupils in comparison with their older brothers? A number of factors would appear to be significant. First, despite the evidence of unemployment and racism in the employment market these boys, unlike Willis' 'lads', were still committed to the notion of a career. Jobs, like dress and ways of handling oneself were clearly bound up with a sense of style and taking a low status job was something to be ashamed of.

> **J.F.:** Well what sort to jobs do you think are good?
> **Leroy:** Well, clerical and mechanical. You can say you're something, not just a factory worker or on the dole. Anything mechanical.
> **Tony:** Say someone asks you, like what's your job? You can say a mechanic, right? You can say it straight out right? Or your mum if she's talking to her friend, she can say "My son's a mechanic". You know, "Working for a firm" and all that, "British Airways" or something. But if you say "My son's working down the factory" that's nothing to boast about is it?

All of the jobs to which these boys aspired demanded considerable entrance qualifications and there was therefore an essential congruence between what the school felt it could offer them by way of certification and the sorts of jobs to which they aspired; but it is here that the heart of the contradiction lies. Although the boys aspired to employment that demanded entrance qualifications and therefore examination passes, a reputation for style within the school could not be gained by being conformist and settling down to work. Even the most ambitious black boy seemed to engage in a precarious balancing act. If they were to maintain their own sense of dignity they had to work hard in class *and* flout the rules of the school to develop a reputation as a man. Unlike their white counterparts they did not see unskilled work as an acceptable alternative path to adulthood and independence. Their rejection of school could therefore never be complete; they were always tied to a recognition of its importance.

The boys' concern with a career was not the only factor that maintained their underlying commitment to school. Equally important were their families' attitudes. None of the boys' parents had been educated in this country, and although they were not interviewed directly all of the boys reported that their parents placed considerable emphasis on school achievement. They were committed to the possibility of upward occupational mobility and saw the school as the primary means of achieving this. Such attitudes to education and employment derived from their parental culture provided one important aspect of the context of their school subculture. The specific institutional context and the structure of the school they attended provided another.[5]

The school the boys attended was typical of many modern comprehensives with its liberal rejection of explicit streaming, its policy of wide option choice systems around a common core of subjects (in this case, maths, English and science) and its comparatively open examination system. These factors in combination meant that despite their evident low academic achievement these boys were shielded from the impact of academic stratification until the last possible moment. The boys knew they were not successful *within* the school. Like all pupils they were constantly evaluated against each other every time they answered a question in class and every time they gave their homework in to be marked. They therefore recognized their own lack of ability in relation to their own more successful peers but their school had learned the lessons provided by social science in the 1960s. It had abandoned explicit streaming and had broadened its curriculum and the pupils were, therefore, shielded from the full reality of their *public* evaluation on standards established outside the school by examination boards and employers.

These two factors, their high valuation of education as a potential path to upward occupational and social mobility, and the liberal policy of the modern comprehensive school, provided the fundamental parameters of the boys' educational experience and therefore the context of their particular culture of resistance. They developed a culture of resistance because in one sense they knew they were failing — in comparison with their peers they were less successful and saw this every day — but the full reality of that failure was concealed from them. They therefore needed a culture of resistance that would allow them to maintain the myth of the possibility of success.

In this sense the boys were different from their disaffected white counterparts in the same school. Many white working class boys and girls already know from their parents that unless they are particularly fortunate, education will not provide the path to the alternative future that it promises. Even though they may see certain high status occupations as desirable and recognize that for some education is a means of achieving them, they are willing to accept that if they fail in education there are other paths to alternative futures which they see as equally valuable and which do not demand educational certification.[6] For them the mystification of the modern liberal comprehensive is irrelevant. Many such white pupils decide early on that schooling is not for them and by the time the fifth year comes they have decided to vote with their feet and begun to truant. These low achieving black boys had yet to learn that lesson.

Clearly a movement such as Rastafarianism is significant in providing a voice for disaffected black youth. But it is inappropriate to see such a culture as mechanically transferred to school. As an ideology it is one resource among a range to be drawn on and developed by pupils in specific situations. As Willis argues, cultural production takes place 'specifically, concretely in determinate conditions and in particular oppositions' (1977:59). Given Rastafarianism's explicitly political nature it certainly gives black resistance an added dimension. That resistance is not only a ritual, it also has a language and a politics of its own. But Rasta beliefs and practices for these boys did not stand alone. Rather they overlay and gave expression to more traditional concerns — the achievement of a black masculine style. That unique form of masculinity was potentially challenging to the authority of teachers long before the popular emergence of the Rastafarian movement and is likely to remain so long after its demise. While masculinity has to be forged in the context of educational failure and discrimination black boys will remain a problem for their teachers.

Deviant Girls?

The problem was how to reconcile others' writing about girls' conformity and acquiescence with my own observations of young women at Torville school being actively critical and contemptuous of much that was going on around them in and outside school. Indeed, in regard to many aspects of their current and likely future lives some of the fifth year girls were markedly *more* critical and politically sophisticated than most of the boys. Yet in terms of overt 'symptoms' within the school the girls . . . did not come across as obviously oppositional or troublesome in terms that others describe "troublesome" male pupils. (Fuller, 1983:167)

Social theorists not only study society, they are themselves the product of society (Gouldner, 1970). As a result the theories they create contain explicit and implicit assumptions and beliefs. One of the most persistent beliefs running throughout the literature on school deviance is sexism. Girls' deviant behaviour (or the apparent lack of it) is simply not taken seriously by most theoretical positions. For example, when positivists measure disruption and truancy either through the use of official statistics or through their own rating scales girls appear with considerably less frequency than do boys.[7] As a consequence some studies have concentrated exclusively on boys.[8] while others have lumped the two sexes together in an unexamined way. Either it is assumed that deviant behaviour by girls is so small as not to merit serious attention or that the underlying 'causes' are the same for both sexes (this would lead to the rather odd conclusion that girls are more middle class, more rural and come from more stable family backgrounds than their brothers!). Virtually no positivistic study of school deviance has treated girls as an independent group to be studied alone.[9]

If positivism can be accused of a covert sexism then those working in a Mertonian tradition appear more overtly sexist. Subcultural theory, in particular, with its concentration on one form of deviant expression — the essentially masculine delinquent group — marginalizes girls. The tight-knit adolescent group commends itself to the researcher in a number of ways. It is often highly visible in the school. As a consequence it is easier to observe and teachers have well developed opinions about it. As it is based on a common value system it also lends itself to systematic analysis — the sociogram, the questionnaire. It is therefore not surprising that so many (male) researchers have studied deviant groups both inside and outside schools. However, as a number of writers have argued (McRobbie, 1978; Meyenn, 1980; Davies, 1984), as a cultural phenomena adolescent groups are, in our society, almost exclusively male. Their fundamental concern is often to establish a sense of masculinity and sexist attitudes are part of their stock in trade. Not surprisingly girls seldom participate except in the most subordinate roles, indeed to do so would be to fundamentally challenge what it is to be feminine in our society. The substantive focus of this form of research therefore by definition excludes girls.

In contrast to either positivism or status deprivation theory interactionism is less overtly sexist. Potentially it offers the possibility of exploring the subjective world of any group of pupils and some studies have indeed been made of deviant girls.[10] However, because of the idealist thrust in interactionist thought which leads researchers to concentrate almost exclusively on the classroom and the school, it has been impossible for this sort of research to explain the gender-specific factors underlying deviant behaviour. Interactionist studies can describe the different responses to school of boys and girls (as, for example, Measor and Woods, 1984, do so well) but an *explanation* of gender differences necessarily takes us beyond school into wider issues of culture and social structure. These theoretical concerns are by definition beyond the purview of interactionist thought which has therefore led to their neglect.[11]

It has only been with the importation of various strands of neo-Marxist thought, particularly with the notion that deviance can be seen as a form of cultural production, that the issue of girls and deviance has really surfaced as a necessary and urgent topic for study in its own right.[12] Even so the numbers of studies are extremely small. One of the most important contributions has been made by McRobbie (McRobbie and Garber, 1976; McRobbie, 1978).

A Culture of Femininity

The starting point of McRobbie's work is again the study of popular youth culture. She argues that what evidence there is suggests that girls have been very marginal to the youth cultures that have been so important in post-war Britain (to this extent the positivists are right). Yet, she argues, 'marginality' may not be the best way of explaining that absence; it may be that girls inhabit a structurally different position from boys at home, in their leisure and at school and they therefore create quite different sorts of response.

> The important question then may not be the absence or presence of girls in the male subcultures but the complementary ways in which girls interact amongst themselves and with each other to form a distinctive culture of their own. (McRobbie, 1976:219)

By making a study of a group of adolescent working class girls from a Birmingham estate, McRobbie sketches in some of the dimensions of this alternative structural position and the way girls may respond. McRobbie's girls found their lives constrained in at least three ways. They were *socially* constrained in their leisure, for they seldom went beyond the youth club on the edge of the estate, and their part-time employment, which was exclusively carried out in their homes doing domestic tasks for their parents. They were *sexually* constrained by the overt double standards of morality applied to boys and girls.[13]. The only way they could explore their sexuality and not become a 'slag' was to 'go steady', which most of these girls did from the age of 15 onwards. Finally, they were *educationally* constrained by an overt curriculum designed to prepare them for domesticity and a 'hidden curriculum' which frowned on expressiveness and expected them to be conformist.[14] In all these ways, the experience of these working class girls, McRobbie argues, was significantly different from boys living on the same estate and from their middle class peers at school.[15]

How do girls respond to these sorts of gender and class specific constraints? McRobbie sketches two alternative cultures that girls often develop at different stages in their development. At a younger age (10–15) the 'culture of the bedroom' often predominates. At the time McRobbie was writing this was called the 'Teeny Bopper' culture, a highly manufactured form made available through the pop industry and teenage magazines. The main focus of the culture was, and still is, an obsessional devotion to male pop stars, an obsession displayed by putting posters on bedroom walls and by screaming at rock concerts. Manufactured though this culture may be, McRobbie argues that it 'works' because it can be accommodated within the constraints that young girls experience in their lives. In its obsessions it offers a sharp contrast to the conformity demanded by school but despite its obsessional qualities it is safe. The street corner is not available for socializing as it is for their brothers. The appeal of the Teeny Bopper culture is that it is easily accommodated within the home, 'Requiring only a bedroom, a record player and permission to invite friends' (1976:220). Anybody can join and there are no risks of personal humiliation or degradation so often associated with early contacts with boys. As such it could be seen as a form of defensive retreat but its more positive side also allows the girls to win space for themselves and develop a degree of self-sufficiency within small female groupings. It is therefore a form of cultural production.

If McRobbie's suggestions are true then it would help to explain why younger girls at school seldom feel the need to challenge their teachers. Certainly the constraints imposed on them by their school, their home and their leisure are severe, but it would be inappropriate to see all girls as mere conformists. Just like boys they need to develop a sense of autonomy, and McRobbie's study illustrates one way in which this is achieved. At the younger stage at least it is often achieved largely without challenging the school; it is achieved in the fantasy of the pop world.[16] At a later stage things can be rather different.

One widely noted factor among older girls, particularly from working class families, is that with the onset of adolescence there is often a sudden and sharp deterioration in their school work. Girls who until the age of 13 or 14 have been conformist and relatively high achievers suddenly turn their backs on formal academic work. This was certainly the case with the girls that McRobbie studied. They believed that they could achieve if they wanted to but they were interested in other things. They looked down on the middle class girls who they knew maintained a commitment to school calling them 'swots' or 'snobs'. They condemned their lack of style and 'taste' in boys. They recognized that at school they were considered failures, certainly in comparison with many middle class girls, but in the 'real' world which they inhabited they felt highly successful. This understanding hinged on their ability to work the system and to transform school into a space for developing their social lives, fancying boys, knowing the latest dance and having a smoke together in the lavatories. However, this oppositional stance was seldom based on an overt aggression or conflict as it was in the case of boys. Instead the girls used their developing sexual identities as a form of expression. In other words they challenged the school by asserting their 'femaleness'.[17] They introduced their sexuality and their physical maturity into the classroom; they took great pleasure in wearing makeup to school; they spent vast amounts of time discussing boy friends in loud voices; carved names on desks and combed their hair under the desk lids. They developed a feminine anti-school culture as a way of challenging the official ideology which demanded neatness, diligence, appliance and passivity. Such a response to school was 'superior' because it recognized the 'reality' of the adult world from these girls' perspectives. It was a world where they would be economically dependent on men, a world where the unmarried working class woman is an oddity and a world where by necessity marriage is more important than qualifications.

Once again McRobbie's evidence is only suggestive but if it is true it would help to explain why girls are considered less of a problem at school than boys. They may in reality be no less critical than boys but the cultural forms of expression they adopt to express their criticisms are often less challenging to teachers and are therefore more easily ignored.[18] Girls who spend their lessons writing the names of their boyfriends on their plimsolls or combing their hair under a desk lid are seldom as challenging as aggressive boys. They may not be conforming but they seldom disrupt the work of other pupils and in the private confines of the classroom they do little to challenge the teacher's public reputation.[19] They can be, and often are, ignored.

In her analysis, McRobbie places a strong emphasis on what she calls the 'structural position' of working class girls in exploring their response to school; the present and future constraints they experience as working class women. Necessarily different, because they inhabit a different structural and cultural world, is the position of girls from ethnic minority backgrounds. Fuller (1982, 1983) in her study of a group of Afro-Caribbean girls documents their rather different response to the 'double subordination' of race and gender.

Fuller's study of a group of Afro-Caribbean girls in a London comprehensive began with the observation that their performance challenged the normal correlation between high educational achievement and teacher approval. This group of pupils were all educationally successful, yet they were looked upon as a problem by their teachers. In the classroom they gave all the appearance of being disaffected and while seldom engaging in serious overt conflict frequently took part in activities that irritated and exasperated the staff. Yet despite this, closer analysis revealed that they did not *automatically* define teachers as adversaries nor did they assume that school was irrelevant. Their challenging behaviour often concealed the fact that they worked hard in most classes. In some senses they were highly committed to school but, as in the study of black boys reported above (Furlong, 1984), that commitment in no way implied conformity.

For Fuller, the explanation of this contradictory stance within the school lay in the girls' understanding of their position as black and female. Two factors were particularly important in this context: first, their need to work in the future, and, secondly, their relationship with boys. It was these two constraints, Fuller argues, that were particularly important in their cultural response to school.

All of the girls in Fuller's study recognized that they would probably need to be economically independent for most of their working lives. In this sense their perceptions of their futures were quite different from those of their white working class counterparts. Although they thought they would get married 'at some stage', marriage did not necessarily bring economic dependence. They assumed that they, like their mothers and older sisters, would have to continue working even when they had small children (an observation which is in fact well substantiated by research).[20] Given this vision of their future the type of work they were likely to achieve was of considerable importance to them. If they were going to have to work they were determined to avoid the low status manual labour undertaken by their mothers. If upward mobility was to be achieved in a world of racist and sexist employment practices and in the face of high unemployment then the pursuit of paper qualifications was of critical importance.

However, despite their utilitarian support for school, they were unwilling to be seen as docile conformists. Boys were the main constraint here. To be seen as soft exposed them to the possibility of being mistreated by their boy friends. As one girl put it: 'You know most coloured boys tend to knock their girls about ... they've got this vicious streak in them' (Fuller, 1983:175). As a consequence, developing a reputation as a girl who could stand up for herself was of considerable importance.

School was therefore important in order to achieve instrumental ends, and so long as it was providing these opportunities these girls were prepared to conform nominally within the classroom and maximally in terms of doing the work set. But beyond a certain point, Fuller asserts, they felt constrained by the disapproval of showing enthusiasm for school. School itself they argued, was 'trivial', 'boring', a place in which it was vital to introduce an element of 'liveliness', partly for its own sake but partly also to mask their ambitions.

Once again we can see that the particular cultural response developed by pupils is linked to the constraints they experience in their lives. Fuller argues that these girls felt doubly constrained as women and as blacks. Their response to school was therefore a contradictory one.

Both McRobbie and Fuller would appear to be arguing that girls may be equally critical of school as boys but because they inhabit different structural positions and have at their disposal different cultural resources, their form of expression is necessarily different. Such an observation would corroborate Davies' (1984) finding that girls may be less deviant than boys in terms of overt challenges to the institutional rules of attendance, misbehaviour and damage, but may be more deviant than boys in terms of creating personal time and space around the school. The difference is in the form of expression not the feeling. This

192 The Deviant Pupil

could also be in the interpretation applied to Measor and Woods' (1984) interactionist research. The deviant girls in their sample did little or nothing, implying a very profound detachment from the values and objectives of their teachers. However, an alternative explanation of all of these observations could be, as was suggested in Chapter 4, that girls *are* less disaffected than boys. They may be less committed to their education in the first place and therefore less concerned about failure. As yet the substantive research in this area is too underdeveloped to speculate as to which interpretation may be correct.

Conclusion

All of the studies of different cultural groups described above are to an extent derivative of Willis' work, though none has achieved the subtlety and sophistication of his analysis. *Learning to Labour* is probably the single most important contribution to the sociological study of school deviance since Cohen's *Delinquent Boys* appeared in 1955. Whether or not one agrees with the analysis it represents a considerable intellectual *tour de force* in its attempt to draw on and go beyond many earlier formulations. The notion of cultural production opens up a wide variety of possibilities for research (only a fraction of which have been taken up so far) and we are therefore likely to feel the impact of Willis' work for many years to come. However, the fact that the study is so significant does not put it beyond criticism. One must ask to what extent does the notion of cultural production overcome the difficulties associated with what were termed 'left idealist' accounts of reproduction and resistance; what other difficulties are implied by Willis' more 'voluntaristic' model of reproduction?

Five difficulties associated with left idealist accounts of reproduction and resistance were outlined in the last chapter. They were (a) functionalism; (b) a crude historicism; (c) a lack of institutional specificity; (d) a simplistic and romantic notion of working class culture; and (e) consciousness. It would certainly seem that in many ways these difficulties are at least in part transcended by Willis' work if not always by his followers. For example, his analysis of working class culture is more sophisticated than that of say Corrigan (1979) and in his notion of 'resonances' he offers a more satisfactory conception of the issue of consciousness (unlike McRobbie or Fuller). Willis also argues against the functionalist implications of resistance. If functional consequences do follow from the behaviour of disruptive working class pupils then this is something that is achieved by the pupils themselves in their informal response to schooling rather than something that is formally planned for by schools. The route to reproduction is rather longer and perhaps more uncertain for Willis than for Althusser,Bowles and Gintis or Bourdieu.

Finally, with regard to historical and institutional specificity, Willis' notion of cultural production at least potentially offers the possibility of a more precise analysis than that developed by the left idealists. The issue is related to consciousness. Cultural production is concerned with how people 'creatively occupy particular positions, relations and sets of material possibilities' (Willis, 1983:114) and such constraints vary historically and geographically; they are also mediated at least in part by specific educational institutions. The positions, relations and material possibilities for school leavers in contemporary working class Liverpool are necessarily different from those of the home counties. Such conditions are different yet again from those obtaining in the same communities in different historical periods. Pupils experience specific constraints in concrete settings and their cultural responses will be directed to what they experience and recognize (however dimly). Willis' notion of cultural production therefore directs the analysis to an exploration of the specificities of schools and communities in specific historical periods in perhaps more detail than he himself has undertaken.

However, despite the considerable advances two important problems arise from this more 'voluntaristic' model of reproduction. Willis argues that he is interested in a particular 'moment' within the reproductive process — the creative moment when 'people collectively produce themselves' (1983:111). For Willis that creativity is not simply a byproduct of social structure, but is essentially implicated in the reproduction of that social structure. Like Giddens (1976) in his concept of 'structuration', Willis rightly emphasizes that it is impossible to think about social structure without at the same time thinking of human agency. People have to respond to their structural world as they experience it and in that response recreate that structure. A major difficulty with this approach that emphasizes this creative moment in reproduction is that despite its significance it is universal and therefore in one sense unimportant. Everyone has to creatively respond to the world as they experience it, deviants and conformists alike. It is just as important in trying to understand reproduction to see conformists willingly accepting the authority of their teachers (and therefore recreating that authority)[21]as it is to see deviants creatively reproducing an alternative culture; creativity is at the heart of any human response. Yet the difficulty for the student of deviance is how to distinguish between these creative responses. The fact that they are creative does not necessarily help us distinguish between those who reproduce the *status quo* and those who challenge it.

A further difficulty with Willis' 'celebration' of creativity is that it may encourage one to overlook the determinism of the situation. Willis emphasizes the importance of the voluntary way in which his 'lads' opted for the low status work. But their sense of choice should in no way blind us to the reality of the situation they faced. With no educational qualifications and bad school reports they had no choice but to opt for generalized labour — however they chose to 'understand' their position their fate was in reality already sealed. Such an observation might lead one to reassess Willis' assertion of the importance of human agency in reproduction. Clearly human agency is crucial in how we *understand* and *accommodate* to objective structural realities. It is also central to how we 'realize' the consequences in our own lives. Yet this is not the same thing as suggesting that human consciousness can create or change those structures. The notion of 'cultural production' is a way of understanding how people accommodate to their world, but for the powerless at least, it does not explain why the world is as it is. Willis himself would perhaps claim no more — he is after all interested in one 'moment' among many.

Notes

1. The school the 'lads' attended made considerable efforts in trying to convince them of the importance of career decisions. Teachers generally felt that such career planning was important. This observation, Willis argues, therefore challenges any crude and simple version of reproduction theory. One has to explain why, despite the school's attempts, these boys chose to ignore this advice.
2. See, for example, the Rampton Report (1981) and the Swann Report (1985).
3. See, for example, Taylor (1981).
4. This research formed part of a larger project (see Bird *et al.*, 1981).
5. The importance of the institutional context in influencing the nature and form of deviance is a factor which Willis and many other 'reproduction theorists' underplay. Anyon (1981a,b) is an important exception. She demonstrates how pupils in different schools can have a dramatically different experience of the 'same' curriculum. See Chapter 7.
6. I would argue that contrary to what Willis suggests, many working class children *do* recognize the value of high status jobs. However, they realize that they have little or no possibility of achieving them and therefore explore alternatives.
7. See, for example, I.L.E.A. (1983), Rutter *et al.* (1975), Davie *et al.* (1972).

8. See, for example, Power *et al.* (1967, 1972).

9. An important exception is the work of Davies (1984). Although her study is not primarily a positivist one, she does, by way of introduction, try to measure the different forms of deviant behaviour that boys and girls pursue. See Chapter 3, note 12.

10. See, for example, Bird (1980), Meyenn (1980), Llewellyn (1980), Measor and Woods (1984).

11. The nearest such interactionist work comes to a consideration of these issues is in the recent study by Davies (1984). In her notions of 'scripts' she explicitly recognizes the fact that deviance can have many meanings at a personal, institutional and societal level. However, her study is still fundamentally interactionist at heart. She provides no systematic consideration of the wider factors which structure girls' lives. Her research is once again primarily focused on the institutional and interpersonal dimensions of deviance.

12. I am not arguing that neo-Marxist analyses are the only way in which girls' deviance can be understood. As was argued in Chapter 4, anomie and status deprivation theory could also be productive in this area. However, it is clear that it is those who have been working in the neo-Marxist tradition who have been the most instrumental in establishing the need for such work.

13 For a graphic description of the sexism of adolescent boys see Wood (1984)

14. See for example Sharpe (1976) and Spender and Sarah (1980).

15. For example, boys had broader leisure interests and working experience. They would leave the estate to do part-time work in nearby supermarkets and in their support for football teams they would often travel away from Birmingham for the day. Middle class girls apparently spent less time doing domestic labour for their parents and were often taken to social events in other parts of the city.

16. The fact that such girls do not challenge the school directly does not mean that this pop culture is not carried into the school. As Measor and Woods (1984) demonstrate, pop culture may be used by younger girls as a badge of allegiance to their peers rather than a direct challenge to authority.

17. This observation would corroborate Davies' (1984) findings (see note 9 above).

18. A fact certainly substantiated by Measor and Woods (1984).

19. As Denscombe (1980) has shown, teachers' reputations are built largely on the visibility (or audibility) of deviants in their classrooms. Noise is particularly significant. Many girls may opt out of work but may not be particularly noisy unless challenged. They are therefore less of a threat to their teachers.

20. See Beechey (1983).

21. For an examination of the way in which creativity is involved in the everyday *acceptance* of authority in school, see Edwards and Furlong (1978), especially Chapter 8.

CHAPTER NINE

Conclusion – Reading School Deviance

School deviance has been a major topic of interest within the sociology of education for the last 25 years. The result, as has been demonstrated in the preceding chapters, is that there is now an almost bewildering variety of research 'findings' derived from an almost equally bewildering array of theoretical positions.

For example, individual positivists (see Chapter 2) have sought the causes of disruption and truancy in personal and family pathology, while institutional positivists (see Chapter 3) have pointed to the part played by the internal processes of schools themselves in causing indiscipline. Those working in a Mertonian tradition (see Chapter 4) have also been concerned with the *causes* of deviance but for them the explanation lies with the anomie or status deprivation created by the way schools are internally structured and organized. Schools, at least in part, cause their own problems when they systematically exclude pupils and identify them as failures. As a result, we are told, pupils either 'adapt' (for example, by dropping out or becoming rebellious) or they form their own deviant subculture and confer status on themselves.

Some interactionists (see Chapter 5) have also been concerned with the 'causes' of school deviance but for them those causes are to be sought in the subjective perceptions of pupils themselves; whether teachers can have a 'laugh', whether they are fair or whether they 'understand their pupils'. Other interactionists have been less concerned with causes but instead have focused on the social *processes* through which deviance is negotiated in the classroom – among the pupils themselves or *vis à vis* their teachers. Labelling theorists (see Chapter 6) are also unconcerned with initial causes — for them the crucial factor in understanding school deviance is the way it is responded to by teachers. Labelling, it is argued, has a fundamental impact on the pupils' self-concept, and it is this fact which can initiate or inhibit the development of a deviant career.

Contemporary neo-Marxist accounts of school deviance (see Chapters 7 and 8) take a different stance yet again. They emphasize that deviance, or rather resistance, is a predominantly working class response to school. Pupils are seen as drawing on a variety of cultural resources in order to reassert their autonomy *vis à vis* the school. In so doing they may explicitly or implicitly challenge the reproductive role education plays in our society.

How are we to make sense of these different findings and different explanations of cause and process? In what follows I want to try and outline the beginnings of a synthesis that makes sense of the wide variety of insights into the phenomena of school deviance produced by different theoretical perspectives. Such a synthesis cannot of course be simply additive. In terms of explanations of the causes and processes of school deviance the different theoretical traditions outlined in the previous chapters are in many senses incompatible. The explanations offered by some individual positivists (that deviant behaviour is a form of pathology resulting from inadequate socialization) is of a profoundly different order from that offered by interactionists with their celebration of subjectivity and rationality. Both of these traditions provide explanations which are quite different from those offered by contemporary neo-Marxists. As has been made clear throughout this book, theoretical traditions often differ in fundamental ways and such differences cannot be easily resolved.

However, the incompatibility of these different perspectives need not necessarily be seen as a disadvantage. The strength of such diversity lies in the fact that a wide variety of different dimensions of the topic have been systematically explored. Each theoretical tradition encourages the researcher to pursue particular sorts of questions and prioritises certain sorts of data. As a result we know a great deal about many different dimensions of school deviance. What is lacking is a framework within which that knowledge can be integrated.

Deviance as Cultural Production

The starting point for an integrative framework, I would argue, is Willis' notion of cultural production. To repeat his definition:

> Cultural production is the *process* of the collective creative use of discourses, meanings, materials, practices and group processes to explore, understand and creatively occupy particular positions, relations, and sets of material possibilities. (Willis, 1983:114)

From this point of view school deviance, in all its complexity and different forms, is seen as the product of an *active* social process. Pupils are not passive bearers of ideologies or social structures, neither are they determined by their own biology or personality. Rather the notion of cultural production implies that pupils creatively exploit a variety of different cultural resources available to them in developing their response to the school. However, pupils are not entirely free either. The purpose of this creativity is to explore and come to terms with factors which impose on their lives.[1]

As was argued in the last chapter, this exploration need not necessarily be fully conscious. Certain forms of behaviour, certain styles of dress and music are selected and valued because of their 'resonance' with aspects of pupils lives. Pupils can come to understand *more* about their feelings towards school by experimenting with truancy or disruption. Certain forms of response 'feel right' and 'make sense' and are therefore repeated.

In his own work Willis has concentrated on one particular dimension of cultural production, the relationship between deviance and class. He has examined the response of a group of working class boys to the class relations of schooling. He describes how these boys drew selectively on elements of working class culture, popular culture and institutional procedures in order to create a 'profane culture' of their own. For Willis the most crucial aspect of this profane culture was its 'resonance' with the boys' experience of a class society. Its particular form, he argues, helped them explore, understand and come to terms with their experience of schooling as working class pupils. Most particularly it helped them come to terms with the contradiction between an educational ideology that stressed opportunity for all and an occupation structure that denied that possibility. It is this contradiction more than any other that Willis sees as the focus of the profane culture they produced.

Clearly the relationship between forms of deviant cultural production and the experience of class is of fundamental significance, particularly to researchers interested in questions of cultural and social reproduction. However, deviant cultural production does not always have this focus. The majority of disruptives and truants may be working class, but an important minority are not. Both middle class and working class deviants are engaged in forms of cultural production and it is just as important to develop a framework that can explain the behaviour of those who are middle class as those who are working class. We must also develop a framework that can explain indiscipline among younger children. It is simply inadequate to interpret the difficult behaviour of eight and nine-year-olds purely in the context of social class.

I believe that forms of deviant cultural production at school can have a *variety* of meanings for pupils. These meanings can be personal (for example, as a way of coming to terms with emotional tensions in their lives outside school), they can be institutional (for example, as a way of coming to terms with the experience of educational failure) or they can be societal (for example, as a way of coming to terms with the experience of race, class and gender divisions). Deviance can be used to 'explore, understand and creatively occupy' many different dimensions of pupils' day-to-day lives. Moreover, it can be used to explore more than one set of issues at the same time. Particularly as pupils grow older *the 'resonances' of indiscipline can multiply*.

Many of the research findings reviewed in earlier chapters can be interpreted within this framework. They can be seen as giving an insight into the dimensions of pupils' lives that can be explored and expressed through deviant cultural production. Before examining this process in more detail, it may therefore be useful to review these earlier findings from this point of view. Given the creative perspective I am trying to develop it is inappropriate to see these findings as suggesting the 'causes' of indiscipline. Rather they are topics which research has shown pupils explore and express through their deviant behaviour. (The 'real' causes of indiscipline are to be sought at a deeper level[2]). The findings of existing research can be grouped under the following broad headings; 'personal and family pathology', 'the deviant school', 'deviance in culture and class' and 'fun'.

Dimensions of Deviance

Personal and Family Pathology

One weakness of a great many sociological accounts of school deviance is that they deny the validity of what to many other observers is common sense; the idea that difficult pupils often come from difficult or unhappy homes. The majority of parents and teachers believe that deviant behaviour at school is at least in part related to children's emotional stability at home. Yet so unacceptable would such an idea appear to be to sociologists that, with the exception of the positivists (many of whom are actually psychologists by training!), there is virtually no systematic sociological exploration of this relationship. Yet the evidence of positivistic research clearly supports teachers' and parents' common sense views. Authors such as Farrington (1980), Rutter *et al.* (1975), Hersov (1960) and Tyerman (1958) and many others have consistently provided evidence to show that school deviance is highly correlated with an incidence of parental separation, or marital disharmony. It is also disproportionately associated with factors such as parental unemployment (Farrington, 1980) and overcrowding at home (Tibbenham, 1977). Tyerman (1958), in his classic study of truancy, may have been exaggerating when he concluded that 'Few truants have a happy and secure home influence' (p. 219), but there is clearly some truth in this observation.

As was suggested in Chapter 2 positivists interpret these correlations to support their claim that deviance is a form of pathology. Maladjustment, they argue, arises because the normal process of emotional development is inhibited. Clearly such an over-determinist account is incompatible with a notion of deviance as cultural production, yet the correlations remain to be explained. It is therefore perhaps more appropriate to see school deviance as a vehicle of expression that is often used by pupils facing emotional difficulties. It is well known that family discord, unemployment and overcrowding can all lead to emotional tensions within families. Schools can provide an excellent arena for an exploration and expression of these tensions. Not only is education highly valued by parents, particularly by parents of young children, it is, like the family, fundamentally structured around authority relationships. Children at any age may therefore engage in deviant behaviour at school as a means of expressing and exploring their emotional feelings about authority figures in their lives outside school. Kicking against teachers is usually emotionally much less dangerous than kicking against parents. One sure reality about school is that however hard one kicks it will always be there in the morning.

On a more mundane level, school rejection can be part of the more common process of adolescent conflict with parents. Adolescence, in our society, is a period commonly associated with emotional upheaval. A central focus for struggle by young people often concerns their attempts to achieve autonomy from their parents. Rejecting school is a highly potent weapon in the battle for adolescent autonomy particularly in families where there is a high valuation of education. It is therefore a weapon that middle class children use quite often, if only for a while.

Deviant Schools

(a) Pupils' Expectations of Their Teachers

A great many studies have focused on selective aspects of institutional life which can contribute to pupil disaffection. One dimension highlighted particularly by interactionist research concerns pupils' expectations of their teachers. It would seem that pupils have clear notions of how teachers 'ought' to behave and those who transgress these expectations sacrifice their right to legitimate authority. The issues highlighted by this interactionist work relate to two dimensions of the teacher's role; first, their efficiency in the task of instruction and, secondly, the type of personal relationships they develop with their pupils. For example, it would seem that pupils object to teachers who cannot control a class — these teachers are 'non-starters'. In addition they do not like teachers who consistently run boring lessons, particularly if they can see no utility in what is being taught. Pupils also object to being treated in a way that implies disrespect — they do not like teachers who do not know their names, who show them up in front of their friends, or use sarcasm as a means of control. They dislike teachers who have favourites, who do not apply the rules of the class fairly, and finally they dislike teachers who cannot take a joke or have a laugh with their class.

These findings are largely based on pupils' retrospective accounts of their behaviour and obviously one cannot always take such explanations at face value. Pupils may criticize their teachers as a way of justifying their disruption or truancy. However, it is clear that teachers who are seen as inadequate, on whatever criteria pupils use, are inviting trouble.

The findings of this interactionist research on pupils' expectations of their teachers are closely paralleled by work undertaken in a quite different tradition, that of institutional positivism. Writers such as Rutter *et al.* (1979) and Reynolds (1975, 1976) have used positivistic methodologies in an attempt to identify those aspects of school practice associated with different 'outcomes' of schools, including deviant behaviour. Once again the twin issue of 'efficiency at teaching' and 'personal relationships' emerge as highly significant. For example, Rutter *et al.* (1979) suggest that in schools where teachers are well organized, where they arrive on time and where they mark work regularly there is less likelihood that pupils will engage in disruption, truancy and other forms of delinquency. In schools where teachers publicly express high expectations of pupils, where they are readily available in their free time to discuss pupils problems and where policies are pursued to give pupils both responsibility and autonomy there is also less deviance. Once again it would seem that pupils will withdraw their support from teachers who are incapable of teaching efficiently or where they feel they are not valued as individuals.

Day-to-day relationships at school are based in large part on pupils granting legitimate authority to their teachers. As teachers know only too well, they have little real power to *insist* that their pupils conform. If, in the eyes of some pupils, the teacher does not deserve that respect, then even the most conformist pupils will withdraw support and start to explore deviant alternatives.

(b) The Experience of Academic Failure

Schools, as the reproduction theorists point out, are the places in which individuals are equipped with suitable skills, qualifications and 'ideological orientations' in order to enter the labour market. Yet the world of employment into which most pupils eventually pass is an unequal one; it is hierarchically structured in terms of power and economic and social reward. Some form of selection is therefore essential and in our society the responsibility for that selection is placed, in the first instance, on schools. Schools have a major task in trying to distinguish those pupils who are a 'success' from those who are 'failures'. As has been demonstrated by research time and time again, the experience of failure is a fundamental factor in the genesis of school deviance.

Of course the way in which schools handle academic failure is highly significant. In schools where there is streaming or banding, where those who are 'failures' are publicly labelled and held up for ridicule, and where they are given the worst teachers and less in the way of resources, one would expect the degree of rejection to be exacerbated. It would also seem that herding together large groups of pupils who have the same low status at school encourages them to develop a solidarity in their opposition which it is more difficult for teachers to contain. By contrast, schools which deliberately pursue policies that do not label pupils at an early age, that find alternative means of incorporating the academically unsuccessful (e.g. through extra curricular activities) and adopt grouping policies which distribute those who are less successful throughout the school, are likely to experience less hostility from their pupils.

However, it is important to realize that schools, even if they try hard, cannot protect their pupils from the reality of academic differentiation forever. Primary schools and secondary schools with their younger children may have some room for manoeuvre in the policies they pursue. But as pupils approach the public examinations the experience of failure for some becomes inevitable. Schools clearly have an important role to play in mitigating the effects of failure but what they can do is limited. They must struggle as well as they can within constraints imposed from the outside.

Academic failure is of profound importance when it comes to explaining why many children embark on a deviant career. For some pupils, failure is something they experience from their first days at school. As they grow older, other reasons and justifications for rejecting school may come to have greater significance in their minds but, for many, the experience of academic failure is the first factor that encourages them to question the validity of school; it is this which has the greatest and most persistent 'resonance' for deviant behaviour.

Deviance in Culture and Class

Many studies of school deviance have shown that pupils' perceptions of schooling are to an important degree influenced by the world they inhabit outside the school. A number of factors are important: the perceptions of education that predominates within their families and communities; the degrees of freedom and responsibility they are given at home and in their leisure; the models of masculine and feminine maturity to which they are exposed; the aspirations for their future they are encouraged to hold. All of these factors are highly significant in how children perceive school. Different cultural groups within our society subscribe to quite different beliefs and values on topics that are central to the educational enterprise. These cultural variations are often related directly and indirectly to the structural location of groups themselves. Such variations have a profound effect on the way in which pupils look at their schooling. For example, their evaluation of the curriculum, their willingness to accept a subordinate role as a pupil, even the importance of academic achievement itself.

A number of interactionist studies have explored pupils' varying cultural perspectives on school — a good example is that of Bird *et al.* (1981). The authors describe the way in which the older pupils they spoke to found a growing tension between the independent lives they led out of school and their essentially childlike dependent role they led as pupils. They describe how the boys who were the most confident of finding employment through their family contacts, and the girls who did not intend to pursue a career, progressively dropped out of school after the age of 13 or 14. The authors also describe how some parents apparently rejected the moral authority of the school and overtly or covertly encouraged their children to do the same.

Other interactionist studies provide similar insights into different cultural valuations of schooling. However, the difficulty with these studies, as was pointed out in Chapter 5, is that their authors do not locate their findings in a broader framework. One suspects that what they are describing are different dimensions of working class culture but this is seldom acknowledged and never systematically explored.

It has therefore fallen to the contemporary neo-Marxist theorists to locate this cultural diversity in a wider structural context. This inevitably brings us back to Willis and his recognition that pupils' perceptions of the curriculum and its utility, and their perceptions of the demands of institutional life are forged in a class cultural context. Their values are not simply free floating but are related to the lives they do and will lead after school; the jobs they aspire to, the models of masculine and feminine maturity they struggle to achieve. Many working class children evaluate what is on offer in school in relation to these realities and find it lacking. For them some questioning of schooling is therefore almost inevitable.

It is, however, important to recognize that class is not the only structural dimension that can be explored through school deviance. Pupils' lives at school and at home are structured in other significant ways too. They are structured by race, by gender and (particularly in relation to unemployment) by locality. Forms of deviant cultural production can therefore be developed as ways of understanding and coming to terms with any of these factors as they impinge on pupils' lives.

Fun

Finally, it is important to mention 'fun' as a fundamental constituent of school deviance. Very little research has systematically addressed this aspect of disruption and truancy but it is implicit in many accounts. Disruption and truancy can often be enjoyable activities. The joke or the laugh are positive values in themselves whether or not they are overlaid with other resonances (Woods, 1976). In the dry process of academic analysis we should not lose sight of the simple pleasure of irreverently poking fun at authority figures; the excitement and solidarity of shared illicit experiences and the positive pleasure of spending the day at home or on the streets rather than at school. Deviant behaviour is not only problem solving; it is not only used by pupils who are unhappy or frustrated or angry, it can also be a source of real pleasure in the dull round of daily life at school and at home.

The Meaning of School Deviance

In summary research shows that pupils may develop deviant forms of behaviour such as disruption and truancy for a variety of different reasons. They may, for example, use it to explore and express their own feelings with regard to their parents or other authority figures in their lives. Deviance may be a direct response to the school, the fact that teachers are inadequate or that pupils are humiliated by the experience of academic failure. Alternatively, deviance may originate from a direct cultural conflict between pupils and their teachers on a variety of different counts. Finally, they may enter into forms of deviant behaviour simply for their intrinsic value, because they are fun.

Any one of these areas may be the starting point for pupils to develop a deviant career, but once they begin to question the authority of their teachers there is the possibility that other logics may add force to their rejection. For example, many primary school pupils are naughty at school when they face particularly incompetent teachers. Teachers who are ineffective at classroom control invite pupils to challenge their authority, after all 'mucking about' can be good fun. However, for children who are academically unsuccessful, participating in such misbehaviour will have an additional significance. By challenging the teacher's authority they may come to learn more about their previously unarticulated feelings towards school. If their naughtiness has this added 'resonance' it is likely to be repeated.

The same is true of children who are suffering emotional tensions in their lives outside school. These tensions may have many different origins — family breakup, poverty, overcrowding, personal relationships. By challenging the authority of their teachers, pupils who face such difficulties may start to explore their feelings of anger and insecurity with regard to those in their lives who have perhaps not lived up to their expectations. Once again, these resonances can overlay and give added force to indiscipline that initially had other origins.

The fact that school deviance can be used to explore more than one issue at a time helps to explain why it is more commonly associated with older pupils than with younger ones and why it is more frequently a working class than a middle class phenomenon. Young pupils do reject the authority of their teachers, and occasionally with some force. However, their deviance is usually directed towards a more limited range of issues than it is for older children. With children of primary school age the issues of 'personal and family pathology' and 'the institutional experience of schooling' are the most common.[3]

As they grow older, however, the same children may come to recognize other factors which add force to their rejection; as they move towards the end of their school career issues of structure and culture take on a more pressing significance. What in the past was opaque takes on a new relevance as pupils start to think about leaving school. For example, working class children may come to recognize that they aspire to models of masculine and feminine maturity that are incompatible with a conformist pupil role. They may also start to recognize that there are alternative models of adulthood to the notion of a career, sponsored by the school (marriage, unskilled work, petty crime). These alternatives are real and important for those who are unable to use education as a path to occupational and social mobility. In this context deviance which may have started for quite different reasons can encourage and enable pupils to 'partially penetrate' the realities which structure their lives as working class children destined for a working class world.

In arguing that issues of culture and structure are particularly important for older children I am not suggesting that they are *irrelevant* at an earlier age. Clearly many factors to which pupils respond, even at a younger age, are directly and indirectly related to class, race and gender. For example, educational underachievement, poverty, overcrowding in the home are all factors which are themselves structured by class. However, I would argue that as some children move towards the end of their school career they experience an increasing tension between their lives, structured in specific ways and what they see school is able to offer them. Deviant cultural production is used to explore the gap between the day-to-day experience of lives structured in terms of class, race and gender and what is formally offered by the school.

Working class pupils are of course not the only ones to reject school; middle class children can also challenge the authority of their teachers. However, the logic of that challenge is limited — the possibilities for wider 'penetrations' do not exist to the same degree. School deviance may be used as a form of expression by middle class pupils when they fail academically or when they are suffering from some form of emotional distress. It may also be used in the adolescent contest for autonomy from parents, and in some localities school deviance may have an added force because pupils (even middle class ones) feel unemployment is almost inevitable. But for the middle class child to reject the school is fundamentally to challenge the values of the middle class family and its community; it challenges the means by which the middle class reproduce themselves in our society. Whereas working class children may receive an important cultural charge from their families and communities when they question the role of school (they are penetrating the role of school within working class life) middle class children are struggling against the tide. The logic of resistance is limited.

This then is, I suggest, the most useful model with which to understand deviant cultural production. It is based on the recognition that forms of deviant behaviour can have many meanings for pupils. To be disruptive in the class may, for a working class underachieving adolescent boy, 'make sense' in a host of different ways. The challenge to the teacher's authority may relate to his experience of educational failure and it may *also* involve a real questioning of the role of formal educational qualifications in the life he is likely to lead when he leaves school. In some circumstances it may give expression to his feelings of emotional tension generated through personal relationships outside the school and, depending on his *way* of challenging his teachers, it may also allow him to explore a particular form of masculine maturity. Other groups of pupils (for example, working class girls, middle class boys) may share some of these meanings but also have others of their own. They inhabit different structural and cultural locations and they will necessarily evaluate schooling and deviance in different ways.

Once pupils engage in forms of deviant behaviour, teachers, as the labelling theorists remind us, respond. Their response is significant and can provide further institutional demensions to the challenge pupils issue. All of these meanings, and perhaps many others, can be encapsulated in a particular deviant act. Just as language has many sedimented layers of meaning[4] so too does the symbolic language of indiscipline. By taking part in school deviance pupils are able to explore these meanings, learn new ones and learn new things about themselves. It is therefore not surprising that indiscipline in such a potent and persistent facet of school life.

The Language of Deviant Behaviour

If deviant behaviour can be seen to be directed at a variety of different issues within pupils lives, what form does this behaviour take? In much sociological literature the behaviour of pupils at school is presented in a very simplified if not crude fashion. Pupils are often characterized as either being pro- or anti-school — they are conformists or deviants. As was argued in Chapter 2, positivistic research is fundamentally dependent on segregating the 'maladjusted' from the 'normals', but a great deal of other research has produced equally crude dualisms. For example, Hargreaves (1967) opposes the 'delinquescent' and 'academic' cultures of school, while Willis (1977) is little better with his 'lads', 'ear 'oles' and 'semi-ear 'oles'. The notion that there are two (or at best three) types of pupils who inhabit our schools is all too common. An important exception is that group of writers who have directly or indirectly employed Merton's notion of adaptation to analyse school behaviour. Woods (1979), for example, is able to describe a variety of different types of conformity as well as to distinguish between 'retreatism', 'intransigence' and 'rebellion' as forms of deviance. These are useful categories if only because they speak more directly to the world as teachers know it. There are many different forms of challenging behaviour and it is only on rare occasions that individuals or groups will develop an all out confrontation with their school.

While the Mertonian model is clearly an advance on the simplicities of the dualistic perspective, in many ways it is still unnecessarily limited. Pupils can take up a vast array of different responses to school. While it may be a useful descriptive device to categorize pupils who are conformist, retreatist, intransigent, or rebellious, that in itself does little to advance our understanding. The critical point is to develop a way of looking at forms of deviant cultural production that help us understand their symbolic meaning. We want to know what it is that pupils try to explore and express through the vocabulary of school deviance. There are many different groups of pupils in our schools, they come from different cultural backgrounds, they are heading for different futures, they experience different personal problems. As such we should expect their forms of deviant cultural production to be different. Condensing their deviant behaviour into even a four-fold category system seems unreal and in the end unhelpful.

At first sight it may seem that the vocabulary of deviance is a limited one. Pupils can play truant, they can be disruptive in classrooms, they can be violent or they can opt out of lessons and become 'mental truants'. This limited vocabulary is widely understood among the pupil population. By the age of eight or nine most children will know what it means to challenge the authority of teachers in these symbolic ways even if they have never used these forms of expression themselves. What is fascinating about children's behaviour at school is to watch how they are able to utilize this limited vocabulary to express many subtleties of meaning. School deviance as a symbolic language has a great potentiality to explore and express many nuances of the way children feel about their schools, their teachers, the curriculum, their ambitions, etc. This is something which they do together in groups, in pairs, or in a lone dialogue between themselves and their schools. As writers such as Willis and McRobbie demonstrate, it is particularly important to interpret how children *use* this vocabulary; how they overlay it with other meanings drawn from wider cultural resources. The *way* children are disruptive in the classroom is of profound significance both for their teachers and for themselves. As was argued in Chapter 8, teachers find the working class and black masculine forms of indiscipline particularly challenging; it is therefore not surprising that these groups appear most frequently in official statistics. By contrast they apparently find girls less of a problem. Chosen forms are significant for pupils too. To be seen smoking on the school premises, or to arrive at school in the latest fashion, can be more than just an expression of school rejection; they can also be an exploration of masculine or feminine style.

School deviance, particularly for older children, has more than one meaning and this complex of meanings influences the precise way in which children carry out their challenging behaviour. Meaning can be encapsulated in the way pupils dress, in the way they talk to their teachers, in their punctuality and in their diligence. It is also encapsulated in their communal life together, in the views they espouse and in the values they hold. Learning how to interpret these complex and subtle messages in the language of deviance is just as important for the teacher as it is for the sociologist.

Notes

1. I am therefore arguing that deviance is essentially a form of *response*. Even though pupils are active and creative they are active and creative as a way of responding to factors over which they have relatively little control — family breakup, academic failure, the structure and organization of the school itself, the local employment opportunities structure. Unlike many contemporary authors (Willis, 1977; Giroux, 1983; Apple, 1982) I would therefore argue that deviance has a limited role to play in our understanding of social and cultural reproduction. It helps us understand how some pupils respond to factors which impose on their lives but tells us little about the origins of those factors themselves.

2. They are to be sought in the biological, psychological, institutional and societal factors that structure pupils' lives, lived out in specific, historically given settings. Deviance is therefore merely a cultural phenomena — it is a response to these more fundamental factors which impose on pupils' lives. The perhaps most significant question of why these factors exist in the way that they do is one that is seldom addressed by research in this tradition.

3. There are of course some important exceptions. See Bird *et al.* (1981) for some descriptions of younger pupils who appear to have a more 'fully developed' sense of hostility to school even at quite a young age.

4. See Edwards and Furlong (1978).

Bibliography

Acton, T. A. (1980), Educational Criteria of Success, *Educational Research*, 22:163-9.

Advisory Centre for Education (1980a), Disruptive Units: Labelling a New Generation, *Where*, 158, May

Advisory Centre for Education Survey (1980b), Disruptive Units, *Where*, 158, May.

Althusser, L. (1971), Ideology and Ideological State Apparatuses, in L. A. Althusser, *Lenin and Philosophy and Other Essays*, Monthly Review Press.

Anon. (1973), Truancy: What the Official Figures Don't Show, *Where*, 83:228-9, August.

Anyon, J. (1981a), Social Class and School Knowledge, *Curriculum Inquiry*, 11(1):3-42.

Anyon, J. (1981b), Elementary Schooling and Distinctions of Social Class, *Interchange*, 12(2-3):118-31.

Apple, M. (1982), *Education and Power*, R.K.P.

Ariès, P. (1960), *Centuries of Childhood*, Penguin.

Ashby, M. K. (1961), *Joseph Ashby of Tysoe, 1859-1919*, Cambridge University Press.

Assistant Masters and Mistresses Association (A.M.M.A.) (1984), The Reception Class Today, *Report*, 7(1):6-9.

Baldwin, J. (1972), Delinquent Schools in Tower Hamlets - A Critique, *British Journal of Criminology*, 12:399-40.

Ball, S. (1981), *Beachside Comprehensive*, Cambridge University Press.

Bandura, A. (1971), *Principles of Behaviour Modification*, Holt, Rinehart and Winston.

Bandura, A. and Walters, R. (1969), *Social Learning and Personality Development*, Holt, Rinehart and Winston.

Barton, L. and Meighan, R. (eds) (1979), *Schools, Pupils and Deviance*, Nafferton Books.

Barton, L. and Walker, S. (eds) (1983), *Race, Class and Education*, Croom Helm.

Baum, T. (1978), Surveys of Absenteeism: A Question of Timing, *Educational Research*, 20(3):226-30.

Becker, H. S. (1963), *Outsiders: Studies in the Sociology of Deviance*, Free Press.

Beechey, V. (1983), *Women and Employment*, Open University 221, Unit 10.

Berger, M., Yule, W. and Rutter, M. (1975), Attainment and Adjustment in two Geographical Areas II: The prevalence of Specific Reading Retardation, *British Journal of Psychiatry*, 126:510-19.

Benyon, J. and Delamont, S. (1983), The Sound of Fury: Pupil Perceptions of School Violence, in H. Gault and N. Frude (eds), *Children's Aggression at School*, Wiley

Billington, B. (1978), Patterns of Attendance and Truancy: A Study of Attendance and Truancy Amongst First-Year Comprehensive School Pupils, *Educational Review*, 30(3):221-5.

Bird, C. (1980), Deviant Labelling in Schools - The Pupils' Perspective, in P. Woods (ed.), *Pupil Strategies*, Croom Helm.

Bird, C., Chessum, R., Furlong, V. J. and Johnson, D. (1981), *Disaffected Pupils*, Brunel University.

Blishen, E. (1955), *Roaring Boys*, Thomas and Hudson.

Blumer, H. (1953), The Psychological Import of the Human Group, in M. Sherif and M. Wilson (ed), *Group Relations at the Crossroads*, Harper Row.

Blumer, H. (1962), Society as Symbolic Interaction, in A. Rose (ed.), *Human Behaviour and Social Processes*, R.K.P.

Blumer, H. (1965), The Sociological Implications of the Thought of George Herbert Mead, *American Journal of Sociology*, 71:535-44.

Bourdieu, P. (1977), *Outline of Theory and Practice*, Cambridge University Press.

Bourdieu, P. and Passeron, J. (1977), *Reproduction in Education, Society and Culture*, Sage.

Bowlby, J. (1953), *Child Care and the Growth of Love*, Penguin.

Bowlby, J. (1971), *Attachment and Loss, Vol. 1: Attachment*, Hogarth Press.

Bowlby, J. (1973), *Attachment and Loss, Vol 2: Separation, Anxiety and Anger*, Hogarth Press.

Bowles, S. and Gintis, H, (1976), *Schooling in Capitalist America*, Basic Books.

Boyson, R. (1975), *The Crisis in Education*, Woburn Press.

Braithwaite, E. R. (1955), *To Sir With Love*, Bodley Head.

Brake, M. (1980), *The Sociology of Youth Culture and Youth Subculture*, R.K.P.

Burgess, R. (1973), *Experiencing Comprehensive Education: A Study of Bishop McGreggor School*, Methuen.

Burrell, G. and Morgan, G. (1979), *Sociological Paradigms and Organisational Analysis*, Heinemann.

Byrne, D., Williamson, B. and Fletcher, B. (1975), *The Poverty of Education*, Martin Robertson.

Carroll, H. (1977), *Absenteeism in South Wales*, Faculty of Education, University College of Swansea.

Carson, W. C. and Wiles, T. (1971), *Crime and Delinquency in Britain*, Martin Robertson.

Cahsmore, E. and Troyna, B. (1982a), Growing up in Babylon, in E. Cashmore and B. Troyna (eds), *Black Youth in Crisis*, George Allen and Unwin.

Cashmore, E. and Troyna, B. (eds) (1982b), *Black Youth in Crisis*, George Allen and Unwin.

Cashmore, E. and Troyna, B. (1983), *Introduction to Race Relations*, R.K.P.

Caspari, I. (1976), *Troublesome Children in Class*, R.K.P.

Castle, E. B. (1958), *Moral Education in Christian Times*, George Allen and Unwin.

Chessum, R. (1980), Teacher Ideologies and Pupil Disaffection, in L. Barton, R. Meighan and S. Walker (eds) *Schooling, Ideology and the Curriculum*, Falmer Press.

Cicourel, A. (1968), *The Social Organisation of Juvenile Justice*, Wiley.

Cicourel, A. and Kitsuse, J. (1963), *The Educational Decision Makers*, Bobbs-Merrill.

Clarke, J., Hall, S., Jefferson, T. and Roberts, B. (1967), Subcultures, Cultures and Class: A Theoretical Overview, in S. Hall and T. Jefferson (eds), *Resistance Through Rituals*, Hutchinson

Clarke, J. and Jefferson, T. (1976), Working Class Youth Cultures in G. Mungham and G. Pearson (eds), *Working Class Youth Culture*, R.K.P.

Cloward, R. and Ohlin, L. (1960), *Delinquency and Opportunity: A Theory of Delinquent Gangs*, Free Press.

Coard, B. (1971), *How the West Indian Child is Made Educationally Sub-normal in the British School System*, New Beacon Books.

Cohen, A. (1955), *Delinquent Boys: The Culture of the Gang*, Free Press.

Cohen, A. (1965), The Sociology of the Deviant Act: Anomie Theory and Beyond, *American Sociological Review*, 30(1):5-14.

Cohen, P. (1972), Subcultural Conflict and Working Class Community, *Working Papers in Cultural Studies*, 2 (Spring), C.C.C.S., University of Birmingham

Cohen, S. (1973), *Folk Devils and Moral Panics*, Paladin.
Coleman, J. (1961), *The Adolescent Society*, Free Press.
Corrigan, P. (1979), *Schooling the Smash Street Kids*, Macmillan.
Croft, I.J. and Grugier, T. G. (1956), Social Relations of Truants and Juvenile Delinquents, *Human Relations*, 9:439–46
Croft, M. (1954), *Spare the Rod*, Longmans.
Dale, R. (1974), Phenomenological Perspectives and the Sociology of the School, in M. Flude and J. Ahier, (eds), *Educability, Schools and Ideology*, Croom Helm.
Davie, R., Butler, N. and Goldstein, H. (1972), *From Birth to Seven*, Longmans.
Davies, L. (1979), Deadlier than the Male?: Girls' Conformity and Deviance in School, in L. Barton and R. Meighan (eds), *Schools, Pupils and Deviance*, Nafferton Books.
Davies, L. (1984), *Pupil Power: Deviance and Gender at School*, Falmer Press.
Deem, R. (ed.) (1980), *Schooling for Women's Work*, R.K.P.
Denscombe, M. (1980), Keeping 'em Quiet, in P. Woods (ed.), *Pupil Strategies*, Croom Helm.
Department of Education and Science (1973), *Survey of Violence, Indiscipline and Vandalism in Schools*, D.E.S.
Department of Education and Science (1975), *Survey of Absence from Secondary and Middle Schools in England and Wales on Thursday 17th January 1974*, D.E.S.
Dhondy, F. (1974), The Black Explosion in Schools, *Race Today*, Feb.:44–7.
Dierenfield, R. (1982), All You Need to Know About Disruption, *T.E.S.*, 29.1.82:4.
Dockar-Drysdale, B. E. (1968), *Therapy in Child Care*, Longman.
Donajgrodski, A. P. (ed.) (1977), *Social Control in Nineteenth Century Britain*, Croom Helm.
Douglas, J. W. B. (1964), *The Home and the School*, Panther.
Douglas, J. W. B. and Ross, J. M. (1964), Adjustment and Educational Progress, *British Journal of Educational Psychology*, 38:2–4.
Douglas, J. W. B. and Ross, J. M. (1965), The Effects of Absence on Primary School Performance, *British Journal of Educational Psychology*, 35:28–40
Downes, D. (1966), *The Delinquent Solution*, R.K.P.
Downes, D. and Rock, P. (1982) *Understanding Deviance*, Clarendon Press.
Durkheim, E. (1951), *Suicide*, Free Press.
Durkheim, E. (1966), *The Rules of Sociological Method*, Free Press.
Eaton, M. J. (1979), A Study of Some Factors Associated with Early Identification of Persistent Absenteeism, *Educational Review*, 31(3):233–42.
Edwards, A. D. and Furlong, V. J. (1978), *The Language of Teaching*, Heinemann Educational Books.
Eillis, A. (1973), Influences on School Attendance in Early Victorian England, *British Journal of Educational Studies*, 2(3):313–26.
Engels, F. (1969), *The Condition of the Working Class in England*, Panther.
Evans, M. (ed.) (1980), *Disruptive Pupils*, Schools Council Publications.
Eysenk, H. (1977), *Crime and Personality*, Paladin.
Farrington, D. (1972), Delinquency Begins at Home, *New Society*, 21:495–7.
Farrington, D. (1980), Truancy, Delinquency, the Home and the School, in L. Hersov and I. Berg (eds). *Out of School*, Wiley.
Finlayson, D. J. and Loughram, J. L. (1976), Pupils' Perceptions of High and Low Delinquency Schools, *Educational Research*, 18:138–45.
Fisher, G. (1983), Language in a Political Context: The Case of West Indians in Britain, *Oxford Review of Education*, 9(2):123–31.
Fitzgerald, M. (1980), *Sociologies of Crime and Deviance*, Open University D207 Block 1 (9).
Fogelman, K. (ed.) (1976), *Britain's Sixteen Year Olds*, National Children's Bureau.
Fogelman, K. (1978), School Attendance, Attainment and Behaviour, *British Journal of Educational Psychology*, 48:148–78.
Fogelman, K. and Richardson, K. (1974), School Attendance: Some Results from the National Child Development Study, in B. Turner (ed.), *Truancy*, Ward Lock.
Fogelman, K., Tibbenham, A. and Lambert, L. (1980), Absence from School: Findings

from the National Child Development Study, in L Hersov and I. Berg (eds) *Out of School*, Wiley.

Ford, J., Mongon, D. and Whelan, M. (1982), *Special Education and Social Control: Invisible Disasters*, R.K.P.

Francis, P. (1975), *Beyond Control*, George Allen and Unwin.

Fuller, M. (1980), Black Girls in a London Comprehensive School, in R. Deem (ed.) *Schooling for Women's Work*, R.K.P.

Fuller, M. (1982), Young, Female and Black, in E. Cashmore and B. Troyna (eds), *Black Youth in Crisis*, George Allen and Unwin.

Fuller, M. (1983), Qualified Criticism, Critical Qualifications, in L. Barton and S. Walker (eds), *Race, Class and Education*, Croom Helm.

Furlong, V. J. (1976), Interaction Sets in the Classroom, in M. Stubbs and S. Delamont (eds), *Explorations in Classroom Observation*, Wiley.

Furlong, V. J. (1977), Anancy goes to School: A Case Study of Pupils' Knowledge of Their Teachers, in P. Woods and M. Hammersley (eds), *School Experience*, Croom Helm.

Furlong, V. J. (1984) Black Resistance in the Liberal Comprehensive, in S. Delamont (ed.), *Readings on Interaction in the Classroom*, Methuen.

Furlong, V. J. and Bird, C. (1981), How Can We Cope with Karen?, *New Society*, 56(959):12–4, April.

Galloway, D. (1976), Size of School, Socio-Economic Hardship, Suspension Rates and Persistent Unjustified Absence from School, *British Journal of Educational Psychology*, 46:40–7.

Galloway, D. (1980), Problems in the Assessment and Management of Persistent Absence from School, in L. Hersov and I. Berg (eds), *Out of School*, Wiley.

Galloway, D., Ball, T., Bloomfield, D. and Seyed, R. (1982), *Schools and Disruptive Pupils*, Longmans.

Gannaway, H. (1976), Making Sense of School, in M. Stubbs and S. Delamont (eds), *Explorations in Classroom Observation*, Wiley.

Garrison, L. (1979), *Black Youth, Rastafarianism and the Identity Crisis in Britain*, A.C.E.R. Project.

Giddens, A. (1976), *New Rules of Sociological Method: A Positive Critique of Interpretative Sociologies*, Hutchinson.

Giddens, A. (1979), *Central Problems in Social Theory: Action, Structure and Contradiction in Social Analysis*, Macmillan.

Gillham, B. (ed.) (1980), *Problem Behaviour in Secondary Schools: A Systems Approach*, Croom Helm.

Giroux, G. (1981), Hegemony, Resistance and the Paradox of Educational Reform, *Interchange*, 12(2–3):3–26.

Giroux, H. (1983), *Theory and Resistance in Education*, Heinemann Educational Books.

Goldstein, H. (1980), The Statistical Procedures, in B. Tizard *et al.* (eds), *Fifteen Thousand Hours: A Discussion*, University of London Institute of Education.

Goodsen, P. (1969), *How They Were Taught*, Blackwell.

Gouldner, A. (1970), *The Coming Crisis in Western Sociology*, Heinemann Educational Books.

Grace, G. (1978), *Teachers, Ideology and Control*, R.K.P.

Graham, P. and Rutter, M. (1970), Selection of Children with Psychiatric Disorder, in M. Rutter, J. Tizard and K. Whitmore (eds), *Education, Health and Behaviour*, Longmans.

Gramsci, A. (1973), *Selections from Prison Notebooks*, Lawrence and Wishart.

Grunsell, R. (1978), *Absent from School*, Writers and Readers.

Grunsell, R. (1979), Suspensions and the Sin Bin Boom, *Where*, 153:307–9.

Grunsell, R. (1980), *Beyond Control: Schools and Suspension*, Writers and Readers.

Hall, S. and Jefferson, T. (1976), *Resistance Through Rituals*, Hutchinson.

Hammersley, M. and Atkinson, P. (1983), *Ethnography: Principals and Practice*, Tavistock.

Hammersley, M. and Woods, P. (eds) (1976), *The Process of Schooling*, O.U.P./R.K.P.

Hargreaves, A. (1978), Towards a Theory of Classroom Coping Strategies, in L. Barton and R. Meighan (eds), *Sociological Interpretations of Schooling and Classrooms*, Nafferton Books.

Hargreaves, A. (1980), Review of Fifteen Thousand Hours, *British Journal of Sociology of Education* 1:211-6.

Hargreaves, A. (1982), Resistance and Relative Autonomy Theories, *British Journal of Sociology of Education*, 3(2):107-26.

Hargreaves, D. H. (1967), *Social Relations in a Secondary School*, R.K.P.

Hargreaves, D. H. (1976), Reactions to Labelling, in M. Hammersley and P. Woods (eds), *The Process of Schooling*, O.U.P./R.K.P.

Hargreaves, D. H. (1980), Classrooms, Schools and Juvenile Delinquency, *Educational Analysis*, 2(2):75-87.

Hargreaves, D. H. (1983), *The Challenge for the Comprehensive*, R.K.P.

Hargreaves, D. H., Hester, S. K. and Mellor, F. (1975), *Deviance in Classrooms*, R.K.P.

Hebdige, D. (1979), *Subculture: The Meaning of Style*, Methuen.

Her Majesty's Inspectorate (1978a), *Behavioural Units: A Survey of Special Units for Pupils with Behavioural Problems*, D.E.S.

Her Majesty's Inspectorate (1978b), *Truancy and Behaviour Problems in Some Urban Schools*, D.E.S.

Hersov, L. (1960), Refusal to go to Schools, *Journal of Child Psychology and Psychiatry*, 1:137-45.

Hersov, L. and Berg, I. (eds) (1980), *Out of School*, Wiley.

Highfield, M. E. and Pinsent, A. (1952), *A Survey of Rewards and Punishments in School*, Newnes Educational Publishing Co.

Hollinshead, A. B. (1949), *Elmstown's Youth*, Wiley.

Homans, G. (1951), *The Human Group*, R.K.P.

Horney, K. (1949), *Our Inner Conflicts*, R.K.P.

Humphries, S. (1981), *Hooligans or Rebels? An Oral History of Working Class Childhood and Youth 1889-1939*, Basil Blackwell.

Inner London Education Authority (1973), *Literacy Survey: Children's Behaviour at School*, I.L.E.A.

Inner London Education Authority (1983), *1983 Attendance Survey (RS 895/83)*, I.L.E.A.

Jackson, B. and Marsden, D. (1962), *Education and the Working Class*, Penguin.

Johnson, D., Ransom, E., Packwood, T., Bowden, E. and Kogan, M. (1980), *Secondary Schools and the Welfare Network*, Unwin Educational Books.

Johnson, R. (1970), Educational Policy and Social Control in Early Victorian England, *Past and Present*, 49:96-119.

Jones, N. J. (1975), Emotionally Disturbed Children in Ordinary Schools: Concepts, Prevalence and Management, *British Journal of Guidance and Counselling*, 3(2):146-59.

Jones-Davies, C. and Cave, R. (eds) (1976), *The Disruptive Pupil in the Secondary School*, Ward Lock Educational.

Keddie, N. (1971), Classroom Knowledge, in M. F. D. Young (ed.), *Knowledge and Control: New Directions for the Sociology of Education*, Collier-Macmillan.

Kitsuse, J. C. (1962), Social Reactions to Deviant Behaviour: Problems of Theory and Method, *Social Problems*, 9:247-57.

Klein, M. (1960), Our Adult World and Its Roots in Infancy, *Tavistock Pamphlet No.2*, Tavistock.

Kuhn, T. (1970), The Logic of Discovery or Psychology of Research, in I. Lakatoz and A. Musgrave (eds), *Criticism and Growth of Knowledge*, Cambridge University Press.

Lacey, C. (1970), *Hightown Grammar*, Manchester University Press.

Lancaster, J. (1805), *Improvements in Education*, Darton and Harvey.

Laqueur, T. W. (1976), Working-Class Demand and the Growth of English Elementary Education, 1750-1850, in L. Stone (ed.), *Schooling and Society: Studies in the History of Education*, John Hopkins University Press.

Laslett, R. (1977a), *Educating Maladjusted Children*, Granada.
Laslett, R. (1977b), Disruptive and Violent Pupils: The Facts and the Fallacies, *Educational Review*, 29:152–62.
Lawrence, J., Steed, D. and Young, P. (1977), Disruptive Behaviour in a Secondary School, *Educational Studies Monograph*, University of London, Goldsmith's College.
Lawrence, J. *et al.* (1981), *Dialogue on Disruptive Behaviour: A Study of a Secondary School*, P.J.D. Press.
Leach, D. and Raybould, E. (1977), *Learning and Behaviour Difficulties in School*, Open Books.
Lemert, E. M. (1951), *Social Pathology*, McGraw-Hill.
Lemert, E. M. (1967), *Human Deviance: Social Problems and Social Control*, Prentice-Hall.
Llewellyn, M. (1980), Studying Girls at School: The Implications of Confusion, in R. Deem (ed.), *Schooling for Women's Work*, R.K.P.
Lowenstein, L. F. (1975), *Violent and Disruptive Behaviour in Schools*, National Association of Schoolmasters.
Lunzer, E. A. (1960), Aggressive and Withdrawing Children in Normal School I:Disparity in Attainment, *British Journal of Educational Psychology*, 30:119–23.
McFie, B. (1934), Behaviour, Personality and Difficulties in Schools, *British Journal Of Educational Psychology*, 4(1):34–6.
McRobbie, A. (1978), Working Class Girls and the Culture of Femininity, in Women's Studies Group, C.C.C.S. University of Birmingham, *Women Take Issue*, Hutchinson.
McRobbie, A. and Garber, J. (1976), Girls and Subcultures, in S. Hall and T. Jefferson (eds), *Resistance Through Rituals*, Hutchinson.
Manis, J. and Meltzer, B. N. (eds) 1967, *Symbolic Interactionism; A Reader in Social Psychology*, Allyn and Bacon.
Marsh, P., Rosser, E. and Harre, R. (1978), *The Rules of Disorder*, R.K.P.
Marx, K and Engels, F. (1969), Manifesto of the Communist Party, in *K. Marx and F. Engels, Selected Works Vol. 1*, Progressive Publishers.
Matza, D. (1964), *Delinquency and Drift*, Wiley.
Matza, D. (1969), *Becoming Deviant*, Prentice-Hall.
Mays, B. (1962), *Education and the Urban Child*, Liverpool University Press.
Measor, L. and Woods, P. (1984), *Changing Schools*, Open University Press.
Meltzer, B. N. and Petras, J. W. (1967), The Chicago and Iowa Schools of Symbolic Interactionism, in J. Manis and B. N. Meltzer (eds), *Symbolic Interactionism: A Reader in Social Psychology*, Allyn and Bacon.
Merton, R. K. (1938), Social Structure and Anomie, *American Sociological Review*, 3:672–82.
Merton, R. K. (1967), Anomie, Anomia and Social Interaction, in M. B. Clinard (ed.), *Anomie and Deviant Behaviour*, Free Press.
Meyenn, R. (1980), School Girl's Peer Groups, in P. Woods (ed.), *Pupil Strategies*, Croom Helm.
Miller, W. (1958), Lower Class Culture as a Generating Millieu of Gang Delinquency, *Journal of Social Issues*, 15:5–19.
Mills, W. C. (1976), *The Seriously Disruptive Behaviour of Pupils in Secondary Schools in One Local Education Authority*, Unpublished M. Ed. Thesis, Birmingham University.
Milner, M. (1938), *The Human Problem in Schools*, Methuen.
Mitchell, S. (1972), The Absentees, *Education in the North*, 9:22–8.
Mitchell, S. and Shepherd, M. (1980), Reluctance to go to School, in L. Hersov and I. Berg (eds), *Out of School*, Wiley.
Mortimore, P., Davies, J., Varlaam, A. and West, A. (1983), *Behaviour Problems in Schools*, Croom Helm.
Mungham, G. and Pearson, G. (eds) (1976), *Working Class Youth Culture*, R.K.P.
Murdock, G. and McCron, R. L. (1976), Youth and Class: The Career of Confusion, in G. Mungham and G. Pearson (eds), *Working Class Youth Culture*, R.K.P.
National Association of Schoolmasters (1974), *Discipline in Schools*, N.A.S.

National Association of Schoolmasters (1976), *Retreat from Authority*, N.A.S.
Newsom, J. (1963), (The Newsom Report), *Half Our Future*, H.M.S.O.
Ogilvie, V. (1953), *The English Public School*, Batsford.
Pack, D. C. (1977), (The Pack Report), *Truancy and Indiscipline in Scotland*, H.M.S.O./S.E.D.
Pallister, R. (1969), The Determinants of Elementary School Attendance About 1850, *Durham Research Review*, 23:384–98.
Partridge, J. (1968), *Life in a Secondary Modern School*, Penguin.
Pearson, G. (1980), *The Deviant Imagination*, Macmillan.
Pearson, G. (1983), *Hooligan: A History of Respectable Fears*, Macmillan.
Pearson, K. (1882), *The Grammar of Science*, Dent.
Phillipson, C. M. (1971), Juvenile Delinquency and the School, in W. G. Carson and P. Wiles (eds), *Crime and Delinquency in Britain*, Martin Robertson.
Plummer, K. (1979), Misunderstanding Labelling Perspectives, in D. Downes and P. Rock (eds), *Deviant Interpretations*, Martin Robertson.
Pollard, A. (1979), Negotiating and Deviance and 'Getting Done' in Primary Classrooms, in L. Barton and R. Meighan (eds), *Schools, Pupils and Deviance*, Nafferton Books.
Popper, K. (1963), *Conjectures and Refutations; The Growth of Scientific Knowledge*, R.K.P.
Poteet, J. A. (1974), *Behaviour Modification; A Practical Guide for Teachers*, University of London Press.
Power, M. J., Alderson, M. R., Phillipson, C. M., Shoenberg, E. and Morris, J. N. (1967), Delinquent Schools, *New Society*, 19 Oct.:542.
Power, M. J., Benn, R. T. and Morris, J. N. (1972), Neighbourhood, Schools and Juveniles Before the Courts, *British Journal of Criminology*, 12:111-32.
Pringle, M. (1974), *The Needs of Children*, Hutchinson.
Pringle, M., Butler, N. and Davie, R. (1966), *11,000 Seven Year Olds*, Longman
Rampton, A. (1981), (The Rampton Report), *West Indian Children in Our Schools*, H.M.S.O.
Rex, J. (1982), West Indian and Asian Youth, in E. Cashmore and B. Troyna (eds), *Black Youth in Crisis*, George Allen and Unwin.
Reynolds, D. (1976a), When Teachers and Pupils Refuse a Truce, in G. Mungham and G. Pearson (eds), *Working Class Youth Culture*, R.K.P.
Reynolds, D. (1976b), The Delinquent School, in M. Hammersley and P. Woods, (eds), *The Process of Schooling*, O.U.P./R.K.P.
Reynolds, D. and Murgatroyd, S. (1974), Being Absent from School, *British Journal of Law and Society*, 1:78-81
Reynolds, D. and Murgatroyd, S. (1977), The Sociology of Schooling and the Absent Pupil, in H. Carroll (ed.), *Absenteeism in South Wales*, Faculty of Education, University of Swansea.
Reynolds, D. and Sullivan, M. (1979), Bringing Schools Back In, in L. Barton and R. Meighan, *Schools, Pupils and Deviance*, Nafferton Books.
Reynolds, D., Jones, D., St. Leger, S. and Murgatroyd, D. (1980), School Factors in Truancy, in L. Hersov and I. Berg (eds), *Out of School*, Wiley.
Rist, R. (1970), Student Social Class and Teacher Expectations: The Self Fulfilling Prophecy in Ghetto Education, *Harvard Educational Review*, 40:411-50.
Rose, A. (1962), A Systematic Summary of Symbolic Interactionism Theory, in A. M. Rose (ed.), *Human Behaviour and Social Processes*, R.K.P.
Rosser, E. and Harre, R. (1976), The Meaning of Disorder, in M. Hammersley and P. Woods (eds), *The Process of Schooling*, O.U.P./R.K.P.
Rubington, E. and Weinberg, M. (1973), *Deviance: The Interactionist Perspective*, Macmillan.
Rubington, E. and Weinberg, M. (1977), *The Study of Social Problems*, Oxford University Press.
Rutter, M. (1967), A Children's Behaviour Questionnaire for Completion by Teachers: Preliminary Findings, *Journal of Child Psychology and Psychiatry*, 8:1-11.
Rutter, M. (1972), *Maternal Deprivation Reassessed*, Penguin.

Rutter, M. (1975), *Helping Troubled Children*, Penguin.
Rutter, M., Yule, W., Berger, M., Yule, B., Morton, J. and Bagley, C. (1974), Children of West Indian Immigrants. I: Rates of Behavioural Deviance and Psychiatric Disorder, *Journal of Psychology and Psychiatry*, 15:214-62.
Rutter, M. , Cox, A., Tupling, C., Berger, M. and Yule, W. (1975), Attainment and Adjustment in Two Geographical Areas. I: The Prevalence of Psychiatric Disorder, *British Journal of Psychiatry*, 126:493-509.
Rutter, M., Maughan, B., Mortimore, P. and Ouston, J. (1979), *Fifteen Thousand Hours: Secondary Schools and their Effects on Children*, Open Books.
Sharp, R. and Green, A. (1975), *Education and Social Control*, R.K.P.
Sharpe, S. (1976), *Just Like a Girl*, Penguin.
Shepherd, M., Oppenheim, B. and Mitchell, S. (1971), *Childhood Behaviour and Mental Health*, University of London Press.
Smith, F. (1923), *The Life and Times of Sir James Kay Shuttleworth*, John Murray.
Spender, D. and Sarah, E. (1980), *Learning to Loose*, The Women's Press.
Stebbins, R. (1970), The Meaning of Disorderly Behaviour, *Sociology of Education*, 44:217-36.
Stott, D. H. (1963), *The Social Adjustment of Children*, University of London Press.
Stott, D. (1982), *Helping the Maladjusted Child*, Open University Press.
Stubbs, M. and Delamont, S. (eds), (1976), *Explorations in Classroom Observation*, Wiley.
Sugarman, B. (1976), Involvement in Youth Culture, Academic Achievement and Conformity in School, *British Journal of Sociology*, 58:157-64.
Sully, J. (1896), *Studies of Childhood*, Longman.
Sully, J. (1913), *The Teacher's Handbook of Psychology*, Longman.
Sutherland, E. and Cressy, D. (1966), *Principles of Criminology*, J. P. Lippincott.
Swann, M. (1985), (The Swann Report), *Education for All*, H.M.S.O.
Sykes, G. M. and Matza, D. (1957), Techniques of Neutralisation: A Theory of Delinquency, *American Sociological Review*, 22:664-70.
Tattum, D. (1982), *Disruptive Pupils in Schools and Units*, Wiley.
Taylor, I., Walton, P. and Young, J. (1973), *The New Criminology: For a Social Theory of Deviance*, R.K.P.
Taylor, L. (1971), *Deviance and Society*, Michael Joseph.
Taylor, M. (1981), *Caught Between: A Review of Research into the Education of Pupils of West Indian Origin*, N.F.E.R. Nelson.
Taylor, W. (1963), *The Secondary Modern School*, Faber.
Thomas, E. (1956), *T.E.S.*, April 6, 1956:1031.
Tibbenham, A. (1977), Housing and Truants, *New Society*, 10 March, 39(735):501-2.
Topping, K. (1983), *Education System Systems for Disruptive Pupils*, Croom Helm.
Troyna, B. (1978), Race and Streaming: A Case Study, *Educational Review*, 30(1).
Turner, B. (ed.) (1974), *Truancy*, Ward Lock.
Turner, G. (1983), *The Social World of the Comprehensive School*, Croom Helm.
Tyerman, M. (1958), A Research into Truancy, *British Journal of Educational Psychology*, 28(3):217-25.
Tyerman, M. (1968), *Truancy*, University of London Press.
Underwood, J. (1955), (The Underwood Report), *Report of the Committee on Maladjusted Behaviour*, H.M.S.O.
Wadsworth, M. (1979), *Roots of Delinquency: Infancy, Adolescence and Crime*, Martin Robertson.
Wakeford, J. (1969), *The Cloistered Elite: A Sociological Analysis of the English Public Boarding School*, Macmillan.
Werthman, C. (1963), Delinquency in Schools: A Test for the Legitimacy of Authority, *Berkley Journal of Sociology*, 8(1):39-60. Reprinted in B. Cosin *et al.* (eds) (1971), *Schools and Society*, R.K.P.
Werthman, C. (1970), The Function of Social Definitions in the Development of Delinquent Careers, in P. E. Garbedian and D. C. Gibbons (eds), *Becoming Delinquent*, Aldine.

West, D. J. (1982), *Delinquency, its Roots, Careers and Prospects*, Heinemann.

West, D. J. and Farrington, D. P. (1973), *Who Becomes Delinquent?*, Heinemann.

West, W. G. (1979), Adolescent Autonomy, Education and Pupil Deviance, in L. Barton and R. Meighan (eds), *Schools, Pupils and Deviance*, Nafferton Books.

Whitehead, J. M. and Williams, P. (1976), Teachers' Perceptions of Behaviour Problems: A Partial Replication of Wickman's Study, Unpublished. Discussed in Cashdan, A. (1976), *Problems of Adjustment and Learning*, Open University Block 9 E201.

Williams, P. (1974), Collecting Figures, in B. Turner (ed.), *Truancy*, Ward Lock.

Williams, R. (1961), *The Long Revolution*, Chatto and Windis.

Willis, P. (1977), *Learning to Labour*, Saxon House.

Willis, P. (1978), *Profane Culture*, R.K.P.

Willis, P. (1981), Cultural Production is Different from Cultural Reproduction is Different from Social Reproduction is Different from Reproduction, *Interchange*, 12(2-3):48-67.

Willis, P. (1983), Cultural Production and Theories of Reproduction, in L. Barton and S. Walker (eds), *Race, Class and Education*, Croom Helm.

Wilson, M. and Evans, P. (1980), *Education of Disturbed Children*, Methuen.

Wilson, P. (1969), Reputation and Respectability: A Suggestion for Caribbean Ethnography, *Man*, 4:70-84.

Winnicott, D. W. (1957), *The Child and the Family*, Hogarth Press.

Wood, J. (1984), Groping Towards Sexism; Boys' Sex Talk, in A. McRobbie and M. Nava, *Gender and Generation*, Macmillan.

Woods, P. (1975), Showing 'em Up, in G. Channon and S. Delamont, *The Frontiers of Classroom Research*, N.F.E.R.

Woods, P. (1976), Having a Laugh — An Antidote to Schooling, in M. Hammersley and P. Woods (eds), *The Process of Schooling*, O.U.P./R.K.P.

Woods, P. (1979), *The Divided School*, R.K.P.

Woods, P. (1980a), *Pupils Strategies*, Croom Helm.

Woods, P. (1980b), *Teacher Strategies*, Croom Helm.

Woods, P. (1981), *Schools and Deviance*, Open University E200, Unit 17.

Woods, P. and Hammersley, M. (eds) (1977), *School Experience*, Croom Helm.

Worsley, H. (1849), *Juvenile Depravity*, Gilpin.

Wright, N. (1977), *Progress in Education*, Croom Helm.

York, R., Heron, J. M. and Wolff, S. (1972), Exclusion from Schools, *Journal of Child Psychology and Psychiatry*, 13:259-66.

Young, J. (1971), The Role of the Police as Amplifiers of Deviancy, Negotiators of Reality and Translators of Fantasy: Some Consequences of our Present System of Drug Control as Seen in Notting Hill, in S. Cohen (ed.), *Images of Deviance*, Penguin.

Young, J. (1979), Left Idealism, Reform and Beyond: From New Criminology to Marxism, in National Deviancy Conference, *Capitalism and the Rule of Law*, Hutchinson.

Young, J. (1981), Thinking Seriously about Crime, in M. Fitzgerald, G. McLennan and J. Pawson (eds), *Crime and Society: Readings in History and Theory*: R.K.P.

Young, M. F. D. (1971), *Knowledge and Control: New Directions for the Sociology of Education*, Collier-Macmillan.

Subject Index

Author Index